Zippy and Me

My life inside Britain's most infamous puppet

Ronnie Le Drew

with Duncan Barrett and Nuala Calvi

unbound

First published in 2019

Unbound
6th Floor Mutual House, 70 Conduit Street, London W1S 2GF
www.unbound.com
All rights reserved

© Ronnie Le Drew, Duncan Barrett & Nuala Calvi, 2019

Text design by PDQ

A CIP record for this book is available from the British Library

ISBN 978-1-78352-698-7 (paperback)
ISBN 978-1-78352-700-7 (ebook)

Printed in Great Britain by Clays Ltd, Elcograf S.p.A.

For my grandchildren Daisy, Theo, Olive and Felix

Contents

Foreword

By Richard Herring

I once met Zippy from *Rainbow*. At least I think I did. Because if memory serves me right, just seconds before the encounter I'd been cycling at speed through the streets of London on a tandem tricycle being steered by John Bishop, before careering through some doors into a TV studio where I was showered in confetti like at the end of *Who Wants To Be a Millionaire*.

So there's a chance that it was just a dream.

This was all for a non-broadcast pilot of a late night TV show and the guests they'd managed to get were me, Richard Herring (probably best known for playing a police officer on *Ant and Dec Unzipped*) and Zippy from *Rainbow*. I don't know what list they'd got us from, but I don't think it was the A-one. If it was the Z-list then, alphabetically at least, Zippy would be right at the end of it. The barrel had been scraped and we'd both been found clinging to the bottom.

And I didn't actually meet Zippy. I just stood next to

him, too dumbfounded by his presence to introduce myself. Because even though I was nearly fifty years old, Zippy still meant as much to me as he did when I had first seen him shouting out of my television set when I was six.

I was always attracted to anarchy in comedy: the flan-flinging antics of the *Tiswas* team, the tomato-ketchup squirting, black-pudding thumping Goodies, the dangerous driving of the Banana Splits. And Zippy was right up there. Because he was anarchic and transgressive within the bounds of what, at first appearance at least, was a traditional happy-clappy kids TV show. George was soppy, Bungle naïve and confused, Geoffrey just another in a long line of ever-cheery presenters that we knew from Play School.

But then there was Zippy. Rude, brash, often angry and frustrated. So much so that people could only shut him up by pulling his mouth shut with a zip. What kind of creature has a zip in their mouth? No creature does. That zip had been stitched in there by someone. This wasn't normal.

And if Zippy wasn't normal then maybe the show wasn't either. What was Rod, Jane and Freddie's real relationship (we could never have guessed quite how complex)? How had Geoffrey, Bungle, George and Zippy even got together in the first place when they had so little in common? How old would Geoffrey actually get before he decided he should move on? Why did their house have no walls? Was George smarter than he seemed? Was Bungle more calculating and selfish? Why did he wear pyjamas when he never wore clothes? Was Geoffrey actually squeaky clean or was there something darker lurking underneath? Was he just one step away from getting out his twanger and showing it to everyone? And was there somewhere, deep in the recesses of all of our brains, some memory of the hideous horror show that was the original Bungle, whose head seemed too small for his (or any) body, like it had been ripped from a bear, left to rot and then attached like an ursine Frankenstein's monster to a body that it simply didn't fit with?

Zippy and his zip mouth being zipped shut was one of the first things that made me laugh (and also slightly scared, as I was also a mouthy child – would someone stitch a zip on to me too?) and one of my earliest memories.

So now, as a grown up, I was more than star struck to be so close to one of my childhood heroes. The young man in charge of the social media part of the team on this never-to-be-broadcast show we were guesting on said, 'So this is the puppet thing, is it?' – aptly enough as the segment was about things that would mean nothing to millennials. I was so aghast I almost punched him for his rudeness. It's fucking Zippy from *Rainbow*, you prick. Have some respect.

I really wanted a selfie with Zippy, but just like the time I met Bryan Cranston, I was too embarrassed to ask (Zippy must be sick of it after all – let him live his life). I can't be the only one to compare Zippy to Walter White.

But John Bishop had no such shame and got photos as the puppeteer hid quite badly behind him. Why didn't I ask too? Imagine having that picture. You don't get opportunities like that twice.

And it's interesting because, even though for most of the time I was with him, Zippy was inanimate, and when he moved, it was only with assistance, it is only him that I really remember. The curse of the puppeteer, and maybe the triumph too, is that you are invisible. I was in the company of the great Ronnie Le Drew, but because he is so great he was practically invisible. I only saw Zippy.

It's certainly the case that many puppeteers and ventriloquists have strange relationships with their puppets. Hopefully not quite THAT strange, though I wouldn't put it past some of them. Apparently Harry Corbett used to take Sooty on holiday and once had to turn the car around because he'd left him Home Alone (now that would be a film – I mean it really would – I might give that a crack). Whereas Rod Hull so resented the fact that his success was tied up with his Emu that he started to hate the puppet (he appeared on our show *Fist of Fun* precisely because we'd asked for him alone and not 'the bird' as he called him, practically spitting the words out).

Either way, Ronnie keeps Zippy in an IKEA bag. Which

makes me think he might be that rare thing: a sane puppeteer. Perhaps this book will prove otherwise.

Either way, it's finally time for the invisible man behind the puppet to rise up above the *Rainbow* kitchen counter. He must remove his hand from Zippy's backside, give it a wash, zip the puppet's mouth shut and lock it with a padlock, and tell us his side of the story. Given that most of it was spent crouching behind scenery I can't imagine he saw very much, but maybe we get a better perspective of things from the background if everyone else has forgotten we're even there.

Thank you, Ronnie, for making me so in awe of a piece of felt that I couldn't bring myself to even ask for a photo. Thank you for bringing this monster to life.

I know I speak for a lot of middle-aged children.

Curtain up

July 1961. Stockwell Gardens council estate, South London.

Crouched behind a cardboard box, I wait impatiently for the audience to settle. I sneak a glance round the side of my brand-new Pollock's toy theatre. Rows of little girls in knee-high socks sit cross-legged on the floor as their brothers jostle for space at the back.

I have summoned them to a performance on the landing of our block of flats, instructing them very clearly not to cross the crack in the concrete that delineates the stage.

I clear my throat importantly, and the rabble quietens down a little. 'The Tragical History of Hamlet, Prince of Denmark, by William Shakespeare,' I announce in the lowest possible tones my thirteen-year-old voice box can muster, prodding Bonnie, my twin sister, to start the wind-up gramophone. I wince as the strains of 'I'm a Lonely Little Petunia in an Onion Patch' begin, to the accompaniment of sniggers. Hardly the grand orchestral music I would have wished, but since it's the only record we own, it will have to do.

1

I take a last, lingering glance at the shiny photograph of Laurence Olivier, resplendent as the Dane in the 1959 film of *Hamlet*, in the book that Benjamin Pollock's toy shop has helpfully provided as part of its Regency Theatre kit. It has taken me eight weeks to save the money to buy it from the Pollock's shop on Monmouth Street, and it is my pride and joy. The wooden stage is exquisitely made, with a little round pit containing a painted orchestra, a battery-operated spotlight, and cardboard scenery and characters lovingly cut out and coloured in by Bonnie and me.

With a nod from me, she now lifts the little wooden curtain and the lights come up; down goes the ghost of Hamlet's father on a piece of cotton thread, uttering the immortal line: 'O horrible! O horrible! Most horrible!' I'm soon well into my stride, moving Hamlet and Horatio around the ramparts and concentrating hard to make sure I get every word right. The audience is completely silent, apparently transfixed by the drama onstage.

After a couple of scenes it's too much – the desire for applause overwhelms me and I pull the curtain down with a flourish, announcing, 'You may clap now!'

As dead silence greets us, Bonnie and I stand up and look over the top of the theatre.

There is no one there. Each and every child has quietly crept away and we have been performing to ourselves.

It is the best lesson I will ever learn as a puppeteer.

Chapter 1: A teenage dolly-waggler

Not that I considered myself a puppeteer then, of course. I was just a kid from a South London council estate, dreaming of a more glamorous existence. Really I wanted to *be* Laurence Olivier, but the next best thing was waggling his cardboard effigy on a little stick.

For now, I had to make do with a distinctly unglamorous home life. My sister, my parents and I lived in a tiny flat, with furniture mostly consisting of old packing crates that Dad had knocked together and painted. We had come over to England from Canada when Bonnie and I were just three so that my father could study to become a teacher. But the circumstances of our arrival were hardly a good omen: the RMS *Empress of Canada*, which had carried us across the Atlantic, took on water on the lower decks and all our worldly possessions were ruined. So we began our new life in the Old World with little more than the clothes on our backs.

My father eventually got a job teaching science at a local secondary school. He always seemed to be busy with his marking, sitting in his favourite armchair surrounded by a cloud of smoke as he puffed away on his Senior Service cigarettes. My mother worked in the accounts department of the Guardian Royal Exchange insurance company, so Bonnie and I were more or less latchkey kids. We would come home briefly to do our chores then spend the rest of our time outside, exploring the bombed-out houses that even in the early sixties surrounded the estate, or setting up our puppet shows in the stairwell.

As it grew dark my sister and I would reluctantly come home, usually to find our parents arguing in the living room. As soon as they realised we were there, they would suddenly fall silent and my mother would fix her face into an exaggerated smile. 'Hello, darlings!' she would say brightly. 'How are you?'

One morning in the summer holidays, Bonnie and I were playing with some puppets when my father called us into the flat. 'Your mother and I have something to tell you,' he said.

We grudgingly followed him inside and took our places on the sofa. My mother was sitting in a chair to one side, while my father stood over her. Mum had her familiar strained smile on her face. 'Dad's decided to leave,' she told us, her voice wavering. 'He's going away for a while.'

I glanced at my father, but his face betrayed no

emotion. At first I thought he must be taking a holiday somewhere – or perhaps a field trip. After all, he was a science teacher. It took me a few moments to realise that my parents were what you called 'separating'.

'Who would you like to live with? Your father or me?' Mum asked.

Bonnie and I looked at each other. 'Mum,' we said, in unison.

Not long afterwards, Dad was at the door with a suitcase in his hand, stiffly wishing us farewell. 'Good luck, Ronald,' he said. 'Look after your mother, and we'll see each other again soon.'

But as the weeks and months passed we wouldn't see him, or have any idea where he had gone.

I was glad to escape to school during term time, and put my efforts into trying to impress my form teacher, the gorgeous Miss Gedney. I was madly in love with her, and diligently memorised a little poem she had taught us:

> Good, better, best,
> Never let it rest,
> 'Til your good is better
> And your better best.

I tried hard to live by those words but my grades spoke for themselves: 18 per cent in technical drawing, 39 per cent in geography, 36 per cent in maths and, most embarrassingly for the son of a science teacher, 24 per cent in science.

My popularity rating wasn't great either, thanks to my extracurricular activities on the stairwell. Most teenage boys dismissed my hobby as 'dolly-waggling' and regarded it as distinctly uncool. But if I felt down, I could always take myself to the Pollock's Toy Theatre shop in Covent Garden and gaze lovingly at the window displays, like Audrey Hepburn on one of her early-morning visits to Tiffany's.

At fourteen I had finally got up the courage to audition for the school drama club, which was putting on a play about Alexander the Great. At that age I was so weedy I looked more like a ten-year-old, and one look at me convinced the teacher I would be perfect for the part of Unnamed Slave. I dutifully came on stage, delivered my single line – 'The envoy of the king of Macedon awaits your pleasure' – then walked off, trying to remind myself that there were no small parts, only small actors.

As it turned out, that was the end of my career as an actor; I was never invited back to drama club. But with my puppets my weediness was not a setback – I could be anything from a mouse to a lion – and so puppetry increasingly became my personal obsession.

Like most kids, I had grown up watching the fairly traditional puppets on children's television: Bill and Ben, Andy Pandy, Sooty and Muffin the Mule. This was in the day before we had a television of our own, so we used to gather around the tiny little box at my Great Uncle Len's house in Streatham every Sunday afternoon, peering at the grainy, black-and-white image. But the puppets I was most excited about were the stars of Gerry Anderson's early black-and-white 'Supermarionation' shows *Supercar* and *Fireball XL5*. These had a lot in common with Anderson's later series *Thunderbirds*: brave heroes with fantastic flying machines, battles in space and under the oceans, and stunning ladies with elaborate blonde hairdos.

In my evenings I had begun hanging out at the Educational Puppetry Association – an organisation based in Holborn that ran courses, mainly for teachers, on how to make and perform puppets – and was beside myself with excitement when I discovered that one of its members, John Blundall, had designed Robert the Robot and some of the other *Fireball* characters.

Inspired, I set out to craft some puppets of my own, but I soon discovered I was a bit of a disaster as a puppet-maker. Seeing that everything I built fell apart, the couple who ran the EPA, the Philpotts, eventually took pity on me and offered to help. Violet Philpott, a lovely woman in her forties with slightly mad, wavy hair, offered me a spare puppet from one of her previous shows. He was a freckly young boy who looked a little bit like me, and I decided to call him Snitchity Titch. I came up with a story about how 'Snitch' would go to sea, his boat would sink and he'd be washed up on a desert island. Violet's husband, who was known as Panto – a very distinguished older man with twinkly dark eyes, whom I regarded as something of a puppetry guru – sat me down and gave me a lesson in characterisation. He told me that I would need a foil for Snitch, someone with a contrasting personality. He suggested a dodo as the perfect complement to the energetic young boy: an ancient, weary and very serious character who spoke with an upper-class accent. Dodo would tell Snitch about his illustrious family line, including his great uncle who lived in a glass cabinet in the Natural History Museum.

Violet kindly made the dodo puppet, which had a carved polystyrene head and beak, and grey fur for its body. Then I spent many happy hours painting the head and sticking bits of fluff and feathers onto it along with a pair of green teddy-bear eyes (unfortunately I couldn't find two that matched). Holding up the puppet in the mirror to see how it looked, I was satisfied that Dodo cut quite a fine figure.

Next I needed a theatre to perform in. Panto built me a beautiful puppet booth, tailor-made for my short arms, and I would sit hidden behind it on a chair and perform my show to my heart's content. Soon a boy a couple of years younger than me, Nigel Plaskitt, joined the EPA too. At last I had a friend around my own age who shared my obsession and didn't think I was just a 'dolly-waggler'.

As I spent more time at the EPA and around puppeteers, I started to realise for the first time that perhaps my hobby could actually become a career. Unlike my teachers at school, who had all but given up on me, Panto and Violet seemed to think I had a real talent, and seeing how seriously they took puppetry encouraged me to think of it as a worthwhile pursuit. I started borrowing books from the EPA library to learn more about the history and theory of puppetry, finding, to my surprise, that Panto had written half of them himself.

To me, Panto was just a kindly old man who had allowed me to practice my favourite hobby in front of a receptive audience, but to most puppeteers at the time he was seen as the grandfather of the industry – the editor of the *Puppet Post*, author of the *Dictionary of Puppetry* and a respected philosopher of puppetry in all its forms. It was a testament to his gentle, unassuming personality that his status as a puppet luminary had gone completely over my head. He was a man who was interested in everyone and gave his complete attention to each person he met – especially children, whom he treated with genuine respect.

The more I read about the history of puppetry the more determined I was to become a puppeteer myself. Now that I had turned fifteen, Panto and Violet told me I should look for opportunities for professional training, but since there were no formal teaching programmes or puppet schools at the time, what I needed was an apprenticeship. I sent off a flurry of letters to anyone and everyone I could think of who might be able to help, and eventually one of my pleas paid off. I received a reply from Bob Pelham, owner of the toy marionette company Pelham Puppets, offering some very useful advice:

27 June 1963

Dear Ronald,

Thank you for your letter of 24 June. I suggest you contact Mr John Wright at the Little Angel Theatre, 14 Dagmar Passage, Islington, who may be able to help you. Mr Wright is running a permanent puppet theatre at the Little Angel.

Yours sincerely,

Bob Pelham

A permanent puppet theatre was almost unheard of in those days. Most puppeteers worked in small teams – often husband-and-wife pairs such as Violet and Panto – touring the country on the Variety circuit. But now someone had built a permanent home for puppetry, right here in London. I was desperate to find out more.

I had been to a few meetings of the British Puppet and Model Theatre Guild, so next time I was there I asked if anyone knew about John Wright and his new marionette theatre. It turned out that Edith Murray, an

Australian puppeteer in her sixties who was lecturing in London, was an old friend of John's, and she offered to introduce me.

A few days later I received a letter from Edith to say she had reserved tickets for us to see a show at the Little Angel and that she would meet me there on Saturday afternoon. She had drawn me a little map with directions of how to get there, which was just as well since the Little Angel was in deepest, darkest North London – further from home than I had ever ventured on my own. Not only that but it was in Islington, then a grimy, run-down area that most people did their best to avoid.

That Saturday I took the tube from Stockwell all the way to Angel and did my best to follow Edith's scrawled directions. When I got there I was a little surprised – the Little Angel was far from the grand theatre that I had imagined. It was an old, converted temperance hall set back from the main road, in a small square next to a graveyard. The building had sustained heavy damage during the war and had been bought for a song by John Wright after the roof caved in. The auditorium looked like a barn, with music-hall seats laid out in rows, and at the far end was a letterbox stage – the traditional style for marionette performances. There was a distinct smell of mothballs in the air, but as the house lights dimmed a shiver of excitement ran down my spine. I had never seen a full-length puppet play before.

The show we saw that day was *The Little Mermaid,* which Edith told me was one of John Wright's signature productions. Before settling in London he had spent years touring the world with a troupe of travelling puppeteers, she explained, surviving like gypsies from one day to the next. Shows like this had been their bread and butter.

As the lights went up, a gorgeous classical overture filled the auditorium and the mermaid appeared centre stage, floating magically behind a layer of gauze representing the sea. As she moved gently with the waves, her cheek pressed against the figurehead of her prince's sunken boat, the plummiest voice I had ever heard began the narration: 'This is the story of a mermaid – no ordinary mermaid, but a princess.' It was Barry Smith, a respected puppeteer who also worked as a voice teacher at RADA – where he spent six months coaching Laurence Olivier to lower his voice by an octave in preparation for playing Othello. Barry's own rich, fruity cadences were a mainstay of the Little Angel's repertoire.

The underwater lighting was exquisite, conjuring a universe of beautiful blues and greens. As a storm broke above her, the lights flashed and the mermaid became caught up in a whirlpool, spinning and thrashing about under the force of the invisible water. Bits of boat started sinking down, followed by the anchor, nearly knocking out the mermaid, and finally the drowning prince with his arms flailing. The mermaid saw the prince, forced her way out of the swirling vortex and approached him. As she looked into his eyes, I could have sworn I saw the expression on her wooden face change.

It was the most beautiful thing I had ever seen, a magical ballet with dancers who could float and fly. The show had everything: action, romance, special effects (including a magnificent witch's cauldron which smoked and bubbled underwater) and a heart-breaking ending – none of Disney's happily-ever-after. From beginning to end I was spellbound, transported into a realm of pure beauty and wonder.

After the show, Edith and I waited in the foyer until Mr Wright emerged. He was a solid, well-built man who looked about my father's age, with wisps of grey streaking his dark-brown hair. He was wearing an old brown pullover – worn through at the elbows – over a white cotton shirt and corduroy trousers, and around his neck hung a pair of reading glasses suspended from a frayed bit of string.

'John, this is Ronnie,' Edith told him. 'The budding puppeteer I spoke to you about on the phone.'

'Pleased to meet you, Ronnie,' John replied warmly, extending a muscular hand for me to shake. His voice was surprisingly gentle, with not a hint of his South African origins. 'So, what did you think of the show?'

'It was brilliant!' I blurted out, wishing I could find the words to explain the effect the performance had had on me.

John smiled. 'Would you like to come and have a look backstage?'

He led me through a door to the backstage area. It was surprisingly cramped and makeshift behind the stage curtain, quite the opposite of the ornate, perfect world I had seen in the show. The lights which had dazzled me sitting in the auditorium turned out to have been held in place by empty beer cans. But to me, it was an Aladdin's cave.

'That's the bridge where the puppeteers stand,' John told me, pointing up a rickety little ladder to a raised walkway above our heads. I could see microphones hanging down from the ceiling, which were used to perform the characters' voices. Below the bridge and off to one side was the witch's cauldron, with a pipe running to it from the wings through which the smoke could be blown.

'Give me a hand, would you, Ronnie?' John said, tossing a couple of bags in my direction. 'We need to get the puppets bagged up.' He gestured to some little hooks on the wall behind me, where the mermaid and the sea witch hung lifeless.

Gingerly, I lifted the sea witch and placed her in one of the little bags before carefully passing her up to John, who was already halfway up the ladder to the bridge. I then did the same for the mermaid, running my hand along her beautiful sequin-covered tail. I couldn't quite believe that I had been allowed to touch such exquisite creations.

When we had put all the puppets to bed, John turned to me. 'So, what can I do for you, Ronnie?' he asked. 'Edith tells me you're looking for somewhere to train.'

'Yes,' I replied. 'I've written to everyone I can think of but no one can help.'

'Well, we may be able to help you,' he said. 'We're only a small family business, so we can't offer paid work, but if you're willing to help out around the theatre I think we can provide you with some training.'

I was so ecstatic at the thought of coming back to the theatre that money was the last thing on my mind. 'That's amazing!' I gushed. 'When can I start?'

'I think you'd better discuss it with your parents first,' John replied. 'Why don't you write to me once you've spoken to them, and we can take it from there?'

He led me back to the foyer, where Edith was waiting, and gave me another firm handshake. 'I hope to hear from you soon, Ronnie,' he said.

All the way back home on the Tube I was in a daze, swept up in reveries about that shimmering mermaid and her magical world. When I got out at Stockwell station I ran all the way home, shooting up the steps of the flats, two at a time, ready to burst with the news I was about to deliver to my poor old mum. As she looked up from her newspaper, I confidently announced: 'Mum, I've made up my mind. I'm leaving school – I'm going to be a puppeteer!'

The enraptured reception I had expected failed to materialise. Instead, my sister Bonnie's stifled laughter in the corner of the room was the only sound that greeted me. My mother simply raised her eyebrows.

I tried to explain about the Little Angel, how there had never been anywhere for young performers like me to get a grounding in puppetry before, but that it was all changing now. John Wright had started a permanent puppet theatre in London and I simply had to be a part of it.

After a torrent of pleading, Mum promised to write to Mr Raggett, my headmaster, to see what he had to say about me leaving school. I felt sure he would have no hesitation in congratulating me on my good fortune and assure her that there was really no need for me to sit my upcoming O levels.

My mother kept her word and wrote to the head immediately. After an agonising wait, Mr Raggett's reply landed on the doormat:

8 July 1963

Dear Mrs Le Drew,

Thank you for your letter. I can entirely see your point of view. For my part, I merely endeavour to get young people to think both deeply and widely about their choice of career. In this connection it is difficult for them to take the long view as they have little knowledge of life. Aristotle tackled this question over 2,000 years

16

ago. One of the important questions in taking the long view is prospects. That was the particular point which worried me about Ronald's choice.

Yours sincerely,

Mr Raggett
Stockwell Manor School

I couldn't believe it. Mr Raggett and some ancient philosopher were conspiring to sabotage my plans. Mum squeezed my hand apologetically. Couldn't I wait until after my exams, she suggested, and then see if Mr Wright would be willing to take me on? My answer was the slamming of the door as I promptly stormed out.

A day or two into my ensuing sulk, my ambitions faced an even more formidable opponent. After more than a year of absence, Dad was back.

The full story of what he got up to in that time would not emerge for years to come, and when it did it would send shock waves through our family. But as it was, there was no explanation. When he telephoned out of the blue one day and asked to come home, Mum simply said yes. Back he came with the same suitcase he had packed the day he left, as if he'd merely been on an extended holiday. Family life reverted to normal – except that Dad now slept in the living room.

When I told Dad about my offer of training, he wasn't best pleased. Not only did it irk him that my mother was considering removing me from school without his permission, but the idea of me, a teacher's son, leaving with no qualifications, was particularly galling to him.

The next morning, I waited outside the living room door, listening to the old, familiar sound of my parents arguing – all the worse because this time I was the cause.

Finally, my father's voice summoned me.

As I waited on the sofa to hear my fate, I felt almost sick with longing – longing to get away from the dreary flats, the arguments and the disappointments of school, and to escape to the magical world I had caught such a tantalising glimpse of at the Little Angel.

'Your mum and I have made a decision,' Dad announced. 'You can try this puppetry lark for six months but, at the end of that, if they don't offer you a paid position you're going to have to get a proper job.'

I didn't wait to hear any more. I rushed straight out of the door and back on the Tube to Islington.

Chapter 2: Up on the bridge

As I strode across the square to the Little Angel, I felt that my time had finally come: at long last, I was going to be a real puppeteer. I took a few seconds to savour the richness of the moment, drew a deep breath and stepped boldly up to the door.

There was no knocker, so I tried rattling the letterbox instead. When that got no response, I put my face up to the flap to see if there was anyone inside.

A mouth suddenly appeared, causing me to take a step backwards.

'Hellew?' it said in a crisp, clipped voice, like a BBC newsreader. 'Ken I help yew?'

I had never heard anyone speak like that outside the telly, so I didn't know how to respond. In my nervousness the performer in me took over, and before I could think, I replied – in my best Noël Coward voice: 'I doo hewp sew.'

The door swung open to reveal a short, sturdy woman of about fifty, wearing a patterned knitted jumper and a

19

silk scarf. There was an awkward silence as she looked me up and down, her nose wrinkling in distaste.

'Um, hello,' I said, reverting to my normal accent. 'I'm here to see John Wright.'

Without taking her eyes off me, she shouted at an ear-piercing volume: 'John! Theer's a boy hyeer to see yew.'

'Has he got his mother with him?' I heard John Wright reply, from somewhere within the depths of the theatre.

'Nyeoh,' replied the lady on the doorstep.

'Oh good, then I shan't change my trousers.'

Moments later, John's burly frame appeared in the doorway, dressed in a pair of scruffy brown cords that were covered in sawdust and wood shavings.

'Ronnie, do come in,' he said. 'Have you met Joyce Wren? You might remember her as the sea witch.'

'Come inside, my pretty,' rasped Joyce, suddenly in character, as she beckoned me into the theatre.

I was astounded. The refined BBC newsreader was none other than the evil sea witch! (As it turned out, Joyce the Voice, as she was known at the theatre, had also performed the innocent mermaid. Thanks to her versatile range of voices, she often spent whole scenes talking to herself.)

John ushered me backstage into the theatre workshop, where three young people were busily painting puppets of knights and monsters for a forthcoming show. 'This is my niece, Mary Kenny,' John said, waving to a slim, freckled woman with long, blonde hair. 'This is Lyndie Parker'

– he gestured to a tall brunette who looked only about nineteen or twenty. 'And this is Christopher Leith, one of our lead puppeteers.' A tall and intelligent-looking man in his mid-twenties smiled and waved at me.

I approached the little gang and shook hands with each in turn, feeling very much like the new kid at school. They were only a few years older than me, but here they were: professional puppeteers.

John turned to me. 'So, Ronnie, what would you like to do?'

'Everything!' I replied enthusiastically. A knight or a monster – I didn't mind, as long as I could be part of the Little Angel's new show.

'That's a good lad,' he said. 'We'll get you kitted out with a broom and you can start by sweeping the floor.'

One of my first roles at the theatre, aside from a regular stint as Cinderella with the broom, was helping with the scene changes on *The Little Mermaid*. I was extremely excited to be working on the show that had made such a strong impression on me. Previously Joyce had done all the scene-changes herself, running down the ladder from the bridge to shift things around on stage, and then rushing back up again to speak into the microphones. Now, with me doing the bulk of the 'downstairs' work, she could concentrate on what needed doing up top, only occasionally helping me out with the more complex and involved bits of the show.

At least, that was the idea. In reality, things weren't quite that simple. Joyce clearly thought a kids' puppet theatre was no place for a child, and the more I tried to prove her wrong the clumsier I became. She was quite intimidated by John, and was at pains to make sure she didn't get the blame for my mistakes. When I inevitably dropped a prop or knocked over a bit of scenery, she would hurriedly whisper up to the bridge, 'John! John! It was Ronnie, darling! It wasn't me!' John, for his part, always remained utterly unfazed, peering down at us with a serene look on his face. That was very much his style as a puppeteer: precise, calm and unruffled.

I practised hard at my scene-changes, and just before my first performance of *The Little Mermaid*, John came up and tapped me on the shoulder. 'Got one more little job for you,' he whispered in my ear. 'Mary normally comes down the ladder to do the smoke for the witch's cauldron, but I thought since you're down there anyway you might as well do it.' He looked me in the eye. 'You do smoke, don't you?'

'Yes, of course,' I lied.

'All right, then,' said John. 'Just take a few puffs and then blow them through the pipe over there. It should come out nice and smooth on stage.'

The show got off to a good start, and when it came to the witch's scene I snuck over to where the end of the pipe trailed into the wings, lit up the cigarette that had been left there for me and took a deep draw of smoke into my lungs.

I instantly felt an unbearable itchiness in my throat, and to my horror I realised I was about to choke. I grabbed wildly for the end of the pipe, stuffed it into my mouth and coughed and spluttered the contents of my lungs into it. Instead of the subtle stream of smoke that I had seen rising from the cauldron when I was in the auditorium, what emerged on stage was a sudden, dense, explosive cloud. John, seeing the commotion onstage and hearing my muffled choking in the wings, calmly improvised, jerking the mermaid's head back as though she too was reacting to the overpowering smoke and it was her strangled gasps that the audience could hear, not mine. I heard a peal of laughter from the auditorium and hung my head in shame. I had ruined a beautiful moment of theatre.

After the show finished I went and found John, anxious to apologise. 'I'm so sorry about the smoke,' I said. 'I ruined it.'

'Oh, I don't know,' he replied, with a twinkle in his eye. 'I rather liked it.'

From then on, the coughing mermaid became a regular part of the show.

As the months passed, I settled into my role as general theatre dogsbody and John continued to find new tasks to keep me occupied: making tea, sorting nuts and bolts in the workshop, even carving a 'biscuit' (the waist section) for a new marionette – everything, in fact, except learning how to operate the puppets. I would have a go with them in my lunch breaks, doing my best to copy what I had seen the other puppeteers do, and occasionally, when John was out of the theatre, Christopher and Lyndie would give me a quick tutorial on the sly. But for the most part, although I was working full-time in a puppet theatre, my dreams of actually being a puppeteer remained stubbornly unfulfilled.

None the less, I was settling into the Little Angel family and spending far more time with them than with the family I had at home. I adored Lyndie and idolised Christopher, and even Joyce had genuinely warmed to me, and no longer referred to me behind my back as 'that vile little child'.

For my part, I did my best to ingratiate myself with Joyce. An old-school luvvie, she was always dropping Shakespearean quotations into conversation, which went right over my head. One day, to my horror, she asked me what my favourite poem was. I wracked my brains, trying to think of something that would impress her, but the only poem I could come up with from my unsatisfactory education was the little rhyme Miss Gedney had taught me at school. I figured it was better than nothing, so in my best classical voice I declaimed:

Good, better, best,
Never let it rest,

'Til your good is better
And your better best.

Joyce looked at me for a moment in complete bewilderment and then a smile spread across her face. She didn't say anything, but after that she took me under her wing a little more, offering me lessons in vocal technique and projection. I began to realise why everyone at the theatre held her in such high esteem.

Eventually John said he thought it was time I did one of the 'turns'. These were brief divertissement acts that were used to extend the playing time of the shorter shows and were the perfect training ground for a wannabe puppeteer. My favourite turn was a silent sketch called 'Baby Sweetheart'. A nanny walks into a park with a baby in a pram, she falls asleep on a park bench and the baby climbs out. A dog jumps into the pram, taking the baby's place, then Nanny wakes up and pushes the pram away with the dog in it.

John told me that he would let me work the dog puppet. 'Come up on the bridge and we'll do a few rehearsals before the show,' he said.

I climbed the ladder nervously, desperate to show John that I could do a good job. He handed me the marionette and we began the act. With his trademark precision, John carefully brought the baby up out of the pram; I walked the dog onto the stage, made it sit by the foot of the pram, and the baby came over and patted it. John muttered something under his breath, which I hoped was an expression of approval.

Then came the tricky part: as the baby crawled off stage left, the dog had to pass behind it to get to the pram, which meant that I had to pass behind John without losing control of the puppet. But when I tried to pass the dog from hand to hand around John, I found it was physically impossible. My scrawny little arms couldn't reach around his waist, and try as I might I just couldn't get the controller into my other hand. With my head pushed right up against John's back and my arms desperately trying to meet in front of his belly, I was forced to admit defeat.

'Oh dear,' said John, setting down his controller and putting a hand on my shoulder. 'Perhaps you're not quite ready after all.'

I hung the dog puppet back up in its place and climbed down the ladder, trying desperately not to let myself cry in front of John. It looked like I would be staying at the foot of the bridge for the foreseeable future.

The six months my parents had given me to make my mark as a puppeteer were fast running out, and my prospects were not looking good. What's more, at home I had other, much more serious, worries.

One night after a performance of *The Little Mermaid* I came home late to find Dad waiting up for me in the living room. 'What sort of time do you call this, Ronnie?' he demanded. 'Your mum and I have been worried sick.'

'I was just out with some friends from the theatre,' I replied.

'You ought to have told your mother,' he snapped. 'You know how she worries. Didn't I tell you to take care of her?'

I half-heartedly argued with him for a bit, before agreeing that if I was staying out late in future I would make sure to call. Then I said goodnight and went to bed.

That night, I woke up in the small hours to the sound of voices in the flat and rattling on the walkway outside. I crept out of my room and along to the living room door, but for some reason a voice in my head told me not to open it. Half asleep, I shuffled back to bed.

The next morning Mum came in with my breakfast on a tray. I thought it was odd, since she only usually did that on my birthday.

'Ronnie,' she said, 'you're going to have to be brave.'

'Why?' I asked. 'What's happened?'

'You're the man of the house now,' she replied quietly. 'Dad died last night.'

My father had suffered a massive heart attack in the early hours of the morning. The rattling I had heard on the walkway was the sound of the paramedics wheeling him away. He had died before they made it to hospital.

When Bonnie found out she immediately burst into tears, and there was much wailing and howling from her in the days that followed, but I didn't say much and neither did Mum. I think we were both equally in shock. Outwardly, I must have seemed to take the news pretty well, but as I took the Tube to work that day, the rhythm of the train seemed to be repeating the words, 'Dad is dead, Dad is dead, Dad is dead.' At the theatre I did my best to act like everything was normal, but before long Lyndie found out what had happened and she and John told me to take time off.

I didn't cry for almost a week, but on the day of the funeral I finally let go. It was a cremation, and after the coffin had disappeared behind the curtain and Bonnie, Mum and I had tottered back out into the daylight, all the teachers who had worked with my father lined up in a row to shake my hand. All I could think was, 'Why did this happen to me?'

With Dad gone, Mum coped admirably on her own – but then she'd had some practice. Bonnie and I did our best to help make ends meet, donating shillings out of our pocket money to feed the electric meter. As time went on, we learned once more to manage without our father, but I bitterly regretted that my last ever conversation with him had been an argument.

In those difficult days, the Little Angel was my solace. My allotted six months came to an end, but after Dad's death I don't think Mum had the heart to make me quit so I stayed on, bagging and sweeping and shifting the scenery around, still desperately keen to perform. Since the financial situation at home had taken a major turn for the worse, John told me he had decided to pay me a modest salary, enough to keep Mum from panicking for the time being. But then he dropped a real bombshell.

As he explained in a letter to my mother:

10 April 1964

Dear Mrs Le Drew,

Last Sunday I had a talk with Ronnie about his future work. I gather that the financial position is becoming rather critical. I've agreed to pay him two pounds a week as of last week in order to assist with his fares, lunches etc, until the company disperses on May 3rd. In the summer the company will be reorganised and I'm afraid I will not be able to include Ronnie in the set-up. I have therefore suggested to him that he uses this intervening period of time to find himself some well-paid work so that he may benefit from all that he has learned recently. I will of course help him in any way I can.

Yours sincerely,

John Wright

I was devastated. The Little Angel had become my life and working there was a dream come true. Now that dream had come crashing down around me before I had even performed a single puppet. My final weeks at the theatre went by all too quickly, then I bade my colleagues a tearful farewell.

It had been almost nine months now since Mum and Dad had made their deal with me, and the prospect of the dreaded 'proper job' hovered like a hawk over my fledgling puppetry career. In the cold light of day I was starting to look suspiciously like a teenager with no qualifications and – as Aristotle had apparently predicted – no prospects.

But like all performers, my deliverance was announced by the sound of the telephone ringing. My mother handed me the receiver.

'Hello, is that Ronald Le Drew?' a formal, rather upper-class voice demanded. 'It's Jan Bussell here.'

Jan Bussell – of The Hogarth Puppets, creators of Muffin the Mule! My heart was in my mouth.

'We're doing a little caravan show in the summer,' he said, 'and we need someone as a stage manager who can also do a bit of puppetry. Are you interested?'

The question was hardly necessary – Jan and his wife Ann Hogarth were the most famous puppeteers in Britain at the time. He was an old professional rival of John

Wright's, renowned not only for Muffin but for decades of high-quality international touring work. Apparently they had been passed my name by some kind soul at the British Puppet and Model Theatre Guild.

'Yes!' I cried.

When I received a letter of confirmation of my employment, asking me to start work on 20 July 1964, I had to resist a strong urge to frame it and nail it above the mantelpiece. Here was proof, finally, that my puppetry was no longer mere 'dolly-waggling' – it was a profession that paid, even if it was a mere £10 a week.

The production I was working on was called *The Toyshop Ballet*. We gave three shows a day in various parks, performed from The Hogarth Puppets' specially adapted caravan. My job was to help set up the little theatre for each performance and to roll up the curtain when Muffin and various other acts took their turns.

Frankly, the position of curtain-roller for the Hogarths would have been honour enough for me, and after eight months as general dogsbody at the Little Angel I didn't dare hope for more. But Jan insisted I start working the puppets right away, believing that the best way to learn was by doing. My years of performance in the stairwell stood me in good stead and I felt like Olivier himself as Jan called out, in his plummy voice, 'That's wonderful, Ronald, marvellous!'

Once I had a few performances under my belt I decided

31

it was time for my fan base to attend, so my mother and sister, as well as Violet Philpott and John Blundall from the EPA, were duly summoned to a park in Hackney to see the show.

Jan started playing his ukulele, I rolled up the curtain excitedly and Muffin began to dance in Ann's expert hands. The performance was well underway and going perfectly when suddenly there was a large *Thwack!* on the side of the caravan, making Jan strike a random chord in surprise. We endeavoured to battle on, but seconds later it happened again: *Thwack!*

Jan peered over the top to see what was happening. 'Ann!' he shouted. 'They're throwing eggs at us!'

'Good God!' said Ann. She promptly grabbed her husband around the waist and yanked him back into the caravan, while I hastily unravelled the curtain. The three of us stood there, trapped, wondering what to do.

After a while we crept timidly out of the caravan to assess the damage. The perpetrators were long gone, and none of the puppets had been harmed, but one side of the caravan was completely covered in raw egg. We scrubbed it as best we could with soapy water, but for years to come the stain could still be seen – a terrifying reminder of what became known as The Egg and Muffin Incident.

I was mortified to face my friends and family after that, but they were all incredibly supportive and assured me that my professional debut had nevertheless been a great success. I could tell that my mother was impressed I had actually found paid employment as a puppeteer. Still, a part of me felt dissatisfied – I hadn't had the chance to prove it to my father.

Jan's faith in me was genuine, however, and I was thrilled when he offered me the lead role in the following summer's touring show. I was to operate the Waterman in his adaptation of the eponymous eighteenth-century comic opera by Charles Dibdin, as well as Count Bougars de Valance in the French romance *Aucassin and Nicolette*. And best of all I had got my young friend Nigel Plaskitt from the EPA a stint helping out with the company in his school holidays. It promised to be a great summer.

In the meantime, however, I would have to come back down to earth. Now that I was sixteen I had at least one toe, if not yet a foot, in reality, and I was starting to understand the responsibility I had to my family with Dad no longer around. With no puppetry work on the horizon for at least a year, I began scanning the jobs pages every morning – a depressing routine that lasted several months.

Eventually, a friend of my mum's managed to swing me a temporary job in a debt recovery service in Clapham, which marked a whole new low in my young life. The role was Chief Envelope Stuffer, dispatching awful letters informing people that the bailiffs were on their way, and each time I lined up a name in the plastic window of an envelope a little pang of guilt shot through me.

Eventually my miserable face got me a new task, operating the Gestetner – a kind of early photocopier – which was kept in its own special room in the office. I was instructed to put the ink in here, turn the handle there, print out the copies like that – and then suddenly I was alone in the room without a clue what I was supposed to do. Minutes later there was ink-splodged paper flying everywhere and the machine was making some extraordinary noises. I was convinced I had wrecked this precious piece of technology and certain that I would be fired. Sick with nervousness, I hid in the room for almost two hours, until my colleagues began to get worried and came looking for me. I was relieved to discover that they thought it an amusing, rather than sackable, offence – until it dawned on me this meant I was back on envelopes.

The experience at the debt collectors' had made me more desperate than ever to return to the puppetry world, and terrified that if I didn't manage to do so I would be doomed to a miserable future. I took to ringing the Hogarths frequently, begging them to take me on in advance of the summer season. 'Sorry, Ronnie,' the reply would come, 'we're off on tour to America,' then 'sorry, we're heading to the Arctic Circle to perform to the Inuit community.' That donkey really seemed to get around!

Unsurprisingly, by May I had worn Jan down with my phone campaign and was allowed to rejoin the Hogarths early. Once I was back in work it was much easier to hear about other opportunities, and I followed my stint with Jan and Ann with a job as a puppeteer for Clifford Heap's Miniature Theatre Company. This was a thirteen-week marionette tour going to proper theatres – not a caravan in sight. This is it, I thought: I'm a star.

The reality of touring life soon hit home, however. I discovered that my pitiful salary couldn't even cover the cost of decent digs – while we were in Birmingham, I and the rest of the performers ended up staying in a brothel; when the madam decided she needed our room one evening, we were told to quickly vacate it while a client went in to be serviced.

I returned home completely exhausted and rather disillusioned. But just as I was wearily contemplating a return to envelope-stuffing, I was once again rescued by the sound of the telephone ringing. I picked it up, and a familiar voice said matter-of-factly, 'We want you back.'

John Wright had his own tour coming up, the Little Angel's production of *Hans the Bell Ringer*, a lovely Christmas story with beautiful sets and costumes designed by Lyndie. My recent memories of touring evaporated and I said yes immediately. This was the Little Angel, after all – the place I really wanted to work – and surely now that I had performed with the famous Hogarths and Clifford Heap, John would finally let me be a puppeteer for him too.

'We need someone to do the lights,' he explained.

On the plus side, John was willing to offer me £15 a week. I swallowed my disappointment and travelled up to Oxford for the start of a two-week run there, dutifully lighting the show each night and watching enviously as Christopher did a wonderful job of operating Hans.

At the end of the first week, I was bagging the puppets after a performance when I heard raised voices coming from the dressing room. I couldn't make out what was being said, but I recognised the voices as belonging to John and Christopher. The next morning John called us all in for a meeting at the theatre, and I noticed that his niece Mary was there too. That's odd, I thought – what's she doing up in Oxford? I also noticed that Christopher was missing.

John was completely calm and collected as he announced: 'Last night, Christopher decided to part company with us. He is no longer working on this show. Mary has come up from London to help us out.' Thank God, I thought – the show had been saved by Mary. She was an experienced puppeteer and could easily take over from Christopher.

'Ronnie, up on the bridge, please,' John said, in the same no-nonsense tone. 'You're operating Hans now. Mary is going to take over the lights.'

Slowly the meaning of the words sunk in: John was asking me to operate a puppet – and not just any puppet, but the lead! What's more, we only had a few hours before the performance was due to start and scores of little children arrived, expecting their Christmas treat. Hans would be up on stage non-stop for an hour and a quarter, and I would have to master the entire thing in time for curtain-up.

That day, I finally got my first puppetry lesson from John. Suddenly all the knowledge and learning of this master puppeteer was available to me and I drank it in, eager to prove to him that I was worth the enormous gamble he was taking on me. He was a very exacting teacher, giving me lots of technical notes. Nevertheless, I think he was impressed by how many of the moves I already seemed to know – of course, I'd memorised them all from my nightly position at the lighting board at the side of the stage.

As the children filed into the theatre I waited backstage, trembling with nerves. This was my big moment – the opportunity I'd been begging for ever since I first knocked on the door of the Little Angel. If I disappointed John now, I might forever be consigned to the lighting desk and making tea. I had to prove to him that I could be a professional puppeteer.

The curtain went up and the performance began. Hans was accosted by Satan, who promised him riches beyond his wildest dreams in exchange for the sweet sound of his bells – not to mention a beautiful red-and-gold cloak that would help him win the hand of his beloved Famke. I was concentrating so hard that I began to sweat profusely, droplets literally dripping off my face and splashing onto the stage. I could only hope the audience would think it was meant to be rain.

Halfway through the performance, I somehow still hadn't made a single mistake, but I knew my biggest challenge was yet to come. Hans was about to accept the cloak, at which point the devil would cackle, 'Ah ha! You're with me now – the bells won't ring this Christmas!' When I'd seen the show performed in London, the curtain would immediately drop for the interval, giving us plenty of time to get the cloak, which was full of fiddly little hooks, onto the Hans puppet. However, in the touring version there was no interval – the curtain came down for just a minute or two while a short piece of music was played. My fingers trembled as I hung up the puppet, got the cloak and tried to fasten the hooks. I was shaking so much that the strings kept getting tangled up, and I had visions of the curtain rising and the children being faced with a terrifying, twisted mess of puppet limbs with half a cloak dangling off them. I recognised the last few bars of the melody – my time was nearly up! I gave the strings one last desperate yank and suddenly they untangled themselves. The curtain went up, Hans was cloaked and ready to face the devil, and I had faced my own demons too.

Backstage after the show I went back over every single move in my head, worrying that I had made a mistake somewhere or other. I avoided John's eye, terrified of seeing disappointment there. But as I was bagging up the puppets I felt a hand on my shoulder and he said quietly, 'You didn't get the puppet tangled up. You didn't drop it. Well done.'

Coming from John, I knew that was high praise indeed.

Chapter 3: New beginnings

After the *Hans* tour, John kept me on, no longer as a general theatre dogsbody but as the Little Angel's lead puppeteer, both at the Islington base and on tour. He took the more dramatic character parts, such as the villains, as well as the heroines, who suited his poised, precise style – but I played the eager young heroes. Many of the roles were familiar to me from watching Christopher perform them, so I fitted into the repertoire very easily. It was a dream time for me – finally, I was right where I wanted to be: up on the bridge. My scrawny arms had grown considerably and were now long enough to stretch around even the most prodigious belly.

As a fully fledged member of the team, I was now earning the princely sum of £18 a week – quite a step up from the £2 pay packet I had received towards the end of my previous stint there. In fact, I was even able to help out another young puppeteer. When I first met John Thirtle he was an Economics student in Southampton, where we were performing one of our shows. He'd offered to give us a hand constructing our touring stage, and he and I hit it off immediately thanks to our mutual obsession with puppets. After the show we stayed in touch, and he told me how much he would love to come and work at the Little Angel once he'd finished his studies. I put in a word for him with John Wright, who managed to get a grant for a student bursary so that he and another young hopeful could come to work with us for a year as formal apprentices.

When John first moved to London he initially stayed with my family in Stockwell and Mum more or less adopted him. She loved having another young man about the house and John got on very well with her. But before long he started telling me he thought it was time I left home: I was seventeen now and I had a good job paying a decent enough wage, so why was I still living with my mum?

I didn't take much convincing but, swept up in my own excitement, I didn't stop to think about Mum's feelings. 'John and I are moving out,' I announced. 'We're going to look for a flat of our own.'

She didn't take the news very well. After Dad walking out on us then dying so suddenly after his return, she saw this as yet another abandonment. For the first month or so after John and I left she would barely speak to me on the phone.

I was sad that things had deteriorated between Mum and

me, but I loved the freedom of having my own place. John and I were living in a basement flat not far from the Little Angel, so we could walk to work every day. We had an Irish landlady who told me that, as a Catholic, she had a strict rule against tenants swearing. The word 'feck' evidently didn't count as far as she was concerned, since she seemed to use it in practically every sentence.

We lived, like students, on meals from a packet, and the flat was always full of sawdust from John's puppet-making but we couldn't have been happier and ended up living together for several years. One night in the summer of 1969 the two of us were huddled around our little black-and-white television into the small hours to watch the first grainy images beamed back from the lunar surface. Little did we know that one day John would go on to populate the lunar landscape with puppets, in his legendary kids' TV series *Button Moon*.

One day I was at the Little Angel when Joyce asked me to help move some of Lyndie's belongings into John's cottage, which was next door to the theatre. I helpfully obliged, carting trunks and boxes up the stairs, until after an hour or two it occurred to me to ask what was going on. Joyce was incredulous. 'Don't you know, Ronnie? John and Lyndie have been together for ages!'

'Oh, right,' I murmured. I had obviously been too obsessed with the puppets to take notice of what the human beings around me were up to. I couldn't help feeling a little taken aback: John was in his late fifties – ancient in my young eyes – while Lyndie was only a few years older than me. In those days, however, it wasn't unusual for female apprentices to marry their puppetry teachers. The age gap between my friends Violet and Panto was almost as big.

Before long Lyndie was pregnant, and after their daughter Sarah was born she and John decided to tie the knot. On the day of the wedding, Joyce and I manned the theatre while John and Lyndie went off to the registry office. I had never seen Joyce so excited – she couldn't wait to see the bride and groom return and she kept a constant vigil in the doorway, expectantly scanning the little square outside the theatre. When the box office phone rang, her impeccable front-of-house demeanour, sustained for so many years, suddenly flew out the window. She rushed over to the desk, grabbed the receiver and shrieked: 'Can't you call back in ten minutes? The director is just getting married!'

I was delighted when I learned that John and Lyndie were expecting another child, and baby Joe soon became a popular addition to the Little Angel family. But I was even more excited by another new arrival at the theatre. Valerie Heberden was a shy young puppeteer, but she turned heads wherever she went, with stunning, dark-brown hair that cascaded down her back in perfect curls.

She was a wonderful performer, holding the audience transfixed in her first Little Angel production, *Cupid and Psyche*, in which she took the role of Venus.

To me, Valerie really was the goddess of love. That she was a spellbinding puppeteer as well as an attractive young woman only added to her charms, and I was smitten.

'You were wonderful,' I gushed to her on the show's opening night.

'Thanks, Ronnie,' Valerie replied, smiling. 'That means a lot, coming from someone so experienced.'

I was determined to ask Valerie out at the first opportunity. One day I overheard her chatting to Lucinda, one of the theatre's volunteer administrators, about how much she loved music. I rushed out immediately and booked some tickets to see a local string quartet.

'I wondered if you'd like to go to a concert together,' I said, the next time we were alone in the theatre.

'Yeah, that would be great,' Valerie replied. 'I think David Bowie's playing in Camden.'

I could have kicked myself. It was rock music she loved, not classical.

'Oh, actually I've already booked this,' I said awkwardly, showing Valerie the tickets.

A momentary look of disappointment flashed across her face, but she quickly dispelled it with a smile. 'That would be lovely,' she replied.

All through our date, I was giddy with excitement. I was so transfixed by my companion, I could barely concentrate on the performance.

'That was a lovely concert, Ronnie,' Valerie told me later as we stood together on the doorstep of her flat. 'I'm really glad you invited me.'

'Oh, that's alright,' I replied, wondering whether it was too soon to go in for a kiss.

'It's so nice to make a new friend,' she continued, offering me a quick peck on the cheek.

I felt winded. Of course, I told myself, a girl like Valerie would never have fancied me. I was the 'nice guy', not boyfriend material. What an idiot I had been to imagine otherwise.

'Oh, me too,' I replied. 'Well, I'll see you at work tomorrow.' I walked home feeling utterly dejected.

Being around Valerie day in, day out, it was hard not to get my hopes up again, even though I knew her feelings weren't going to change. She seemed to have plenty of time on her hands, though, and we soon began seeing each other more and more outside work, going to the cinema or to see plays. Sooner or later I knew she would get a boyfriend and her free evenings would suddenly dry up, but in the meantime it was bliss merely being in her presence.

The moment I had dreaded arrived sooner than I'd expected. One afternoon backstage, when I suggested a trip to the cinema, Valerie replied, 'I'm really sorry, Ronnie, but

I can't. I've agreed to spend this evening with someone else.'

Lucinda soon filled me in on the gossip. 'Valerie's got a date with my brother Jolien,' she told me cheerily.

'Oh, right,' I replied, trying my best to hide how I felt. Jolien was a lorry driver who made iron sculptures as a hobby, including the metal angel which hung above the main entrance to the theatre. He was both an artist and a 'real man', I thought ruefully – no wonder Valerie had chosen him over me. My mind flashed back to a Charles Atlas advert I had seen as a child, of a weedy man on the beach unable to stand up to a bully kicking sand in his face.

The next day I was dreading seeing Valerie again, worried about how I would cope with the awkwardness of the situation. I needn't have worried. 'Oh hello, Ronnie,' she called brightly as she arrived at the theatre. Her natural warmth cut through the embarrassment I was feeling, and I realised that nothing between us had really changed. We could still remain friends, and that meant a lot to me.

As it turned out, Valerie soon left the Little Angel to work on a new television puppet series, *The Adventures of Rupert the Bear*. But it wouldn't be long before our paths crossed again.

Meanwhile my own work at the Little Angel was opening doors to the glamorous world of television and film. Every so often, John Wright would be called upon to provide some puppetry expertise for a new screen production and would kindly bring me along with him to take part in the filming. In 1966 I made my screen debut in a BBC film called *A Touch of Don Juan* in which a puppet was required to portray the statue that sends the titular character to hell. John did all the real puppetry, of course – I just had to lift the statue's arm at the right moment – but it was a thrill just to see the inside of BBC Television Centre, and my mum was suitably impressed when I told her I was going to be on the telly.

A few years later I was given my own starring role in the Cold War spy thriller *A Dandy in Aspic* – or at least in the credit sequence which ran before the film proper began. The director had a vision of a helpless marionette caught up in the tussle between East and West, dragged this way and that across the screen by sinister, unseen puppetmasters. I was delighted to be offered the chance to operate the marionette, although the work went against almost everything John had taught me – I had to violently yank the poor puppet back and forth until it was tangled in its own strings, while the director egged me on from behind the camera, bellowing, 'Go mad! Pull it harder!' Despite my professional discomfort, I did as I was told, but eventually I reached my limit: when the man demanded I throw the puppet on the floor, I point-blank refused. As far as I was concerned, it was like asking a violinist to drop their instrument.

Despite my protest the director was happy with the footage and when the film went on general release several months later I rushed to the Odeon at Elephant and Castle to see it. I'm afraid I couldn't tell you a thing about the complex machinations of the espionage plot – all I remember from that trip to the cinema was the intense excitement of those first couple of minutes, seeing my puppet several metres tall, up on the screen. To me, that was far more thrilling than anything that happened in the movie.

While I was being seduced by the silver screen, John Wright had his sights set on mainstream respectability. Unlike many puppeteers, he had always seen himself more as an artist than an entertainer – the Little Angel shows might have been designed primarily for kids, but as far as he was concerned that was no reason not to produce high-quality, serious work. If the adults in the audience weren't equally enthralled then, in John's eyes, we had failed in our job.

Understandably, then, he was delighted when, after years building up a solid local following in Islington, the Little Angel was asked to participate in a major new music festival at the Queen Elizabeth Hall on London's South Bank. We would be performing a puppet version of Stravinsky's ballet *The Soldier's Tale*, with Daniel Barenboim conducting the orchestra. It was to be by far the biggest production the Little Angel had ever mounted, and we were given almost a year to pull it all together. We had to hire a whole new workshop to make the incredible puppets which Lyndie had designed, including the Devil and a horde of near-life-size flying horses.

It was a so-called black-theatre production, so the puppeteers were dressed head-to-toe in black on a black stage, with the lights carefully arranged so that the puppets were clearly visible as we moved around but we remained hidden in shadow. The style had become popular among Czech puppeteers but was still seen as radically avant-garde in England.

We used giant rod puppets, some of them more than 6 ft high, and the stage we performed on had a huge 50 ft proscenium arch. Christopher Leith returned to the Little Angel for the first time since his argument with John and the two of us operated the large soldier puppet together. It was my ideal job: a sweeping, classical performance in a full-size theatre, not just the cramped confines of the Little Angel.

The show was a tremendous success and was feted in all the national papers. The *Guardian* reviewer even commented that our puppets performed their parts better than any human beings could have. The festival organisers were so pleased that they invited us back for two more shows in the following years: an adaptation of Quentin Blake's story *Angelo*, in the Purcell Room, and Gian Carlo Menotti's opera *Amahl and the Night Visitors* in the Queen Elizabeth Hall. Puppetry, it seemed, was suddenly being accepted into the theatrical mainstream, and the Little Angel was at the heart of the action.

One day I was in the Little Angel workshop helping to make some puppets for our new show, *The Hubble Bubbles*, when we were paid a surprise visit by two rather superior women from Thames Television, a franchise of ITV. They told John they were researching a new series called *Rainbow*, which they hoped would be the British answer to *Sesame Street*. My ears pricked up immediately: the American preschool programme, which used Jim Henson's Muppet characters, had already made waves among British puppeteers and was ITV's most popular kids' import. (The BBC had refused to touch it because it felt that using advertising techniques, such as jingles, in a children's programme was 'immoral'.)

The elder of our two visitors was a producer called Pamela Lonsdale, who had been behind a very successful television adaptation of *The Lion, the Witch and the Wardrobe*. Thames had given Pamela an open brief to devise their new flagship preschool programme, which would be one of four being produced by different ITV franchises – the others were ATV's *Inigo Pipkin*, featuring an elderly puppet-maker in his workshop, Yorkshire Television's *Mr Trimble*, about a man who lived in an attic with a puppet goldfish, and *Hickory House* from Granada, about a woman with a grouchy mop head and a talking cushion. Pamela had also decided that puppets would be a central part of her programme and had brought her researcher, Sue Hansen, along to the Little Angel with her to explore their potential. When John ushered them into the workshop I was working on one of my *Hubble Bubbles*, which had a head shaped like a potato and a zip across its mouth. I could have sworn I saw a flicker of interest in Sue's eyes but she quickly turned her attention back to John, who was giving them his grand tour, demonstrating the different types of puppets through the ages.

As they got ready to leave, Pamela turned to John and said, 'We'll be looking for one or two puppeteers to work on the programme. I don't suppose you have anybody who might be interested?'

I was about to jump out of my chair and shout 'Take me! Take me!' when John replied, in a slightly condescending manner, 'Oh no, I don't think so. We do much more sophisticated work here.' Pamela nodded politely, and she and her companion walked out of the door.

I didn't dare say anything to John, but inwardly I was fuming. This could have been my big break: a regular television job – on the British answer to *Sesame Street*, no less. I felt I had missed out on a golden opportunity.

As it turned out, my loss was someone else's gain – and I owed that someone a favour, in any case. A few months after the researchers had been to visit the Little

Angel, I had a call from my old friend Violet Philpott at the EPA. She told me that she had been asked to provide the puppetry for a series called *Rainbow* which was about to begin filming in Teddington, south-west London. There were to be three puppets: Moony and Sunshine, a pair of sock-type glove puppets who would provide little inset comedy moments, and Zippy, a larger, orange creature who would comment on the goings-on in the *Rainbow* house. Violet was already hard at work making the puppets in preparation for the pilot episode.

I thought back to that visit at the Little Angel and remembered the *Hubble Bubbles* puppet that I had been working on at the time.

'Sorry, Violet, what was that last one called again?' I asked.

'Zippy. It has a kind of zip across its mouth.'

Oh, really, I thought to myself.

It was in the autumn of 1972, around the time of my twenty-fifth birthday, that *Rainbow* was first released upon an unsuspecting audience. By then, Pamela Lonsdale had already made some changes in personnel. The pilot episode, which featured a 6 ft bear called Rainbow and used largely improvised dialogue, had not met her high standards so she had brought in an established writer, John Kershaw, along with a human presenter, David Cook, to try again. The bear character, now christened Bungle, was played by John Leeson, who later provided the voice of Doctor Who's robot dog K9.

I tuned in to watch the first episode, partly because I knew it was a big deal for Violet, and partly to wonder ruefully about the job that might have been. My jealousy faded pretty quickly. The presenter was very nice but he was about as wooden as a puppet himself: 'Hello [pause]. We're drawing circles [pause]. Can you do that?' *Rainbow* was hardly the equal of the high-energy *Sesame Street*, with its vivid, extravagant Muppets.

To make matters worse, the Bungle character, though introduced as a bear, looked more like a demented fox. Its head was too small for its body, with freaky, monster eyes that didn't suit its pleasant, old-school-BBC demeanour, and its fur was made of mangy nylon.

Meanwhile, the supposed comic relief provided by Moony and Sunshine was distinctly unfunny:

Sunshine: If a square has got four sides and a triangle has got three sides, how many sides have you got, Moony?

Moony: I don't know. How many?

Sunshine: Two – *inside* and *outside*. Ha, ha, ha.

Telltale, the band who had been hired to provide the music, had done a good job with the show's theme tune but they weren't exactly pop stars – more like a pair of young hippies and their balding, moustachioed uncle. The lyrics of their songs hardly inspired confidence, either:

> I know a shape, it's just right for me,
> I'd be a square, that's what I'd be.

But the biggest disappointment for me was Zippy. Violet had made him as a lip-sync puppet in the Muppet style, but his bottom lip was attached to a string that she had to pull on, rather than being part of the main glove. This meant that whenever he spoke it looked like he was sticking out his tongue to catch flies. Then there was the voice. Zippy had a rather kind, thoughtful tone, courtesy of Peter Hawkins, who had previously provided the voices for *Watch With Mother* favourites Bill and Ben. What's more, he was perpetually stuck outside the house, peering in through a window; the smaller puppets Sunshine and Moony (voiced by Peter and Violet respectively) suffered similar treatment and were relegated to a blank tabletop. It seemed as if the producers didn't really understand what puppets could do, so they had kept them at arm's length (so to speak), outside the main action.

Of course, I told Violet that I absolutely loved it, but secretly I felt I'd had a lucky escape. There was no doubt in my mind that the show would be axed within the month.

Around this time, John Thirtle decided to move in with his boyfriend, another puppeteer called Ian Allen, so I took a room above a restaurant called The Tasty Palate on Islington's Essex Road, just around the corner from the Little Angel. The rent was extremely cheap but it turned out there were a couple of catches. The first was that I was expected to sweep the floor of the restaurant every night. The second was that I was repeatedly asked to attend meetings held by the building's owners, who were a pair of committed spiritualists. Terrified that they might offer to put my father on the line, I always made my excuses, and did my best to avoid bumping into them on the stairs.

John and Ian began making a mark together with their company Playboard Puppets, and before long I heard that John had been called in by Thames Television to take over from Violet because she had suffered a back injury. Poor Violet had been having a rough time in the *Rainbow* studio. Crouching behind the window for hours at a time, she had been increasingly uncomfortable but, ever the obliging puppeteer, she hadn't dared to say anything. She had eventually asked if they could change the set at all, but was told it would be far too expensive. Not long after that she slipped a disc, which left her bedridden for nearly a year.

While Violet's puppetry duties went to John, her voice was still needed for Moony, the morose, mauve glove puppet who appeared in the less than hilarious comedy inserts. This meant that Peter Hawkins, who voiced

Sunshine, had to go round to her flat every week with the sound crew to record their dialogue. Violet would be lying on the floor, trying to keep her spine in alignment, all the while reciting the rather feeble comedy routines – a grim fate for such a talented puppeteer.

Violet's back eventually recovered, but unsurprisingly she had no desire to return to work on *Rainbow* so John took over full time. Around the same period, my friend Nigel Plaskitt from the EPA, who was now working as a puppeteer in his own right, scored a job on one of *Rainbow*'s sister shows, *Inigo Pipkin*. I was starting to feel like I had been left behind by the telly train, while all my friends were hopping aboard. I began to feel the green-eyed monster creeping up on me. And there was more – before long, I learned that Valerie Heberden (the gorgeous brunette whom I had moped over at the Little Angel) had been brought in to *Rainbow* to operate a new character that John Thirtle was busy making.

I consoled myself with the thought that I had a good job of my own at the Little Angel, and in any case *Rainbow* was hardly a classic. I still had hopes that one day I would pick up the phone to hear Gerry Anderson's grave voice summoning me to lend my talents to International Rescue.

Curious to see what my friends were up to, I decided to tune in to *Rainbow* once again. What I saw could have been a completely different programme. In place of David Cook, with his rather prim persona, was the young and easy-going Geoffrey Hayes. Geoffrey had landed the job by accident. A semi-regular on the BBC's cop series *Z Cars*, he had been shooting a bit part in a soap opera at Thames when he ran into John Leeson, alias Bungle, in the corridor. The two knew each other from regional repertory theatre. At that point both John and David Cook were planning to leave the show, and John told Geoffrey the producer was in the middle of casting their replacements. Before Geoffrey could stop and think, he had agreed to let John take him to Pamela's office to try out for the part. She liked what she saw in the attractive blond young man, and Geoffrey took the job, thinking it would just be a stopgap for a few months before his next hard-hitting drama series.

As well as having a new presenter, the revamped *Rainbow* had a new musical troupe, Telltale having been replaced by the much cooler trio of Julian Littman, Karl Johnson and Charmian Dore. Moony and Sunshine had been ditched altogether, and Bungle was almost unrecognisable, with soft, teddy-bear fur in place of the cheap nylon, and a head much more in proportion with his body. Meanwhile, inside the suit was a new actor, Stanley Bates.

But the biggest change I noticed was in the puppets. John Thirtle had completely remade Zippy, with a proper lip-sync mouth instead of Violet's string arrangement, and the improvement was huge. His voice had changed too, with Roy Skelton – best known as the voice of the Daleks in *Doctor Who* – having taken over from Peter Hawkins. Cheekier and more sarcastic, Zippy was at last allowed to have a bit of character and get involved in the stories rather than just politely commenting as events unfolded.

Though Moony had gone, the soft, quiet and gentle aspects of her character had gone into the new puppet, George, a pink fluffy hippo with long, batting eyelashes on a nifty finger control, designed from scratch by John and, like Zippy, voiced by Roy. The two puppets had a wonderful dynamic between them, with George's niceness allowing Zippy even more scope to be naughty. Even better, the puppets were no longer forced to remain behind a window, but could pop up from behind the kitchen table as well (always tastefully dressed with a tablecloth to hide the puppeteers underneath). Evidently, someone had decided that puppets could be house-trained.

Each character now had his own clearly defined personality: the bungling bear, the simpering hippo, the arrogant... well, whatever Zippy was. As a result, a much more interesting dynamic had begun to develop between them, with Geoffrey playing the role not just of presenter, but of long-suffering parent figure to a rabble of (presumably adopted) children.

The show was still pursuing an educational agenda,

but with genuine character comedy thrown into the mix, entertaining as well as educating its audience. There was a lot more energy than in the first episode I had seen, and even the odd moment of slapstick, such as Bungle getting over-excited and accidentally tripping Geoffrey up, much to Zippy's delight.

In less than a year, *Rainbow* had transformed from a dull, humourless failure into a real triumph. Once again, I could feel the pangs of jealousy beginning to strike.

One day in October 1973 I was sweeping the floor of the restaurant when I heard the phone ringing upstairs in my flat. I put down my broom and ran up to answer the call, hoping not to encounter my spiritualist landlords on the way.

'Hello?' I panted into the receiver.

'Hi, Ronnie, it's John Thirtle,' came the reply. 'Are you alright to talk?'

'Yes, of course, John,' I said. 'What's up?'

'Well, you know this programme *Rainbow* that I've been doing?'

'Oh, yes?' I tried my best to sound nonchalant, as if my friend's TV stardom had barely made an impression.

'Well, the thing is, I've been offered some other work I want to do that clashes.'

'Oh, right,' I said. 'Congratulations.' Some people seemed to have all the luck.

'They asked if I could recommend anyone.'

There was a pause while the cogs in my brain turned ever so slowly, taking in what John was saying.

'I put your name down. I hope that's alright.'

I was speechless: from nowhere, right out of the blue, I had landed my own telly gig, on a programme that was already a roaring success. And John said I didn't even need to audition, just turn up that Thursday to meet everyone. 'Don't worry,' he told me. 'Just make sure when you meet our producer, Pamela, that you name-drop Muffin the Mule – that'll impress her.'

'Right,' I replied, still in shock.

As soon as I hung up the phone, a terrifying thought struck me and I began to panic. I grabbed the receiver again and swiftly dialled John's number. Mercifully, he answered right away.

'John!' I said, urgently. 'What should I wear?'

'Don't worry, Ronnie,' John laughed. 'They couldn't care less about that. Just be yourself, and I promise you'll be fine.'

Chapter 4: Into the Rainbow

For the next few days I tuned in religiously at noon to catch the latest episode of *Rainbow*, studying John's operation of Zippy like an obsessive fan and committing his every move to memory. By the time Thursday came around the show had assumed an iconic status in my mind, and the thought of meeting these television idols made me feel like a star-struck teenager.

On Thursday morning I made the train journey to Teddington, sitting nervously among the suited commuters, who were no doubt on their way to 'proper' jobs. From the station I walked the half-mile to Teddington Studios, a rather nondescript, modern building complex with a little white portico out front, and made my way straight to reception. Above the desk was a board displaying the shooting schedule for the day: Studio One – *The Tommy Cooper Hour*; Studio Two – *The Tomorrow People*; and there, in big bold letters, 'Studio Three – *Rainbow*'.

I told the lady behind the desk that I was here to see Pamela Lonsdale and before long a researcher was dispatched to fetch me. We walked past an imposing pair of double doors labelled Studio Three, with a red 'Do Not Enter' light above them, and into an antechamber with a large glass panel in the wall that looked directly onto the studio's control room.

Inside the control room was a wall of TV screens with a bank of desks in front, where an array of people were pointing and conferring with each other. I spotted a perfectly coiffed short, blonde hairdo and recognised Pamela. She turned around and mimed at me through the glass: 'Good to see you – we'll speak later.'

On the screens I could see what was happening inside the studio. Recording had not yet begun and everyone was bustling around, setting things up. I caught a glimpse of John Thirtle with the Zippy puppet draped over his arm and watched as the stagehands jovially shifted scenery, passing out of one monitor and into another. At the very edge of one of the screens I could see a man in his early forties sitting in a little booth with a microphone, puffing away on a cigar. I guessed that this must be Roy Skelton, who did the voices for Zippy and George – then the camera moved slightly and he was gone. On another screen, Geoffrey Hayes was chatting to a floor manager – only it wasn't quite Geoffrey as I'd seen him on TV. This was the real man behind the *Rainbow* persona, looking serious and thoughtful as he carefully walked through his movements for the scene. Then someone shouted 'Action!' and it was as if a switch had flicked: suddenly, there was the charming, energetic guy I had seen on the programme, chatting away with Bungle, while Zippy and George popped up from behind the kitchen table.

After each shot, the two puppets would drop back down behind the table and Bungle would whisk off his head to reveal Stanley Bates, a short, dark-haired fellow who looked exhausted and was dripping with sweat. When the director was ready to go again Stanley would reluctantly don the bear-head and suddenly Bungle would be back.

An hour or so after I had arrived, the first episode of the day was in the can and the cast were told they could break for lunch. Zippy and George disappeared, and from behind the table popped up John and the gorgeous Valerie. I made my way down to the corridor and waited for them to emerge from the door marked 'Green Room'. John appeared first, followed by Valerie.

'Hi, Ronnie. We're all going for lunch in the restaurant,' he said. 'I think Pamela must be doing it in your honour because normally we eat in the canteen.'

Valerie could see I was nervous so she whispered to me, 'Don't worry, they're all very nice.'

John grabbed my arm. 'But first, let me introduce you to someone,' he said. He led me through the green room – waving briefly to Geoffrey and Stanley, who were getting changed – and onto the studio floor. It was smaller than I had imagined, but that did nothing to dampen my excitement. There were the various cameras on their tracks and the rack of lights up above, while the set for the *Rainbow* house took up about half the floor space. Behind it, a huge cyclorama cut across the middle of the studio; on the other side of this was where the musicians would record their performances.

John led me behind the kitchen table. 'Ronnie, meet Zippy,' he said, picking up a limp bundle of orange towelling with an incongruous rugby-ball shape at one end.

'May I?' I asked, taking the puppet from John's hands.

'Of course.'

Zippy was lighter than I had expected. I reached my arm inside and took hold of the lip-sync mechanism. 'Hello, John,' I said, in my best imitation of Roy's voice work.

'That's good,' John told me. 'But make sure you keep your wrist at a right angle. It's a bit painful after a while but it looks much better on camera.'

I adjusted my wrist, looking at the puppet as I did so. He was right – if I let my wrist relax and straighten even slightly, Zippy seemed to look up at the ceiling.

John then produced another bit of orange towelling from beneath the table. 'And this,' he said proudly, 'is the arm.'

Watching the show, I had always assumed that the arm was just part of the main puppet, but it turned out to be a separate piece entirely, essentially just a long three-fingered orange glove. 'You need to make sure you don't stretch too far or he'll end up looking like an octopus,' John advised me.

I knelt down on the floor, so that my body was hidden behind the table, and started working the puppet, one hand in the head and the other in the arm. John stepped around to the front of the table to get a better view.

'Does this look alright?' I asked him.

'You can see for yourself.' John came back behind the table, crouched down next to me and switched on a small monitor by my knees. 'Can you leave Camera Three on, please?' he shouted to a chap across the studio.

A tiny black-and-white image fizzled into life on the screen. There it was, plain as day: Zippy, behind the table – and I was operating him.

'It's reverse-scan, which makes it easier,' John informed me. 'Just imagine you're doing it in front of a mirror.' I practised some more, while he peered at the monitor over my shoulder. 'Good work,' he said encouragingly. 'Now all you have to master is the lip-sync.'

A little affronted, I brought Zippy around to look John in the face. 'I'm perfectly good at that, thank you very much!' the puppet rebuked him. Perhaps Zippy's arrogance was already rubbing off on me.

'Ah, but that's easy,' replied John. 'The trick is to do it when Roy's the one speaking, not you.'

'Right,' I said quietly, reverting to my normal voice.

67

'So, any questions?' asked John.

'Just one,' I said, my knees creaking as I stood up and set Zippy down on the table. 'Did you never think of asking for a cushion?'

In the restaurant, John introduced me to the rest of the cast. Geoffrey, as I had already observed from the control room, was a quiet and reserved character in person. He said a polite 'How do you do?' and we left it at that. Roy, Zippy's voice man, couldn't have been more different. I was aware of the lingering aroma of his cigar as he shook my hand, proclaiming, 'Oh, hello darling.' Roy, was charming and a true luvvie in every respect, from the fruity RADA voice to the endless name-dropping. 'You know, *Larry* and I were very close,' he told me, when I mentioned my fondness for Olivier. Stanley Bates, the sweaty fellow who played Bungle, was in his early thirties and less overwhelming than Roy, but equally warm and welcoming. Then there were the musicians: Julian, Charmian ('Charlie') and Karl. Charlie was gorgeous – with long, straight, brown hair, she looked a bit like an American folk singer – and all three of them were very friendly to me. Finally, in strode Pamela Lonsdale: the big cheese. She had the demeanour of a prim headmistress from the 1950s – kind, but very firm.

The 'interview' itself was a fairly relaxed affair, at least for everyone else – I was pretty nervous, talking to a table of TV celebrities. Pamela asked what sort of work I had done previously, so I took her through the highlights of my career at the Little Angel and the tour with Clifford Heap's Miniature Theatre Company.

'Ah, the life of the open road,' Roy sighed, nostalgically.

Then I remembered John Thirtle's advice. 'Oh, and I worked with Muffin the Mule,' I said hastily, hoping that the name-dropping didn't sound too obvious. It evidently worked, as I saw an approving look pass across Pamela's face.

She never asked to see me operate a puppet, which I thought rather odd. John and Valerie must have both vouched for me, but I suspect Muffin was the referee who really got me the job. At any rate, when the lunch plates were cleared away, Pamela took a quick glance around the table, lingering ever so slightly on Geoffrey, before turning back and extending her hand towards me.

'Ronnie,' she said, 'I'd like you to start as soon as possible.'

'Thank you!' I replied, beaming. 'I'd love to.'

'Wonderful. How does tomorrow sound?'

The next morning morning I sat on the train to Teddington, feeling a peculiar mixture of excitement and guilt. The night before, I had broken the news about the job to John Wright at the Little Angel and been met with a subdued response. I didn't want to sever my ties with the theatre – as I told him, this *Rainbow* lark would probably only last six weeks – so I reassured him that I fully intended to keep performing in his weekend marionette shows. 'You do still have to rehearse you know, Ronnie,' had been the reply. In the end we had struck a deal: I had discovered that Fridays at *Rainbow* were normally a half day so I would come to the Little Angel after lunch, rehearse until six o'clock and do the performances the next day – after all, having spent several years reprising the theatre's back catalogue, it wasn't as if I needed much practice.

Friday mornings at *Rainbow* were dedicated to a read-through of the new scripts for the following week. After the relative glamour of Studio Three, arriving at the rehearsal space for the first time was something of a shock: my directions had taken me to a yacht club. I went up a flight of stairs and into a draughty hall, worrying that I had got it wrong and was about to intrude on an amateur dramatics society. But no, there were the *Rainbow* gang in all their morning glory: Geoffrey, staring rather morosely into a cup of tea; Roy, spluttering over a cigar he was trying to light; Stanley, looking smaller without his Bungle suit; and a head of curly brown hair that turned around to reveal Valerie's smiling face.

I made a beeline for Valerie and she offered me a cup of tea to steady my obvious nerves. 'This is Daphne Shadwell,' she said, introducing me to a woman standing next to her, 'our director for next week.' Daphne was a lovely lady in her late forties and would become one of the most prolific directors of *Rainbow*. I was lucky to have such a safe pair of hands for my first day on the show. Each series of *Rainbow* usually had three directors on rotation, which meant that the style of programme could vary wildly within each series – as could the rehearsal process. Since it was a puppet show there were quite a few directors with a Variety background, and their attitude was more or less 'You go on and do your act, darling.' By contrast, someone like Daryl Blake, a serious theatre and television drama director, would agonise over the scripts, turning to a perplexed Bungle or Zippy and asking, 'Now, what is the thought process behind that line?'

Some directors were assigned to *Rainbow* as a training ground and didn't have a single clue what they were doing. Daphne, however, had been in the business for years and was very experienced in children's television. Her approach was that of a sweet-natured auntie, and she made me feel like one of the team straight away. 'Just listen to Roy in the read-through, dear, and if you've got any questions, feel free to ask,' she told me.

At that moment, in marched our producer, Pamela, closely followed by her PA, and the writer, John Kershaw – a friendly, easy-going chap who penned many of the early *Rainbow* scripts. Like a roomful of naughty schoolchildren, everyone jumped to attention. Geoffrey suddenly became animated, looking up from his tea with an obliging smile, and we all scuttled over to take our seats around a large table.

The scripts for next week's filming were handed round: three shows about different occupations, entitled 'Bus Driver', 'Police' and 'Nurse'. Valerie and I followed them silently as the others began to read out their lines. Suddenly, it was as if Zippy, George and Bungle were in the room with us, talking and arguing just as they did on television – only they were nowhere to be seen. Instead, their voices were coming out of two very normal-looking gentlemen, one of whom appeared to be having a conversation with himself, as if he was suffering from multiple-personality disorder. I tried hard to repress an overwhelming desire to giggle at this surreal situation, made worse when I peeked over my script at Pamela and saw a look of absolute seriousness and concentration on her face.

Pamela held a stopwatch in her hand and at the end of each script would bark out the running time: 'Twenty minutes – too long! Lose five!' Invariably the problem was that there was just too much material, and the disappointed writer would be told to hack his magnum opus down to size.

Next it was time to work out the blocking – how the characters moved around in each scene – and, to my relief, Pamela and the writer left us alone to get on with it. Tape on the floor roughly marked out the space we had available. There was a table about the same size as the one on the actual set, and two chairs represented the window.

I was starting to wonder if I was in an am-dram production after all.

Valerie and I unzipped the bags containing the puppets. To my horror, what faced me was not the familiar bright-orange rugby-ball head but a tatty, faded, paint-splattered thing that looked like a poor imitation of Zippy. Had John Thirtle made off with the real one on his last day in the studio, and left me with a dud?

Of course, he had done no such thing. Valerie explained that these were the rehearsal puppets, former Zippies and Georges who had served their time on the show and had now been demoted, replaced by newer versions made by John for filming. The rehearsal puppets were much more malleable, she told me. In fact, the new ones were always very stiff to begin with; opening their mouths was hand-achingly difficult, and in between takes they would be seen yawning repeatedly as she and John tried to stretch them into submission.

As we went over the scenes I tried hard to keep up with Zippy's lines, making sure I was opening his mouth at the right time. Looking down at the script while performing the puppet up above me proved very tricky, so after a while I stopped following the words on the page and just listened out for Roy's voice instead. It helped that he usually preceded his lines with little non-verbal cues – a friendly gurgling for George and a grumbling 'Argh, argh, argh' for Zippy. Roy's own script was marked up with a squiggle next to George's lines and a straight line next to Zippy's, and I was amazed how quickly he could switch between the two, all the time puffing away like a chimney on his cigar.

When we reached the end of the third script and Pamela was satisfied with the timings, she cheerfully dismissed us for the weekend. Poor Stanley and Geoffrey had to be sure to learn their lines before Monday morning. Roy, Valerie and I didn't need to, of course, as the cameras never saw us – but desperate to prove myself to Pamela, I spent most of the weekend poring over Zippy's lines anyway, like a little swot hoping to impress the teacher.

Monday and Tuesday were spent back in the yacht club, rehearsing all three shows with just the cast and director present. We always had the deadline of 3 p.m. on Tuesday looming over us – the moment when Pamela would arrive to watch us give a complete run-through. At the end of my first performance, Pamela and Daphne quietly withdrew together and we sat there waiting to hear what their verdict would be. It felt excruciating to me, like awaiting exam results.

'That's fine, everybody,' came the response, finally, and I breathed a sigh of relief.

I didn't sleep at all that night, knowing that tomorrow was my first filming day. We had two episodes to get through by 7:30 p.m. Wednesday and another to film on Thursday morning. I was so anxious not to be late that I got in two hours early and ended up sitting in the Teddington Studios canteen, eating breakfast on my own.

At 9:30 a.m. I joined the others in Studio Three and immediately went over to check that the right Zippy puppet was waiting for me on my chair behind the table. My hand had barely brushed against its furry head when a loud voice shouted, 'Oi! Don't ya dare touch anyfink!' It was Sid, the Studio Three props man, who had been there since 7 a.m. pulling down the set for *Magpie* and putting up ours – and the last thing he wanted was some wet-behind-the-ears puppeteer coming along to mess it up. Thanks to strict union rules, everyone working in television was very protective of their own particular area of expertise and they didn't appreciate anyone else coming in and stepping on their toes; it was very different to the puppetry world, where we all just mucked in with whatever needed doing. I had to keep reminding myself not to move any of my props. If I did, someone would soon whisper in my ear, 'Sid'll do that' and I'd have to put them back the way they were.

Sid was a friendly bloke, however, and a great talker. A cockney geezer to the core, he loved nothing better than a crude joke. Behind Pamela's back he was always remarking what a 'nice pair of Bristols' she had or referring to her as 'Titsalina'. I was terrified that one day she would catch me in conversation with him and assume

I shared his sentiments. He also liked to employ his skills in prop-making by fashioning Plasticine turds and leaving them around the studio. If Pamela ever encountered one she would simply lift her foot and step gracefully over it, her nose held high in the air.

As soon as we started work, however, Sid became the complete professional. His straight-talking, honest approach was much valued by the cast – he had been in the business for years and clearly knew what he was talking about. If Sid said a show had been really good, it was a great compliment, and if he told you it could have been better, you took his words to heart. Eventually Sid became our comrade in arms, sticking up for us if a floor manager or director insisted we use a prop that we all knew looked wrong next to the puppets or made our work too difficult. Giving us a cheeky wink, he would say, 'They wanted you to have this – Pah! – but don't worry, I'll find you a better one.'

As I waited for my first day's filming to begin, I picked up a camera script to have a look at the running order of the shows. The blue front cover of the document had a big red *Rainbow* logo at the top and underneath it, on the cast list, there it was: 'PUPPETEER: RONNIE LE DREW'. While I was busy experiencing a head rush at the mere sight of my name on the script, it was clear from the expressions on the faces of the rest of the cast that they all considered the camera rehearsal a deathly boring experience. They had a point: it usually involved hanging around for at least four hours while the director ran through the technical process of the show, explaining to the cameramen when to zoom in or pan across, with we performers occasionally called upon to run the odd line.

It was a small, stuffy studio, and with all the cast and crew in there under the bright lights it got hotter and hotter with each passing hour. My arm was aching already from holding up Zippy and I tried to snatch a little rest whenever I wasn't needed so that I wouldn't get too sweaty – God forbid that Valerie would notice the spreading wet patches under my arms. Stanley had it much worse – his predecessor had been reduced to taking salt tablets to prevent the worst effects of dehydration caused by the dreaded Bungle suit, and on several occasions had to be sent home in a taxi after almost passing out during some of the more energetic scenes. Stanley was good at standing up for himself, though, and generally refused to wear more than the Bungle head and gloves during camera rehearsals. Daphne was very understanding about this, but every time a new director came in they would demand to see what he looked like in the whole costume and Stanley would once again insist, 'I will not get into that bear until the dress rehearsal.'

After lunch in the canteen, we had one hour's dress rehearsal and then the filming proper began. I was surprised to discover that we didn't get to speak to the director face-to-face during filming. Instead, everything was done through the floor manager, part of whose job was to translate an exasperated director's comments into something more tactful.

The thing I found hardest was making sure Zippy was facing the right camera at the right time – and remembering where on earth I had to be for each scene. At one point I was sitting calmly under the kitchen table when I realised I was about to gatecrash a little moment between Geoffrey and Bungle; meanwhile, Valerie was back behind the window wondering where on earth I had got to. The problem was that, while all the instructions were on my camera script, I had to put this down while I was working Zippy. Inevitably someone would then pick it up or move it, leaving me under the table in a blind panic about where I was meant to be next. In the end my solution was to keep an eye on Roy. If he wasn't in what was referred to as 'Roy's hole' – the little space he sat in with his chair and sound box – it was usually safe to assume that Zippy and George weren't needed in the scene.

When the cast weren't needed for a while – for example, when the musicians were recording their segments – they quickly disappeared to the green room to make the most of the much-needed break. But being the new boy I was too scared to leave the studio for fear of missing something. Fortunately I had a kindred spirit in cameraman number three. A new trainee, he was equally glued to the spot, too scared to leave his camera, so the two of us remained in the boiling hot studio for almost the entire ten-hour day.

As the closing scene of my first show finally drew to an end, Valerie and I were behind the window with Zippy and George, waving goodbye to the *Rainbow* viewers while the credits began to roll, just as I had seen so many times on television. To me, it felt like a huge milestone, and the relief was overwhelming. I stopped waving and stood straight up, mentally congratulating myself on my achievement – when across the studio floor rang out the words, 'Cut! Puppeteer in view!'

I'd only gone and wrecked the scene by standing up before the show was over – potentially destroying the belief of tens of thousands of little children that Zippy was real. Worse still, because of the way the show was filmed, as-live, in the studio, we were forced to rewind the tape and do the whole scene again. As I waved goodbye to the viewers a second time, I felt convinced that I was also waving goodbye to my job on *Rainbow*.

Afterwards we all sat down together with Pamela to watch the episode played back in the control room. First there was the Thames Television ident, with the London landmarks reflected in the river, accompanied by the 'Salute to Thames' tune, which had to be played onto the recording before each show. Next came the *Rainbow* opening sequence: the criss-crossing lines of colour which transformed into a rainbow then opened out like window shutters onto a little town. As the show started, I began to understand why even the most successful of actors often refused to watch their own work. I squirmed in my seat as I noticed Zippy blabbing away before his voice caught up with him or chatting to George while seeming to address some invisible person off in the middle distance. To me, ever the anxious perfectionist, it was full of mistakes, and when the credits rolled my face screwed up even tighter with embarrassment as I remembered how I had wrecked the last scene.

'Ronnie,' Pamela said, in a soothing tone that I assumed she always adopted when firing people.

'Yes?' I replied, quietly, waiting for the inevitable.

'That was marvellous,' she said, smiling. 'Well done.'

And then the ultimate compliment: 'It looked just like John's Zippy.'

I breathed an enormous sigh of relief.

That evening, after my second episode was committed to tape without incident, I returned on the train to Highbury triumphant. My salary on *Rainbow* was £125 per week – almost seven times what I had been earning at the Little Angel – and in anticipation of my first big paycheque I decided to blow all the money left in my bank account on a brand-new colour television. After all, how could I be in a show called *Rainbow* and still be watching it in black and white? When the programme went out,

Mum called immediately to congratulate me, insisting I go over for tea so that all her friends on the estate could coo over her newly famous TV-star son. The listing in that week's *TV Times* had been carefully cut out and put on the mantelpiece as evidence of my success. Finally, my dolly-waggling had become a source of family pride.

Chapter 5: Getting my hand in

As I spent more time on the *Rainbow* set, I became increasingly aware that my most important relationship was with Roy, the actor who provided Zippy's voice. He and I had to learn to perform as a single entity, and over time we developed an unconscious, almost symbiotic connection that meant even without a script I could reflect what he was about to say. This was crucial if one of us had to cover for the other and improvise our way out of a scrape. In one episode Zippy was sporting a wig, and when I got too carried away with a flamboyant movement it fell off his head mid-scene. I was waiting for the director to shout 'Cut!' when Roy suddenly started improvising. 'Pick that up, will you, Bungle?' he demanded, and without realising it I found myself moving Zippy's mouth in sync. Stanley put the wig back on Zippy's head and we finished the scene with no need to rewind the tape. The relationship worked the other way around as well – if I improvised a bored finger-tapping movement in response to Geoffrey or Bungle babbling on, Roy would make a grumbling noise to go with it.

Luckily, Roy and I got on pretty well, but he did rub certain people up the wrong way. He could be a bit of a drama queen if things didn't go according to plan and, just like Zippy, if he got ill you never heard the end of it – a common cold would be treated like tuberculosis. Stanley found him more frustrating than most, complaining about the endlessly repeated stories of the glory days of acting and the constant name-dropping.

One day when Roy had launched into a familiar anecdote about the time he worked with Alfred Hitchcock, I interrupted cheekily, 'Goodness me, Roy! Isn't it the fiftieth time you've told that story?'

Roy huffed a bit and said, in a mock-imperious tone, 'Oh, I'm terribly sorry, am I boring you?' But my gentle prod seemed to work – he didn't mention Hitch for at least a week, much to Stanley's relief.

What bothered me more than the stories, though, were the cigars. Roy smoked everywhere, morning, noon and night, and the whole set reeked of it. A lot of the cast and crew were smokers too, so they didn't mind, but Valerie and I couldn't stand the wretched smell. After a lengthy campaign – and lots of polite little coughs from Valerie – we at least persuaded Roy not to smoke in the windowless green room. However, the result was that he would generously forgo his midday cigar until he got to the canteen, so our lunch would be infused with tobacco instead.

Roy had a rather cheeky sense of humour – in fact his stories were often downright saucy, always laced with innuendo and double entendres, and he had one of those voices that made everything sound faintly suggestive. I once said to him, 'You know, Roy, you're very coarse,' and never heard the end of it. He thought it was hilarious, and for months afterwards if I ever commented on anything he had said or done he would retort, 'Well, what do you expect? I'm so *coarse*!' and burst out laughing. Around Valerie, however, Roy kept his dirty sense of humour in check and was as good as gold. Everyone in the cast loved Valerie – in fact, she gained the nickname The Lovely Valerie – but Roy was particularly fond of her and treated her with a fatherly affection.

Roy was the eldest of the cast by at least a decade and as a result, rather like Zippy, he seemed to view himself as the authority on practically everything. One episode featured a marionette from the Little Angel which I was operating for a brief insert scene. Roy had been in a show with some marionettes a few decades previously, and immediately began talking up his own puppetry skills.

'Oh yes, I'm a marvellous marionettist – everybody said so at the time,' he declared.

'Really, Roy?' I responded. 'Would you like to have a go then?'

Roy took the puppet off me and attempted to walk it across the floor. Its limbs flailed wildly and its strings were soon tangled up.

'Oh, this is different to the ones we used,' he muttered, handing it back to me and strolling off. He took the temporary humiliation entirely in his stride and was back to his old self within moments, offering Geoffrey tips on how to read a story.

Unsurprisingly, Roy's tendency to think he always knew best extended to the scripts as well. No Friday read-through was complete without him adding his own ideas about how a given story could be spiced up, and he occasionally won Pamela's consent for revisions. In particular he was always pushing to give Zippy a bit more of an edge. Here, though, he came up against a formidable opponent: Stephanie Connell, the show's education adviser. It was her job to make sure that every script conformed to Thames's strict requirements: that any art or craft in the programme could be easily copied by our preschool audience, that we only ever used round-nosed scissors and plastic crockery – and, most crucially, that our characters didn't set a bad example to children. This was the toughest bone of contention since Stephanie was highly sensitive to Zippy's bad behaviour, fearing that tens of thousands of children at home would copy his every huff and puff. So while Roy would always want Zippy to storm off in a strop, it would be Stephanie who insisted he came back and apologised.

As a perennial know-it-all, Roy was mortified if he was ever pulled up for a mistake – which made it all the funnier for the rest of us. The bright lights meant the studio always got very hot as the day wore on, and since Roy had a comfy booth to sit in, the afternoon slump would sometimes get the better of him. In the long break while the techies were preparing to shoot, snoring would be heard coming from the little booth. The floor manager would wake him up just in time for the take and Roy, flustered with embarrassment, would grab the first script to hand, often launching with full gusto into the wrong scene, or even the wrong episode.

Roy's other occasional error was to mix up Zippy's and George's lines, despite his special marks next to their names on the script. One time, when Zippy started speaking with George's voice, Valerie and I carried on, trying our best not to giggle. At the end of the scene I walked over to Roy's little booth and said, ever so nonchalantly, 'Did you realise that Zippy and George just swapped voices?'

An ashen look fell on Roy's face. 'Oh *no!*' he cried, leaping from his chair. Then he shouted up to the control room, 'They're telling me I made a mistake!'

'Maybe we should play the tape back, just to be sure,' suggested Stanley, enjoying the moment.

We all gathered round and the tape was duly played, revealing Roy's error. 'Oh *God*!' he wailed, holding his head in his hands. 'I'm *so* sorry, everyone! I made a terrible mistake!'

'OK, let's go for another take,' said the director. Roy skulked back to his booth while the rest of us stifled our laughter.

None of us could claim we didn't contribute our own share of bloopers, however. We kept a tally of how many takes were ruined by each of the programme's various teams, and whenever a mistake occurred someone would call out, 'That's three for Sound,' or 'Number five for Puppets,' or 'Geoffrey's on ten.'

Although we joked about them, an excessive number of mistakes would sour the atmosphere on set. We were on an extremely tight schedule and if things overran on a Wednesday we all went home with a horrible, sinking feeling in our stomachs, aware that we would have to work doubly fast the next day to make up for lost time. No one wanted to be the cause of one of those insanely stressful Thursday-morning shoots.

On a show that was recorded as quickly as *Rainbow*, directors would often go with something we weren't completely happy with, rather than take the time to reshoot it. Hence, every so often, if Geoffrey fluffed a line or Bungle knocked something over, the mistake would make it to broadcast. Ever the perfectionist, however, I took to sabotage to protect my own reputation, deliberately ruining a bad take so it couldn't be used. This was something John Thirtle had recommended to me before he left the show. 'It won't make you popular,' he confided, 'but the puppet is your responsibility and if something looks bad it's your right to do it again.'

I took John's words seriously. I had seen how on one of our sister shows, *Hickory House*, a mop of curly brown hair could sometimes be seen floating behind Humphrey Cushion on the sofa, and I didn't want to be responsible for similar crimes against puppetry. Looking at the monitor by my knees I could see if, for example, a bit of my arm suddenly became visible behind Zippy. As soon as I spotted something amiss, I would always force a cut by standing up and shouting, 'Sorry, I messed that one up,' to a chorus of groans around the studio.

John had also told me that it would be my responsibility to look out for the puppet's wellbeing, and as time went on I became increasingly protective of my little orange friend. I was mortified when one day I got ink on Zippy's fur while he was writing a letter. I put him in the wash but to my horror the dye in his towelling ran, and he came out looking much paler than usual. From then on I insisted that if any 'stunt work' was required, the retired rehearsal model would be called in for a cameo. Even so, such scenes were always a nightmare to film. Painting a picture two feet above your head is not easy, especially when you're watching it in reverse on a monitor wedged between your knees. Many a time would I proudly finish a painting only to discover, when I pulled the paper down to take a proper look, that my horse had mysteriously transformed into a cow. Felt-tip pens were not much better – they had a tendency to dry out under the harsh studio lights, so as I finally got round to drawing the little curly tail on a pig, the director would have to call 'cut' because the pen had run out. After a while the directors wised up to these problems and had pictures pre-drawn so that I only had to do the final stroke; or, even better, they would shoot down over Zippy's shoulder, which meant I could hold the head still and operate just the arm.

You might think that Geoffrey, who had no puppet arms to worry about and no bulky bear-head obscuring his vision, would have contributed fewer bloopers than the rest of us, but in fact he was one of the worst offenders. In his case the problem was almost always with his lines. For some reason, even though he remembered them all in rehearsal, once he was on the studio floor they went right out of his head. I suppose it was difficult for Geoffrey, playing the responsible adult of the show – he was the one who was supposed to be in charge, so he had to be on top of things at all times despite the distracting antics of Zippy, George and Bungle. He was also the only one who had to speak directly to the audience, so he had to remember which camera was on him. There were many times we would slog our way through a long and complicated scene, everyone doing their best to put in a good performance, and then just one or two lines from the end Geoffrey would suddenly dry. His mouth would open but no words would come out. We would all be silently willing him to say the next line, but when the pause had got just too long, the director would be forced to call 'Cut!' and the cameras would reset. 'Sorry, guys,' Geoffrey would say sheepishly, and the rest of us would do our best not to show our frustration.

To make matters worse for Geoffrey, Stanley was always word-perfect. He was one of those actors who merely had to glance at a script to commit it to memory – unlike Geoffrey, who would nervously pore over his words for hours in the green room. Stanley couldn't understand what Geoffrey found so hard about remembering a few simple lines, and, sweating like a pig in his bear suit, he would get frustrated at the resulting delays. 'Could you please try to get it right this time?' he would say after the umpteenth resct. Geoffrey hated to row, so instead he would go very quiet. He would do his best to fake a cheery persona for the cameras, but not always successfully. Under the kitchen table – or, in later years, behind the counter – I would often listen in on 'cans' – the headphones which the techies used to communicate with the control room – and hear the director bellowing to the floor manager, 'Put some life into that fucking presenter!'

With Stanley, the director's comments tended to be the opposite: 'Will someone tell that bear to calm down? He's flapping about like a lunatic!' Perhaps it was hard for Stanley to tell how big some of his gestures were, with the poor vision from inside the bear-head. Or perhaps he just enjoyed upstaging Geoffrey.

Stanley and Geoffrey were chalk and cheese, so maybe it's no surprise that there was a bit of a personality clash between them. Stanley was quite cultured – he had a fabulous flat near the Garrick Theatre in the West End (the Bates Motel, I called it) and was always inviting me to visit an exhibition with him or go to the opera. Like me, he would take on theatre work in the gaps between series, only for Stanley it was the classical repertoire. He was once interviewed in the *TV Times* about going straight from Bungle to a role in *Hamlet* and claimed the bear was the more challenging part.

Geoffrey, meanwhile, considered Stanley a bit of a soft southerner. His own background was in cop shows and he saw himself as a man of the people, proud of his Northern, working-class roots. He lived in a dingy flat with an enormously fat cat and always brought in a packed lunch of tripe and onions rather than eating what they served in the canteen. He was a quiet type, not at all a luvvie like Roy or Stanley, and always seemed happiest when hunched over a copy of the *Guardian* in the corner. It's not that Geoffrey was antisocial exactly but he liked to keep himself to himself; he was a serious, thoughtful person.

By contrast, Stanley was always looking for an opportunity for a bit of mischief: letting Bungle's pyjamas fall down in the middle of a bedroom scene, deliberately moving a prop just out of Zippy or George's reach or scooping one of the puppets into a hug that threatened to reveal the puppeteer beneath. The Bungle suit offered the perfect cover for his pranks, since he could always claim that his blinkered eyes were to blame. He would apparently have no sense of distance, standing uncomfortably close to Geoffrey or bunching the rest of us up at one end of the counter. It became a continual challenge to deal with whatever Stanley would throw at us, while he played the total innocent and made it look as though every mishap was by accident. One of his favourite ruses was to 'accidentally' knock Geoffrey's arm when he was making something. Geoffrey hated demonstrating any kind of art project on the show and seemed to find the most straightforward things impossible on camera. Stanley, even with his bear hands on, could always do them with ease and would often end up helping Geoffrey out – partly from a genuine desire to get things done and partly because he knew it really wound Geoffrey up. Sometimes Roy would wander over as well, and he and Stanley would take great pleasure in showing Geoffrey how easy the task was.

What Geoffrey hated more than anything was being made to look silly, which on a preschool puppet show was a bit of an occupational hazard. In fact, as John Thirtle had warned me when I first started, Geoffrey was not wild about the puppets at all. As far as he was concerned, *Rainbow* was his show – he was the presenter and the one in charge, and he didn't like to feel like the inmates were taking over the asylum. He was afraid of being upstaged by Zippy and George so he always liked to stand where he could keep an eye on them; a three-shot with Geoff in the middle and a puppet on either side of him was guaranteed to put him in an anxious mood.

Usually, it would be up to Pamela to reassure Geoffrey that everything was alright. With him she played the mother hen rather than the stern headmistress that she was with the rest of us. The two of them would frequently be seen having a private chat about some issue that Geoffrey was unhappy about, until she finally talked him into returning to the set. She also knew how to make Geoffrey feel good about himself, complimenting him on the horrifically garish shirts he always seemed to pick out on filming days. (Fashion was the one area in which Geoff's on-screen persona aligned perfectly with his 'real' identity – in fact, whenever he took a fancy to a particularly hideous outfit, the danger was that he'd want to wear it for every episode and would have to be gently coaxed into trying something else.)

Deep down, I'm not sure Geoffrey was ever really comfortable as a presenter because it meant putting himself, rather than a character, in front of the audience. Before *Rainbow* he had always worked as a character actor, and it was in the episodes where he got to dress up and play someone else that you could see his real talent shining through, whether as a pirate or a pantomime dame. With a less skilled actor these routines would have been embarrassing, but Geoffrey threw himself into them and made them a highlight of the show – and funnily enough, in those episodes he never forgot his lines.

After several months working on *Rainbow*, I felt I had got to know my new colleagues and their foibles pretty well. It amused me to watch Stanley teasing Roy and Geoffrey, each of them a little highly strung in their own way and perfect fodder for his sly sense of humour. Stanley always knew which buttons to press, and he soon found mine as well: my professional pride. He began to joke about me being a career 'dolly-waggler' – a phrase from my childhood that I must have inadvertently given him – and when I made the mistake of telling him about the puppet show I had created as a teenager, *Snitchity Titch*, he would always ask me to tell him about my 'Scratch and sniff' routines.

His favourite thing to wind me up about, however, was the black-theatre inserts. These were short, wordless segments in which Valerie and I might operate a pair of caterpillars or a choo-choo train while dressed head to toe in black so that we couldn't be seen on screen. They were only about thirty seconds long, but I would take them very seriously – I was a professional puppeteer, after all! When it was time to film them, Stanley would shout, 'The Black Death is coming!' and the rest of the cast would rush over to watch. The camera would be locked in position and the director would go on a break, so it was up to me to say when I was ready to go. I would psych myself up to give the performance of a lifetime, pull on my black mask and call 'Action!' only for Stanley to shout 'Cut!' before I had even moved a muscle, much to the amusement of my colleagues. When I finally did get going, Stanley would tickle me in the middle of a take or tie my shoelaces together when I wasn't looking – any schoolboy trick he could think of to distract me from the task in hand.

One time, as take after take went by, I became more and more outraged at Stanley's behaviour. As the studio lights beat down on me in my baking-hot black outfit, I felt pure rage bubbling up inside me. 'That's *it*!' I screamed as I flounced out of the studio. 'I've had enough of the black-theatre! I'm never doing it again!' The rest of the cast were in hysterics, and it was left to the ever-diplomatic floor manager to clear the studio and coax me back in.

A few days later, however, Stanley got his karmic comeuppance. He had always used his blinkered vision inside the bear suit as a cover for his pranks, but it turned out the excuse was not entirely unfounded. We were in a camera rehearsal so he was wearing the Bungle head and gloves but not the body. The boom operator had just rested his arm for a moment, letting the microphone hang down a bit lower than usual, and Stanley walked straight into it. It clunked him so hard on the head that he fell to the floor, and we all ran over to check that he was still conscious. 'I'm fine, I'm fine,' Stanley said, rather embarrassed, and insisted that we carry on with the rehearsal. But by the time he took the bear-head off for lunch he was sporting an impressive black eye.

Chapter 6: Climbing high

By the end of my first series of *Rainbow* I felt very much like one of the family, and when we all parted ways for the summer I was sad to say goodbye. I tried my best to concentrate on my work at the Little Angel, but inside I was constantly worrying about whether I would get the call asking me to return to play Zippy in the autumn.

Luckily, John Wright had set me a new challenge – to try my hand at directing for the first time. He and Lyndie were taking the main company off for a summer tour and he had decided to leave me and Joyce to hold the fort. I was to direct *The Nine Pointed Crown*, a recent addition to the Little Angel repertoire created by Frank Wells, son of the famous H.G., featuring a mixture of rod and glove puppets. I was extremely proud and excited to think that John had shown such confidence in me, and determined to prove I was up to the job.

The show was a kind of fairy tale about a king (played by Joyce) whose crown is stolen by a crow. It had been designed for deaf children so there was no dialogue, although it did have a sweeping orchestral score for those who could hear. Unfortunately, performing in a show with no words proved a huge challenge for Joyce The Voice, and for some reason, she just couldn't seem to move her puppet in time with the music. Whenever she made a mistake I had to stop the tape, rewind it and start again, my impatience growing with each repetition. I knew she had a tendency to flap – when John was directing I'd often hear him shout, 'For God's sake, Joyce, can you just get on with it!' – but I forced myself to keep a lid on my growing frustration.

With only a couple of days before the show opened, Joyce was still struggling and I was feeling increasingly panicked; I knew from experience that, although she claimed not to suffer from stage fright, she would only get more flustered as the pre-show nerves kicked in. After we'd had to stop the tape for the umpteenth time, my anxiety and exasperation hit fever pitch.

'For God's sake, Joyce!' I screeched across the auditorium, 'You're driving me up the wall!'

Joyce's head popped up from behind the playboard.

'Well!' she said, visibly bristling. 'I'm sure John has never had a problem with my work.'

This was more than I could cope with – I had spent weeks trying not to lose my temper with Joyce the way John did. I said the first thing that came into my head: 'Oh, you are a silly cow!'

Joyce took a sharp intake of breath. Then she pointedly set her puppet down and said, 'Well, thank you very much.' She marched off the set and straight out of the theatre.

There was an awkward silence and I wondered what the other puppeteers behind the playboard were thinking. 'Um, take an hour for lunch everybody,' I said, rushing out of the theatre just in time to see Joyce storming off up the road. My God, I thought, what have I done?

I desperately needed some advice, but John and Lyndie were away – and in any case I would have been mortified if they had heard I'd lost my leading lady. I decided to call on an old friend of the Wrights who lived opposite the theatre, Vivien Trant. Her girls were the same age as John and Lyndie's daughter, Sarah, and the children would often come and play on the Little Angel's stage when it was closed for the afternoon.

I rushed across the square and knocked urgently on the door. As soon as Vivien opened it I blurted out, 'I called Joyce a silly cow and now she's gone!'

'Oh, hello, Ronnie,' she said, surprised. 'You look a state. Come inside and have a cup of tea.'

I followed her in gratefully and collapsed on the sofa. Vivien listened attentively as I described the nightmare I'd had over the past few weeks and how I'd finally lost my temper.

'Well, it must be very difficult for Joyce, being directed by you,' Vivien said. 'She's been at the theatre for donkey's years, and she probably still thinks of you as a kid.'

'I'm twenty-seven, Viv!' I protested.

'Not to her, you're not.'

I thought back to my first encounter with Joyce, on the doorstep of the Little Angel, when I had cheekily mimicked her accent. Of course! How could I have been so stupid? Taking orders from me must have been a terrible struggle.

'You're right,' I sighed. 'But what am I going to do? We open in two days and she'll never come back now.'

'Ronnie,' Vivien said, 'all you have to do is make Joyce feel important again. Tell her how much you need her – how much the Little Angel needs her. Tell her you can't do the show without her.'

Through the window I could see Joyce striding back across the square towards the theatre.

'Thanks, Vivien,' I said hastily as I rushed out the door and caught up with Joyce.

'Please, Joyce,' I panted, 'can I have a word?'

'I don't think there's much to say,' she retorted.

'Look,' I said, swallowing my pride, 'the reason I lost my temper is that I'm really worried about the show being a success. It's the first one I've directed and I don't want to let John down. I can't do it without you, Joyce – I need your help. You're the most experienced puppeteer on the show.'

Joyce paused, taking a moment to consider this information. I could see a little smile forming at the corner of her mouth.

'Well,' she said. 'In that case we had better get on with rehearsing Act Two.'

As Joyce turned to go back into the theatre I looked over my shoulder and saw Vivien smiling at me from her window.

I went on to direct many other shows at the Little Angel, but I never forgot the lesson I learned that day – and I never lost my temper with a cast member again.

Towards the end of the summer, a call finally came from the casting director at Thames asking me if I was free for the next series of *Rainbow*. I was overjoyed but I didn't want to sound desperate. 'Oh, let me have a look,' I said, leaving an extended pause while I pretended to flick through the pages of my diary. 'Yes, I think I can fit you in.' Over the years that call became a bit of a ritual, as did my imaginary diary-flicking.

Coming back to *Rainbow* was always a bit like returning for a new term at school. None of us really kept in touch much during the summer breaks but each time we got together again it was as if we'd never been apart. We would all excitedly swap stories of what we'd been up to, Roy proudly telling us about voicing the Daleks on *Doctor Who* and Stanley recounting his latest theatre roles. I would always fill them in on my work at the Little Angel but I don't think it made quite the same impression.

Although returning to *Rainbow* after the holidays felt like settling back into a familiar routine, there were often changes since the previous series. The first major shake-up I witnessed was the appointment of three new musicians after Julian, Charmian and Karl decided to leave to pursue more grown-up projects. Jane Tucker, a young jobbing actress, had been called in to audition as one of their replacements. She had rocked up in Pamela's office with some songs that her husband Rod – a former graphic designer who had recently taken up the banjo – had written for her. When Pamela told Jane that she was looking to cast a trio of musicians, Jane suggested she call her other half in from the corridor to try out as well. Pamela was so impressed that she hired the pair on the spot, handing each of them a *Rainbow* badge to seal the deal. Freddy Marks – who would later complete the famous trio Rod, Jane and Freddy – had auditioned separately but missed out this time to Matthew Corbett, son of Sooty creator Harry Corbett.

So, *Rainbow*'s third line up of singers was in place: Rod, Jane and Matthew. They shared out the songwriting equally, but with three episodes being recorded every week that meant they each had to come up with a new tune on a weekly basis too – no mean feat. To make matters worse, because the audio for each song was pre-recorded the week before the episode featuring it was shot, that meant there were always nine songs on the go at any one time: three being written, three going on tape in the recording studio, and three being filmed on set.

Rod was a little older than the other two musicians and a rather serious soul, committed to doing the best possible job with the music. In contrast to her husband, Jane was a bit of a wild child and loved to party. One year she dragged the cast and crew to Stringfellows for her birthday bash. What the other patrons must have thought of a bunch of children's television stars having a night out at an 'adult' establishment I don't know.

Jane's naughty side surfaced most memorably one Wednesday morning during our weekly camera rehearsal. When it was time to run through the latest musical numbers, most of us would generally hang around and watch. This Wednesday, one of the new songs was an innocent little ditty about a ladybird. On came Jane looking as demure as could be with her blonde hair and a neat beige raincoat, but as the song lyrics started, we were surprised to see her slowly and seductively untie the belt of the coat and sling it across the studio floor. Fixing the camera with a smouldering look, she grabbed the sides of the jacket and paused for effect, before throwing the coat open in a flourish to reveal a shiny, tight, leather S&M outfit. As the jaws of the cast and crew collectively dropped, Jane continued singing her cheery tune as if nothing had happened. By the end of the number we were all in hysterics, tears streaming down our faces. I have no idea where she got her kinky get-up – I can only assume she and Rod enjoyed doing rather more in their evenings than just playing the banjo – but from then on she was forever known to us as Miss Whiplash.

The performance must have made a particularly strong impression on Stanley, our own chief joker. A few weeks later, we were rehearsing an episode in which Jane sent Bungle shopping. Stanley had clearly made a few purchases himself: as he recounted the items on Jane's shopping list one by one – 'bread, butter, eggs, flour' – he pulled some rather different items from his basket: whip, mask, vibrator and crotchless knickers.

Matthew Corbett, meanwhile, had his own sense of mischief. Like Jane, his face had a beguiling innocence just right for the cheery *Rainbow* numbers – which was why, when he grinned widely during a camera rehearsal one day to reveal that half his teeth had been blacked out with marker pen, it was such a perfect gag. He was also a real giggler, and once he started it was very hard to get him to stop. The only person who could snap him out of it was our favourite director, Daphne Shadwell. She had worked on *The Sooty Show* with his father, Harry, for years so she was like an auntie to him. 'Now, come on, Peter Matthew,' she would say firmly, using his birth name, which always calmed him down straight away.

Unfortunately Matthew wasn't on *Rainbow* for long. When Harry Corbett suffered a heart attack he was determined to carry on presenting *The Sooty Show*, but Daphne persuaded him that the time had come to hand the reins over to his son. (He was given a little slot – 'Harry Remembers' – in every episode so that he wouldn't feel totally sidelined.) While Matthew went home to take care of the family business, Pamela began the search for a replacement musician.

Once again, Freddy Marks turned up to audition – and this time he impressed Pamela enough to get the job. However, due to some obscure ruling by the entertainment union Equity, he was told that he wasn't allowed to accept it. Freddy went home dejected for a second time, nursing his wounds with the role of Brad Majors in the second London production of *The Rocky Horror Show*. That Tuesday afternoon a chap called Roger Walker auditioned as a singer for *Rainbow* and by Friday morning he was sitting down with us at the yacht club. He was, like Matthew, more of an actor than a singer, but he got on well with everyone.

Although everyone was sad to see Matthew go, his departure had a silver lining for me. He had always combined his commitments to *Rainbow* with operating Sweep on his dad's TV show, which was shot during our summer holiday in the rather grander Studio 2 next door. Now that Matthew was taking over as presenter and operating Sooty himself, there was a vacancy for a second puppeteer. As a result, for the next few years, I spent much of my annual break from Zippy moonlighting as Sweep.

I have to admit I had always been a bit snobbish where *Sooty* was concerned. I had watched the show growing up, back when it was on the BBC. (Harry had moved it to Thames after the Beeb objected to the female panda Soo, played by his wife Marjorie, being introduced as a love interest for Sooty – the director general had grudgingly allowed the new character on condition that the two bears never touched, but the experience had prompted Harry to look for another home for his puppets.) As a teenager I had thought the puppetry on *Sooty* rather unsophisticated, certainly compared to my own favourite puppet programmes, Gerry Anderson's Supermarionation shows *Supercar* and *Fireball XL5*. After all, Sooty and Sweep were just little glove puppets with a finger in their heads.

Meeting Harry Corbett changed my opinion completely. I saw the passion he had for the characters and the care he took to make sure everything was just right. In fact, he was an exacting puppetmaster. When I first started operating Sweep he gave me a reed to put in my mouth to make the character's distinctive squeaking noise. I experimented with it for a while, squeaking the reed while moving the puppet so it looked like he was talking.

'Not bad,' commented Harry, 'but I don't believe he's actually speaking.'

I was a little taken aback. I was blowing into the thing – what more did he want? But according to Harry, while the audience might just hear random squeaking noises, the puppeteer had to know exactly what Sweep was saying, down to the timing and intonation of every word – otherwise it just wouldn't sound authentic. He made me go over the same line again and again, first speaking it myself then attempting to replicate my speech patterns with the reed.

'That's the one!' he announced suddenly, after the twentieth repetition. I felt that I was still just making a series of indistinguishable squeaks, but Harry was satisfied at last.

Harry was a perfectionist, and I suppose that was fair enough since the family pride was at stake. He felt that Sooty and Sweep were following in a time-honoured tradition and that his art was not to be taken lightly. 'I trust you've insured your hands?' he asked me rather seriously one day. I had to admit that the idea had never crossed my mind. 'But all great artists must!' he cried. 'Whether they are concert pianists or puppeteers!' I mumbled that I would look into it, but I never did.

As well as working in the studio, we spent many weeks each summer on location in Dorset. This meant more expenditure for Thames so the directors were always keen to 'show the money', which meant scouting around for dramatic locations so we could have scenes such as Sooty climbing up a cliff-face with a spectacular view behind him of waves crashing to shore.

Harry and his wife, Marjorie, who performed Soo the panda, lived in a beautiful house in the area and they put me up with their friends next door. It was lovely being part of a family troupe and I really felt as though they had adopted me. Marjorie – or Tobes, as Harry and Matthew called her – was incredibly sweet to her husband, always taking care of him and making sure everything was just how he liked it. Her early-onset arthritis meant she found it uncomfortable getting her hand inside Soo so, rather bizarrely, she had to have a control mechanism built to allow her to operate the puppet without ever touching it.

After a few years, one of *The Sooty Show*'s directors suggested that maybe it was time to get a new actress for Soo – rather tactlessly, he said she sounded as if she'd knocked back a few too many glasses of gin. I don't think that was true of Marjorie but she did have quite a deep voice. A lovely young lady called Brenda Longman took over and Soo suddenly seemed to lose several decades.

Sometimes, when Matthew was presenting, Harry would take over Sooty and he and I would work under the table together. I found myself a captive audience for his whispered stories and reminiscences. A favourite yarn was the tale of how he had created the character of Sooty back in the forties. In those days he was working in an ironworks in Yorkshire (where his uncle was the famous fishmonger Harry Ramsden) and performing magic at children's parties in his spare time. One year he and Marjorie went to Blackpool for a holiday. 'I saw a little yellow bear in the window of a shop,' he told me, 'and thought I could use it for my magic show. It only cost me seven and six. I coloured its ears in, black as soot, and when Tobes asked what I was going to call it, I told her, "Sooty!"'

Unfortunately, Harry and I each used different kinds of monitor, which could cause quite a problem. He used a straight-scan monitor whereas I used reverse-scan, so we had to be very careful not to look at each other's screens by accident. If we did we would both get very confused and poor Sooty and Sweep risked a head-on collision.

Stuck beneath the table, Harry and I were the hapless victims of Matthew's mischievous sense of humour. Presenting up above us, he delighted in getting us as messy as possible. Food, paint, water – whatever was at hand in the scene always mysteriously made its way onto our heads. Perhaps exacting revenge on Harry for the years when their positions had been reversed, Matthew would shout disapprovingly, 'Oh, Sooty, look what you've done!' as he knocked yet another gloopy substance off the kitchen counter.

If Matthew didn't get us, then the bathroom scenes would. The Corbetts went to great lengths to ensure the puppets never made contact with water, for fear of damaging them. Instead, the jet of the shower would be carefully angled away from them, meaning that the expendable puppeteer generally got drenched instead. After a while I decided to follow Harry's example and change into a swimming costume before we started shooting.

Each time the director called 'Cut!' at the end of a particularly wet or messy scene, I would give Matthew evil looks from under the table and threaten: 'I'll get you back for that!' Despite my warnings I don't think Matthew ever expected retribution – which made it all the sweeter when my chance finally came. One lunchtime when we were filming at Teddington Studios I found him sitting in the canteen chatting away to a group of employees, with his back to the door. I grabbed a plastic cup from a nearby table, filled it with water, placed a menu on top then flipped it over so the water held the menu in place. As I brought the cup above Matthew's head he suddenly stopped talking and looked up. 'Told you I'd get you back,' I said as I whisked the menu away. The look on his face – shocked, bedraggled and perhaps a tiny bit impressed – was absolutely priceless.

Coming back to *Rainbow* after playing Sweep all summer, I always was reminded how physically demanding it was to operate Zippy. For my friend Violet it had proved literally back-breaking, and with no intention of suffering her fate I had equipped myself with an ergonomic rubber cushion to take the strain off my back. Even so, it could be a difficult job to keep the puppet moving throughout a long scene. Most directors would take this on board, cutting away for at least a few seconds so that Valerie and

I could briefly rest our arms, but some of the younger, less experienced ones were not as accommodating. These 'baby directors', as we called them, often felt they had a lot to prove and would throw their weight around on set.

One time, after a particularly arm-aching scene had been fluffed because of some problem with the camera, the director announced we were going again straight away.

I stood up from behind the counter and said, 'I'm really sorry, but you're going to have to give us a minute to rest.'

To my surprise, the young guy stormed out of the control room and onto the floor to have it out with me.

'What's wrong with you?' he asked. 'This is your job, isn't it?'

The atmosphere in the studio suddenly cooled, and everyone waited to see what would happen.

Very calmly I held out the Zippy puppet to him and asked, 'Would you like to try doing it this time?'

My bluff proved effective and, as I had hoped, the young director backed down immediately. A ten-minute break was called for cast and crew, and when we returned the scene was filmed without a hitch.

Even with the best directors it could be difficult to assert our rights as puppeteers. Hidden behind the counter, Valerie and I were invisible to them – and when the directors came on set they would often give their notes to Roy rather than to us, as though he was telepathically controlling the puppets' movements. Perhaps as a result, I became very sensitive about being overlooked. Things came to a head one day when another 'baby director' was preparing a scene in which Zippy and George drove a sports car. The props department had built a wonderful model car, perfectly scaled to the size of the puppets. There was only one problem: they had failed to allow any space for me and Valerie.

When I pointed this out to the director, he simply replied, 'Oh, that's OK– we'll just stuff the puppets with newspaper and they'll stand up on their own.'

I was incensed. Being forgotten about under the counter was one thing, but being replaced by scrunched-up newspaper was the final straw. I stormed off the studio floor and into the control room, where I found our producer, Pamela.

'You can't let him do this!' I shouted at her. 'You can't have puppets without puppeteers!'

Pamela was clearly taken aback – this was a side of me that she had never seen before.

'For goodness' sake!' she exclaimed. 'Will someone get this puppeteer out of here and give him a cup of tea?'

I didn't wait to be frogmarched from the control room. I turned on my heel and left, walking off my anger until I felt reasonably calm. It was only then that I realised the stupidity of what I had done. Suddenly, I started to panic. I rushed back to the control room, knocked politely this time, and then entered.

'Hello, Pamela, may I speak with you for a moment?' I said, sheepishly.

Pamela raised her eyebrows.

'I'm sorry,' I said. 'I didn't mean to lose my temper. I just feel very strongly about puppets.'

She looked at me for a moment, her face completely serious – but I could swear I saw a twinkle of amusement in her eye. 'Of course you do, dear,' she replied.

I felt mortified, but my angry outburst proved to be effective – the director was forced to find another way to shoot the scene, and no puppets were stuffed in the making of that programme.

Zippy had one distinctive attribute that I'm sure Pamela wished I shared that day: a mouth that could be zipped shut. For some reason, it had taken the *Rainbow* writers several years to realise they could actually use this, but once they did, the gimmick really took off. With Zippy becoming increasingly bolshie and loud-mouthed, particularly with poor old Bungle, he was soon being zipped up in almost every episode. Before long, we started to get letters of complaint from politically correct parents outraged at the idea of apparently 'gagging' a child. Others pointed out anxiously that since Zippy didn't have a nose he must be suffocating.

Their comments were taken surprisingly seriously at

Thames, sending the powers that be into a tizz – and sure enough a memo soon came down from above, putting an embargo on the practice of zipping up Zippy. (It didn't put a stop to it altogether, but it became a less regular activity.)

As it happens, I was a little relieved because using the zip was not very good for the puppet. If Geoffrey did it too quickly or forcefully – as often happened when he was 'acting' his frustration with Zippy – the zip could get stuck and sometimes the ring would break off. (If you watch some of the episodes featuring Zippy's cousin Zippo, you can see that the retired Zippy puppet which was used for the guest character has a broken zip ring from just such an incident.)

Zipping up Zippy was difficult anyway because of the rugby-ball curve of his face, and I got very protective of him if Geoffrey yanked the ring in the wrong way. In the end I realised that I could actually help him by moving Zippy's head in the opposite direction as he pulled the ring across, so although it looked like Zippy was resisting he was actually complicit in his own punishment.

People often asked me why Zippy never unzipped himself. In fact he did on at least one occasion, although that may have been because a new writer's script slipped through the net without the shocking inconsistency being corrected – and, again, a memo from above was the result.

It was not only Zippy who was beginning to misbehave.

Increasingly, our shows were becoming more character-driven, and Zippy, George and Bungle were all behaving increasingly like real children rather than the impeccable role models our education adviser would have wished. Even Geoffrey, the good parent, wasn't always perfect – in one episode he twisted his ankle and when Jane offered to help with the chores he took advantage of her generosity and began to exploit her – before, of course, realising the error of his ways. In other episodes he was depicted as absent, distracted or in a grump (the latter, perhaps, a case of art imitating life).

As the years went by, *Rainbow*'s original educational agenda began to slide further and further out of sight, and our writers and directors looked for ways to bring more fun into the show. One of the most significant developments was the garden set, which offered many opportunities for silliness. It had been a big step for the powers that be to allow the puppets to even enter the house, so letting them out from behind the kitchen counter was even more revolutionary. Since the puppets didn't have legs, there was a limit to their freedom of movement, but once they realised that puppeteers were quite adaptable folk and could easily be hidden away behind a pot plant or under a deckchair, the possibilities suddenly opened up. The garden soon became a regular fixture, which was bad news for Geoffrey since such episodes almost always ended with him getting soaked by a garden hose. He couldn't even retaliate because if Zippy, George or Bungle got wet their fur would run.

On hot days in the garden, George took to wearing a pair of rather camp Dame Edna-style sunglasses and Zippy sported a knotted hankie on his head like a working man at the seaside; Bungle, meanwhile, would produce a pair of inexcusable bright-pink bathing trunks. These were among several items of clothing that Bungle would insist on adopting for particular occasions, while going around the rest of the time apparently naked.

With the focus of the shows shifting towards entertainment and character comedy, *Rainbow*'s popularity was growing year on year. We had already outstripped the success of our sister programmes from the other ITV franchises – *Hickory House* and *Mr Trimble* had fallen by the wayside, and only *Pipkins* continued to give us a run for our money. Our viewing figures were steadily increasing, and press attention was growing alongside them.

One side-effect of this was that photo shoots – for the *TV Times*, the *Rainbow* annuals and even for greetings cards – started to become a regular feature of our work. Geoffrey couldn't get enough of these, displaying his winsome smile for any number of flashbulbs, but for the puppeteers they were a rather dreary, arm-aching affair. Without a monitor it was hard to get the eyelines of the puppets right and the photographers could never understand why Zippy and George often ended up looking at the floor or the ceiling, like bored children in a wedding album.

With greater success and recognition came a higher calibre of guest star, particularly for the storyteller spot. I used to love name-dropping when I went round for tea with my mum.

'Felicity was saying the other day...' I would start, and Mum's eyes would widen in amazement.

'You don't mean Felicity Kendal?' she would ask.

'Oh yes,' I would reply nonchalantly. 'She's a big fan of the show.'

For me, the programme's success also meant financial security. Every year my pay went up, and soon I was also receiving repeat fees on top. While I enjoyed the odd trip to the theatre or ballet I was never extravagant and always put a large portion of my salary into a savings account. After a few years I had enough for a deposit to buy my own flat. It turned out that getting a mortgage wasn't quite as easy as I had hoped, however. The problem was what to put for a job description on the application form. 'Puppeteer' turned out to be a dirty word as far as the bank was concerned, and it wasn't until I settled on 'children's entertainer' that they were prepared to consider my application. Fortunately it was accepted, and I began the search for a new home with the princely sum of £10,000 as my budget.

Vivien Trant, John and Lyndie Wright's friend who

had helped me fix my crisis with Joyce at the Little Angel, insisted on coming flat-hunting with me. This was, she told me, a practical necessity because, left to myself, I would 'probably make a terrible mistake'. We soon found an affordable flat in a fairly new block in Ponder Street, just off Caledonian Road in Islington, sandwiched between the railway line and the prison. The previous owner assured me that the passenger trains stopped at 11 p.m. so there was no question of them keeping me up at night. What he didn't mention until after we had exchanged contracts was that at 11:01 the goods trains took over the line, causing the little flat to vibrate all night long. But I was so pleased to have my own property that I determined to make the best of it, and soon I wondered how I had ever managed to drift off without being rocked to sleep by the incessant rumbling.

Having my own home marked the start of a new era for me, but with it came the end of an old one. I received a call from Violet Philpott telling me that her husband, Panto – my mentor during those very early days at the EPA – had suffered a stroke. I immediately rushed to the hospital in Hampstead where he was being treated and found Violet by his bedside. The consummate puppeteer, Panto believed that, as professionals, we should never appear in public without the tools of our trade, and sure enough he had his favourite red squirrel glove puppet with him. The stroke had rendered him unable to speak but, as he lay in his hospital bed, one arm was still busy working the puppet, to the delight of a child visiting his grandfather in the next bed.

That was the enduring image of Panto – my friend and the man who had first made me believe I could be a puppeteer – that I held on to during his funeral a few days later.

Rainbow was going from strength to strength, finally showing that it could be all Pamela had dreamed of when she first sketched out her ideas for Thames's flagship preschool series. Her success was even recognised by BAFTA when they presented her with the award for best children's programme. Pamela was ecstatic, and each of the cast and crew received a personal letter of congratulation from Sue Turner, Thames's Controller of Children's Programmes. Sue and her mates upstairs in management appropriated the trophy, however, adding it to the horde they kept in their display cabinet.

With *Rainbow*'s ascendancy came a certain celebrity status for the cast, in particular for Geoffrey, who was the only one of us recognisable in person. If we all went out for a meal together, Geoff would have to sit with his back to the door or risk being mobbed by star-struck kids – and their even more star-struck parents. The rest of us would continue our meals in peace, no doubt presumed to be Geoffrey's entourage.

When it came to fan mail, however, it was the puppets

that came up trumps. By this point we were receiving hundreds of letters a week, requiring increasing numbers of badges, photos and stickers to be printed to meet demand. Secretaries at Thames would have to sift through the many unsolicited paintings and drawings sent in by kids, which we started to pin up on the wall in the *Rainbow* house. Inevitably Zippy, George and Bungle received the most, which I think irked Geoffrey a bit. But then he had his own fans: the mums. While the little ones were tuning in to see their favourite puppet characters, a legion of mothers were having their hearts set aflutter by Geoff's blond good looks. I believe some of the letters were rather racy, but being a very private person, Geoffrey would hastily stuff them in his pocket. Other mothers wrote to Geoffrey as sympathetic, similarly brow-beaten parents, telling him how their children were just as difficult to control as Zippy and that they dearly wished they too could zip them up.

From the kids themselves, it was Zippy who received the biggest mailbag of all, and it fell to me or Roy to respond to as many of them as we could. Answering letters from preschool children is an unenviable task, given their fondness for questions – explanations were demanded for everything from Zippy's parentage (*Oh, I can't remember – I was very young when I was born*) to his age (perpetually stuck at five). A popular question was: *What is Zippy's favourite food?* I innocently came up with the answer 'sausages' and never lived it down with Roy, who jumped at the opportunity to turn the tables and taunt me for my own 'terrible coarseness'.

But the hottest question of the day – and one which continues to perplex viewers even today – was: *What is Zippy?* Some believed him to be a frog, although a press release from Thames had randomly referred to him as a tortoise. One TV reviewer labelled him a 'know-it-all snake' – which was rather harsh, I thought. Some children wondered if he was the Gingerbread Man, while others assumed he was an alien, beamed into the *Rainbow* house to live alongside his more earthly companions. In the end, through sheer exasperation, Roy and I decided we had to nail our colours to the mast, and he came up with the answer: Zippy was… 'a Unique'.

Not all of the correspondence we received was quite so frivolous, however. One day, I was contacted by a lady who ran a charity that helped arrange special wishes for sick children. She had been told by the parents of a terminally ill young boy that Zippy was his favourite TV character. We all went out for a meal together and the little boy was thrilled to spend some time with his hero. A few months later I had a letter from the parents telling me their son had died but they wanted me to know how much pleasure he had got from meeting Zippy. That letter was worth more to me than any fan mail.

Before long there was hardly a household in the

land that didn't contain a share of *Rainbow*'s fan base, but we were a little surprised, when going through the postbag one morning early in 1979, to find a letter from Buckingham Palace. The Queen, it turned out, was planning to hold a huge children's party in Hyde Park over two days in May, and Thames had been invited to have its own marquee. Geoffrey would share presenting duties with the team from *Magpie*, and Zippy, George and Bungle were to perform for Her Majesty.

Since kids were constantly begging us to pin the pictures they sent us up on the walls of the *Rainbow* house, we decided to use the Queen's party as an opportunity to run our own art competition, encouraging viewers to paint a portrait of the monarch with the promise that the shortlisted finalists would get an invitation to the party. Before long we were deluged with artworks, and the bagfuls of entries were whittled down to a final fifty by the secretarial staff upstairs. The cast then sat down together to vote for our favourite portrait, and we soon settled on a striking, if unusual, interpretation in which the Queen had been painted with an almost entirely black face.

On the day of the party everyone was incredibly nervous, but Geoffrey did a brilliant job of holding the whole thing together. We ran a quick rehearsal, with a lady-in-waiting standing in for Her Majesty, then a few hours later the monarch herself arrived, stepping out of her car into a blizzard of paparazzi flashes. Even at a distance I felt quite terrified on her behalf, but she was clearly used to the attention and passed them by utterly unfazed. Geoffrey introduced her to the boy who had painted the winning picture, then she and Prince Philip stepped up to see the artwork itself. Her Majesty merely smiled politely, but the Duke of Edinburgh, faced with an image of his wife apparently depicted as an African queen, couldn't help laughing. 'Oh dear, I think you're going to have to change your make-up,' he told her.

Just as *Rainbow* was shining brighter than ever before and gathering fans in high places, we received a shattering piece of news: Pamela, our long-standing producer, would be leaving us. The show she had given birth to was now the most successful preschool programme on television and she felt we didn't need her anymore. Thames Television was promoting Pamela to commissioning producer and someone else would be taking over at *Rainbow*. She took us all out for a meal to say goodbye and I could sense that Geoffrey in particular was struggling to come to terms with her departure; now he would have no mother hen to protect and soothe him.

For the rest of us, mixed with the sadness at seeing Pamela go was a niggling question: could *Rainbow* survive without the woman who had been its champion right from the start?

Chapter 7: X-rated Rainbow

Following Pamela's tightly run regime in *Rainbow*'s early years came a rebellious and turbulent adolescence. Our new helmsman, a tall and dapper producer called Charles Warren, was a very different character to his predecessor – laid-back and easy-going, one of his early diktats was that I should take my first ever holiday. Being so anxious to establish myself in my career, I had been working as a puppeteer for more than fifteen years without a break, first at the Little Angel and for more than half a decade at *Rainbow* as well.

Charles was well respected at Thames – and he knew his puppets, having previously produced *The Sooty Show*. But the greatest measure of his professionalism was his deft handling of Geoffrey. He knew that keeping his presenter happy was a big part of the job, and that if Geoff got upset then his performance would be affected. He didn't attempt to mother him as Pamela had done, but instead responded to Geoffrey's moods by quietly taking him to one side in the bar at the end of the day and asking him what was up. If Geoffrey had a complaint, such as feeling that he hadn't been given a big enough role in a particular episode, Charles would let him get it off his chest – then just ask him to bear with it. Treating him like a grown-up, rather than a child, seemed to do the trick: Geoffrey would be rather quiet the next morning, but over the course of the day his mood would gradually lift.

The loss of our headmistress, however, seemed to bring out the schoolboy in the rest of us, and lewd antics became the order of the day. The boredom of our weekly camera rehearsals was now regularly alleviated by pranks, egged on by our appreciative cameramen. Unfortunately for Geoffrey, he was often required to tuck Zippy, George and Bungle in at night, and these bedroom scenes proved irresistible opportunities. Several times Zippy smuggled a large carrot under the covers that poked up at opportune moments, and he also became very prone to masturbating. Bungle frequently complained that he could see bits of his fur stuck in Zippy's zip, while Zippy would retort that he couldn't sleep next to George because of his bad breath. George would be reprimanded by Bungle for wetting the bed or leaving skid marks on the sheets, and when Geoffrey spoke straight to camera, George and Zippy would often start humping in the background. Personally, I was a bit of a goody-goody by nature but seeing Zippy's antics through my monitor made me feel somehow removed from them. There were many times I caught myself watching him and George copulating and thought to myself, *Oh they are naughty* – before remembering that I was to blame.

As time went on, our behaviour became progressively worse. While our pranks had previously been limited to camera rehearsals, which weren't recorded, they gradually began to creep into the show itself. In the kitchen set we had some model zoo and farm animals on a table, and these rarely made it through a rehearsal without being put in various sexual positions – the more bizarre the coupling, the better – but one scene had to be reshot after the amorous creatures were found to have been accidentally left in position during recording.

The musical numbers became fair game too. If Rod, Jane and Roger were rehearsing a song, the rest of us would take it in turns to walk across the set behind them, waving placards with such helpful suggestions as 'Keep in tune' or 'Get off, you're rubbish.' In return, they wrote little messages into their lyrics – a reference to Charles's notorious 'waggy finger' remained in the final cut of a Hawaiian number during a pirate-themed show. Rehearsals became even more innuendo-laden whenever musical instruments were involved, with Jane asking Zippy if he fancied playing with her maracas, or Zippy and George chatting about plucking each other's 'twangers' – the homemade instruments formed from shoe boxes and rubber bands that we sometimes used in the show.

Charles himself didn't mind a joke, but our exasperated directors could often be heard shouting 'Make them stop!' from the control room – the more serious-minded the director, the more we wound them up. Their worst fear was that one of the top brass would come into the studio and catch us at our games.

The most embarrassing incident occurred when an archbishop came to visit Teddington Studios. With *Rainbow* now one of Thames Television's big success stories, the head of children's output told him all about the programme during his tour of the building, talking up our excellent educational credentials.

When they reached the Studio 3 control room, he proudly flicked on one of the monitors – only to see Zippy mounted upon George, going at it hammer and tongs.

'I'm terribly sorry, I must have got the wrong channel,' the poor man improvised.

An out-of-breath runner appeared on the studio floor moments later, crying, 'Stop it! There's an archbishop watching!'

By Christmas 1979 we were becoming rather proud of our wayward talents, and when the opportunity came to show them off to a wider audience we jumped at the chance.

Little did we know it would be a decision that would change the public perception of *Rainbow* forever.

The tradition of the Christmas tape – a collection of unscreened bloopers from popular shows, edited together for the private enjoyment of television staff at their end-of-year party – began at the BBC in the fifties. When some of the staff left the Beeb to join the newly formed ITV they took the idea with them, and by the late seventies the annual title for the funniest out-takes was hotly contested between the different ITV companies, including Thames. The tapes' comedy value usually lay in seeing the most respectable and serious presenters of the day cursing like fishwives when they forgot their lines – or, better still, newsreaders and weathermen turning red with embarrassment when their autocue failed. But a preschool programme had never entered the fray before.

Rather than simply offering up our own out-takes, our mastermind of coarseness, Roy Skelton, came up with the idea of making a spoof *Rainbow* episode especially for the contest, and approached Charles with the suggestion. It was the kind of thing that even Roy would have blushed to suggest to Pamela, but he had an inkling that Charles might go along with it, and he was right. Our producer had only one caveat: 'You have to do the whole thing in the style of a real *Rainbow* episode – so no swearing!' His insistence on this point was what ultimately made the recording so funny, since we had to rely entirely on innuendo.

Roy and Stanley wrote the script together, making particularly good use of the so-called twangers, and the cast rehearsed it as seriously as we would have for any other episode. When filming finished on Wednesday afternoon we asked the rest of the team if they wouldn't mind staying behind to shoot something extra, assuring them it wouldn't take long. The set was kept exactly as it had been in the real episode we had just been making, with Camera One on a wide shot and Camera Two on the puppets. The lights were left just as they were, and we began.

[George holds a banana, which Zippy peels.]

Zippy: One skin… Two skin… Three skin… Four—

George: Zippy, where's Bungle?

Zippy: Oh, I think Geoffrey's trying to get him up.

[We see the door to the other room and hear Bungle moaning behind it.]

Bungle: Oh, I can't get it in, Geoffrey.

Geoffrey: Well, you managed it last night, Bungle.

Bungle: Yes, I know. Well, let's try it the other way round. Ooh, Geoffrey, have you dropped one? … I've got it in!

[Bungle enters, hammering a nail into a block of wood, followed by Geoffrey.]

Zippy: Hello, Bungle!

Geoffrey: Hello, Zippy, hello, George. *[To camera]* Oh, hello! We're going to talk about playing today.

Bungle: Playing with each other, Geoffrey?

Geoffrey: Yes, Bungle. *[To camera]* Tell me, have you got a special friend that you like to play with?

George: Ooh, Geoffrey, yesterday we played with our balls, didn't we? Are we going to play with our friend's balls today?

Bungle: Yes, and we can play with our twangers as well.

Geoffrey: *[To camera]* Have you seen Bungle's twanger?

Zippy: Oh, I have, yes. I showed him how to pluck with it.

Bungle: Yes, it's my plucking instrument.

Geoffrey: *[To camera]* Can you pluck, like Bungle?

Zippy: I can, I'm the best plucker here.

Geoffrey: Let's get back to Bungle's twanger.

Bungle: Oh, Geoffrey, we could all paint our twangers, couldn't we?

Geoffrey: Well, not now Bungle, it's nearly time for us all to go.

Bungle: But I've just been!

George: I know, let's sing that plucking song again.

Bungle: Ooh, yes, and then Rod and Roger could get their instruments out – and Jane's got two lovely maracas.

Geoffrey: Oh, what a smashing idea. *[Calls]* Jane, Rod, Roger!

[The door to the other room opens again and Jane,

Rod and Roger appear. Rod and Roger are carrying guitars.]

Roger: Hello! We could hear you all banging away.

Rod: Banging can be fun.

Jane: Yes, I was banging away all last night with Rod and Roger.

Roger: *[Looking sad]* Yes, but it broke my plucking instrument.

Geoffrey: Oh well, never mind, Roger. Look, we're all going to sing the plucking song. So come on everybody, get your instruments out.

Rod: *[To Jane]* Do you want to blow my pipe while I'm twanging away?

Jane: Oh no, Rod, I was blowing a lot with Roger last night. But would you like to play my maracas?

Zippy: No, no, let's just pluck away with our twangers.

George: Yes, it doesn't matter what size your twanger is.

Zippy: I've got a big, red one.

George: *[Holding up one finger]* I've only got a tiny twanger *[Zippy looks down towards George's crotch, under the counter]* but it works well and I like to play with it.

Geoffrey: *[To camera]* Well, have you got your twangers out? And remember, you can bounce your balls at the same time if you like. Or, if you haven't got any balls, you could ask a friend if you can play with his. Right, come on then, let's all sing the plucking song.

Zippy: Right, are we all ready? One, two, three – pluck!

Everyone: *[Singing, with Rod and Roger playing the guitar, Jane playing the maracas, Zippy and Geoffrey plucking on twangers and Bungle hitting his wooden block]* Pluck, pluck, pluck away, we're going to pluck all day today. Pluck, pluck, pluck away, we're going to pluck all day.

Geoffrey: It's time for us to go now, but don't forget to get your twangers out, and play with your balls. See you soon. Bye!

Everyone: Bye!

Somehow, we managed to play it straight all the way through and didn't corpse, but as soon the camera stopped rolling we collapsed into giggles. Then we rushed up to the control room to watch it back, feeling rather proud of ourselves. Charles, too, seemed impressed, and it was duly entered into the competition. When it was screened at the ITV Christmas party, the effect of seeing these by-now famous children's TV characters in such a sordid new light was electric. The tape stormed the competition and Thames became the proud winner of that year's contest.

Another instance of bawdy behaviour occurred when the *Rainbow* gang guest-starred on *The Jim Davidson Show*.

Jim had come on to *Rainbow* as a storyteller – he was a rising star of the comedy circuit at the time, and one of our directors, Peter Webb, had seen his act and heard he was a fan of Zippy and George. In fact this turned out to be an understatement – Jim was absolutely obsessed with the two puppets, and the thought of performing on *Rainbow* had the normally cocky lad paralysed with fear. He was sweating buckets as he struggled through the story and kept looking down at the book he was reading from, even though he had learned the words by heart.

Despite his endearing nerves, Stanley and I took an instant dislike to Jim. Roy, on the other hand, felt he had found a kindred spirit who shared his dirty sense of humour. Before he left at the end of his day of filming, Jim made Roy a solemn promise: 'If I ever get my own show, you guys are all coming on it.'

Jim was as good as his word and when, at the ripe old age of twenty-six, he was offered his own weekly show, Zippy, George and Geoffrey found themselves with an invitation to appear. (Poor old Bungle was left off the guest list, but I don't think Stanley was too disappointed.) Roy spoke to Charles about it and was told that we could accept the invitation on one very strict condition: that we must stay in character at all times. 'Just don't do anything that Zippy and George wouldn't do,' Charles warned him, emphasising the word 'don't' with his notorious 'waggy finger'.

Roy did as he was told throughout the filming of the show itself, but the camera rehearsal beforehand was another matter. The atmosphere on set was in line with Jim's own personality, so there was a lot of smutty schoolboy humour and general piss-taking. In one routine, Jim's assistant, Tommy Boyd, asked Zippy and George quiz-show-style questions. 'Here comes the first fucking difficult one,' Tommy began. 'What did Eve say to Adam in the Garden of Eden?'

'Ooh, that's a stiff one,' Roy improvised as George and Jim shook with laughter.

Then Zippy tried to answer the question, if in a rather surreal manner: 'Is it something to do with hover mowers – you know, "a lot less bovver with a hover"?'

Geoffrey, unsurprisingly, was bemused at Roy's response. 'Zippy, what the hell are you talking about?' he replied.

'The fucking Garden of Eden!' Zippy shouted with exasperation, as Jim collapsed on the floor in hysterics.

I had never heard Zippy swear before – not even in our own camera rehearsals – and I found it surprisingly shocking. But as a puppeteer I had to go with whatever came out of Roy's mouth, coarse or otherwise.

Unfortunately, unbeknownst to any of us, a sneaky camera operator had set his tape running throughout the rehearsal – perhaps put up to it by Jim – and the footage was preserved for posterity. It found its way on to another of ITV's Christmas tapes, thus breaking

Charles's edict that the puppets should never be seen to swear.

With the dawn of a new decade came the final reshuffle of *Rainbow*'s musical troupe as Roger Walker left to pursue other projects, including the kids' classic *Bodger and Badger*, the gambling sitcom *Big Deal* and the failed Costa Del Sol soap *Eldorado*, where he was the only cast member with the good sense to terminate his contract before the axe fell.

As the search for Roger's replacement kicked into gear, Freddy Marks was called in to audition for a third time. He was reluctant to put himself through the process again, fearing yet another humiliating rejection, but Jane called him personally to say that she and Rod were rooting for him. With their backing, and the mysterious Equity block removed, he couldn't fail to win over *Rainbow*'s new producer, and sure enough he was soon welcomed into the fold.

Other changes had been going on among the singers too. Rod and Jane had recently got divorced, but they remained close and, placing the good of the band before all else, continued to work together – any disputes they had seemed only ever to be work-related. Freddy's cheeky charm and good looks turned out to be just what Rod and Jane needed in their bid to push the band into true pop-star territory. Their numbers became increasingly ambitious, with their own sets, fancy costumes and elaborate choreography provided by Jane. Some directors were clearly more interested in the musical extravaganzas than the rest of the show, and would spend the lion's share of the time – and budget – on them. John Woods had particular flair and was one of the trio's favourites. Whenever he was slated to direct, we knew that the rest of us would be spending half the day in the green room while the latest musical opus was committed to videotape.

Like the puppets before them, the singers gradually began to sneak into the *Rainbow* house and get more lines in the scripts. This was a fresh challenge for long-suffering Rod, who wasn't a trained actor, although in time he developed into quite a sly and funny performer. By contrast, his ex-wife shone in the spotlight from the get-go. As a result the writers showered her with more and more scenes, oblivious to the fact that Geoffrey was turning green in her shadow.

One Friday morning we were all sitting around in the yacht club for our read-through, looking at a script in which Geoffrey was ill, providing Jane with yet another chance to rule the roost. Geoff was fine with the overall storyline, as it offered some nice hammy moments for his poorly and woebegone character, but when we got to the storytelling part of the episode a cloud passed across his face: it was a *Tat the Cat* story and the scriptwriter had assigned it to Jane. The storytelling segments were one of Geoff's favourite parts of the show, and he loved reading the *Tat the Cat* series in particular because he got to showcase his impressive repertoire of accents: Prunella the posh duck, Oscar the northern dog, Alexander the laconic Scots cat and Emmanuel the cockney fox cub.

As Jane began to read the story, Geoffrey went very quiet and the atmosphere in the room was dreadful. All of us could see what the problem was – apart from the writer, who was blissfully ignorant of his terrible faux pas. In the break, Jane went and asked Charles if there was any way that the script could be changed, but the inserts of the book illustrations had already been filmed so the story couldn't be altered. Geoffrey's attempt to change Charles's mind fell on equally deaf ears – all the producer could offer him was his signature advice: 'Bear with it.'

The weekend did nothing to improve Geoffrey's mood, and all week long poor Jane was dreading the wretched story. Mercifully, Geoffrey went off for a break when the time came to film, so at least she didn't have to read it in front of him.

Meanwhile, the drive to make stars of Rod, Jane and Freddy led to the release of a number of albums, and before long they were offered their own eponymous spin-off show, running alongside *Rainbow* and filmed during our long summer holiday. We even began to include scenes of them writing, recording and rehearsing their songs together, offering the audience a tantalising glimpse at their rock 'n' roll lifestyle.

This being *Rainbow*, there was no getting high on class-A drugs or throwing TV sets out of hotel windows, but the musicians did enjoy getting lashed with Geoffrey after filming wrapped for the week on a Thursday afternoon. Geoff had moved from Hampstead to a flat in Teddington near the studios, and since Rod, Jane and Freddy all lived nearby as well, they would frequently drink the night away together in the local boozer, staggering in for the next day's read-through and desperately clawing at the nearest cup of coffee. When Charles walked in they would sit up to attention and do their best to disguise their hangovers, but as soon as he left they would slump back down into their chairs. The Friday morning rehearsals were often distinctly lacklustre affairs.

It turned out that drinking wasn't all that was going on during those late-night sessions at the pub, and it wasn't long before *Rainbow* was hit by scandal. Freddy had joined the show already married with a child, but soon Jane's blonde good looks and sparkling personality got the better of him. It was obvious the two of them were getting closer, but nobody dared to mention it because it seemed so improbable: Jane flirting with a married man right under the nose of her ex-husband? Surely not!

But if we were slow on the uptake, the press certainly weren't. A mole in our midst had spotted the potential for a salacious story, and one day when I went to the local newsagent I saw to my horror that my co-workers were splashed all over the red tops. 'LOVE SWAP SECRETS OF BUNGLE'S TV STARS' screamed one headline; 'RAINBOW LOVE TRIANGLE' declared another. It was clear how this was going to be spun: as a sordid little ménage à trois at the heart of Britain's best-loved children's show. The coverage was extremely moralistic, especially surrounding Freddy's apparent abandonment of his wife and child, and the focus was all on how they had 'betrayed' *Rainbow*'s young audience. I was frantic – surely this would spell the end of the show – and, with it, my television career. I cursed myself for yet again being too focused on my puppets to take heed of what was happening between the people around me.

The next time we were due to see Rod, Jane and Freddy was at that Friday's read-through. The cast made tea and discussed what our approach should be; we decided the best thing to do was to ignore the tabloid reports and behave as if nothing had happened. Just as we had reached our decision, the door opened and in walked Jane, followed by Rod and a slightly sheepish Freddy. We gathered around the table, the three of them taking seats opposite the rest of us. I felt as if I was attending a bizarre press conference, quickly convened in the unlikely surroundings of the yacht club.

Jane cleared her throat. 'I wanted to say something to you all,' she said, looking straight ahead, her gaze clear. Rod and Freddy looked solemn, their eyes turned downwards. 'We know you've read some things about us in the papers,' she continued, 'but I'm sure you know that not everything you read is true.'

She was going to deny it, I thought. The whole thing must have been a terrible misunderstanding.

'However, from now on I will be living with Freddy.'

My heart sank.

'The three of us will do our best to remain as professional as you've always known us to be. There will be no change in the standard of our performances, and we have no intention of leaving the show. We intend to be here until the end of this series.' She faltered for a moment. 'And hopefully the next.'

I suddenly realised the selfishness of my anxieties – there I was, worrying about myself, when poor Jane must have been tied up in knots over the whole business and facing the very real threat that she and the other two musicians would lose their jobs. How could they withstand the wrath of an education department that had always been so desperate to set the right example to children, when even pointy-nosed scissors had been banned?

As soon as Jane finished speaking, it was as if a great weight had been lifted. There were hugs all round, and we could laugh about what had happened, at least for the time being. We reassured Rod, Jane and Freddy that they had our unwavering support, and that as far as we were concerned, life would go on as usual.

Privately, we all still worried that the axe would fall on

the hapless trio. Nothing happened, however, and when the current series came to an end there was still no word. After the summer holiday I was relieved to see Rod, Jane and Freddy returning to work as normal. If there ever was any fallout upstairs then Charles must have dealt with it pretty swiftly.

In time, the tabloid fuss blew over, and – aside from a brief flare-up a few years later when Rod was issued a speeding ticket (no doubt setting a terrible example to the next generation of drivers) – the press mercifully left the three of them alone to get on with their lives.

Chapter 8: Creative differences

Not long after taking over as producer at *Rainbow*, Charles Warren had an idea which was to change the show forever. By this point the nags and grumblings that would ensue every Friday morning as the cast picked apart the latest script were becoming increasingly virulent, and Roy and Stanley in particular kept complaining that they could do better than the writers. Charles's solution was not one that any of us could have predicted, but it proved effective in silencing their discontent. On the last day of filming before the summer break, he called the entire cast together for a meeting.

'I have an announcement to make,' Charles told us, as we sat round anxiously wondering what this meeting could possibly portend – were we about to be fired? Was the show being cancelled? Were Rod and Freddy running off with each other this time?

'I've decided that since you all have such strong opinions about the scripts, I'm going to let you try writing them.'

I couldn't believe it. Was he trying to call Roy and Stanley's bluff?

But no, the offer was genuine. 'Any one of you is invited to submit a script for the next series,' Charles explained, 'as long as it meets our standards.'

Roy and Stanley immediately offered their services, and I was surprised to see Geoffrey and Freddy following suit. Personally, I couldn't think of anything I'd rather do less than spend the summer holiday writing scripts for *Rainbow*, only to have my efforts scrutinised and torn apart by my fellow castmates. Valerie was of the same opinion.

'Stephanie, our education expert, has prepared a list of episode titles for the next series,' Charles said, producing a piece of paper. 'You can put your names down against the ones that interest you.'

There was a scramble as our budding writers rushed to bag the best titles. I gladly left them to it, heading back to Islington for another summer at the Little Angel.

When it came to the first read-through of the next series, there was a buzz of nervous expectation in the air. Although many of *Rainbow*'s regular writers had been busy penning episodes too, Charles had tactfully made sure that the first week's filming included one script each by Roy, Stanley and Geoffrey (Freddy was less likely to kick up a fuss, so his contribution could wait until later in the series.) As the three brand-new scripts were plonked down on the table in front of me, I noticed something peculiar about them: they varied dramatically in size. Roy's script looked more like a novel, while Geoffrey's was little more than a pamphlet. Only Stanley's resembled our regular scripts in thickness.

The director frowned. 'Roy, I think this might be a little longer than twenty minutes,' he said. 'Is there anything we can leave out?'

Roy huffed a bit before reluctantly taking up his pencil. 'I suppose this could go,' he sighed, striking through a few lines. 'And this bit here…'

While Roy was busy chipping away at his tome, I could see Geoffrey anxiously scribbling extra lines in the margin of his own script in an attempt to bulk it out.

Once we started reading, it quickly became clear that the style of the scripts also varied hugely. Roy's centred on conflict among the inhabitants of the *Rainbow* house, providing plenty of opportunity for bickering between Zippy and the others. Stanley's was grounded in character comedy, with a touch of the absurd, while Geoffrey's was very workmanlike and more educationally driven.

Up until now we had been used to slagging off the latest scripts the moment the writer had left the room, but that was no longer an option. From now on the Friday morning read-throughs were going to require some high-level diplomatic skills. When I wanted to query something,

I had to do it ever so gently: 'I'm so sorry to ask, Stanley, but do you really think Zippy would say this?' or 'Roy, could you possibly explain why Zippy throws the cake at Bungle?' The responses varied according to the individual personality of the writer: Roy argued every point into the ground, while poor Geoffrey would go deathly silent until the critique was over.

After a few more attempts, Geoffrey decided that the writer's life wasn't for him, leaving Roy and Stanley to duke it out in the ongoing *Rainbow* script wars. Each desperate to outshine the other, they eagerly picked holes in their rival's latest offerings. Meanwhile Geoffrey became very sensitive to his treatment in their storylines – if he felt that Roy had sidelined him in a particular episode, focusing too much attention on Zippy and George and not enough on him, he would make his irritation known. He had to be careful, though, because Roy could exact revenge in the next script, giving him a particularly tricky art project to cope with, or showering him with water in the garden.

For my part, I found it complicated my relationship with Roy that he now wrote a large portion of the scenes for our character. After I had spent years arguing against the use of paint and foodstuffs on set, it infuriated me to find Roy, of all people, frequently setting up Zippy for a messy disaster. But if I voiced my concerns in the read-through I would be told dismissively, 'Oh, don't be silly, darling, it's only a paintbrush.' Worse, Roy seemed to have developed a bizarre obsession with sausages, which meant that grease was also a perennial problem. I got quite good at palming them so that the meat never touched the puppet's mouth, but then they always seemed to end up in my lap, much to Roy's amusement.

In fact, Roy's scripts always relied far more on props than anybody else's – perhaps because as a disembodied voice he had no idea how infuriating physical objects could be. (Geoffrey's scripts, less mysteriously, frequently included bacon sandwiches, because he knew he often got peckish during filming.) If Stanley approached him at the read-through saying, 'I'm sorry, Roy, but I can't hold six different cases and open a door at the same time – I can hardly see where I'm going in the suit, as it is,' Roy would blithely pat him on the shoulder and respond, 'You're not the first man to dress up as a bear, you know.'

The people I felt most sorry for under the new system were the 'baby directors', who were still regularly sent to *Rainbow* as a training ground. If they found themselves working on a script by Roy or Stanley, they ran the risk of being taken aside every ten minutes for a chat about 'What I had in mind for this scene…'. It took quite some maturity and confidence to deal with these challenging star writers.

Stephanie, *Rainbow*'s long-suffering education adviser, was horrified at Charles's suggestion that the cast be given a hand in scripting the show – she had enough trouble keeping her regular writers on the straight and narrow; how on earth was she supposed to manage a troupe of actors who were suffering delusions of literary grandeur? Charles promised her that he would smooth over any problems that arose, but Roy, in particular, was always keen to see how much he could get away with. Innuendo was actually pretty rare on *Rainbow* – and it had to be very subtle to get under Stephanie's radar – but on the odd occasion when a double entendre did slip through (the storyline about a neighbour called Mrs Dogfondle losing her pussy, for example), you could bet that either Roy or Stanley was behind it.

For his part, Roy clearly resented Stephanie's meddling. He felt that she eviscerated his scripts, crossing through all his funniest lines in her damning red ink, irrespective of the structure or comedic build-up of a given scene. Sometimes we would get a new script of Roy's at a read-through and he would be on the defensive before we'd even lifted the first page. 'I'm sorry it's ended up so bland,' he would mope. 'I wrote a marvellous fight between Zippy and Bungle but *Stephanie* took out the whole thing!' Other times, uncharacteristic lines would creep in, such as Zippy saying, 'I'm sorry, I didn't mean it,' at the end of an argument. '*Stephanie...*' Roy would mutter through gritted teeth, in response to the collection of raised eyebrows around the table.

At times the battle of wills between writer and education adviser would boil over into outright conflict. One time, Stanley had written a script for a seaside episode which featured a Punch and Judy routine. Stephanie felt that, traditional or not, Mr Punch's pantomime violence had no place on a preschool programme. As far as Stanley was concerned, this was politically-correct nonsense, but Stephanie stuck to her guns. Fortunately, Charles was able to intervene and smooth things over before a real Punch and Judy show ensued between the two of them.

I couldn't help wondering if Charles ever regretted his bold decision to hand over the reins of our storylines to the performers, but if so he gave no sign of it. In terms of the actual episodes we produced, his experiment was undoubtedly a success, helping *Rainbow* to move with the times and providing some wonderful storylines.

As far as I was concerned, one of the most important things to come out of the new approach was convincing the powers that be that the puppets could be trusted on location. I don't know why this had taken so long – after all, little Sooty had been mountaineering for years – but perhaps it was due to the extra bit of ingenuity required to hide the puppeteers, and of course the fact that Zippy and George had no legs.

In any case, our first foray out of the *Rainbow* house was for an episode about camping. This was easy enough, logistically speaking, when the puppeteers could crawl underneath a tent; elsewhere, we had to hide ourselves behind strategically placed haystacks or relocated bushes. No such requirements restricted Bungle, who stole the show as a know-it-all Boy Scout, complete with ridiculous uniform. When he wasn't showing off about his knowledge of camping he was complaining about the countryside's lack of toilet facilities (or lavatories, as Stephanie insisted we call them), eventually running behind a tree in desperation. In Bungle's defence, those scouting shorts did look painfully tight on his large, hairy behind. Stanley certainly found the outfit quite amusing – during one rehearsal he bent over, presenting his giant rear end to the camera, and exclaimed, 'What an enormous spread we've got for tea!'

Eventually, some brave person even decided it would be safe to let Zippy loose on the outside world without the moderating influence of George, to star in a solo adventure in which he fulfilled his lifelong dream (hitherto unmentioned) of becoming a steam-train driver. This involved a day filming on the Romney, Hythe and Dymchurch Railway, with me crouched down in a cramped space in the locomotive while Zippy, in red scarf and cap, maniacally shovelled coal into the furnace.

As they gained confidence in their writing, the cast's imaginations began to run wild. An episode by Stanley entitled 'Lions and Tigers' required a whole forest to be built in Studio Three, designed to emulate Rousseau's

Tiger in a Tropical Storm. The director, Andrew Thomas, did his best to accommodate Stanley's vision but the thing must have cost a fortune.

Soon, elaborate fantasy sequences were being written in which Zippy, George and Bungle set off for the limitless horizons of their own imaginations. In one *Batman*-themed episode, 'Zipman' and his sidekick 'Bobbin the Boy Blunder' (George, in a blue cape and mask with eye holes just big enough to accommodate his heavy lashes) attempted to overthrow 'The Joker Geoffrey' and 'Sour-Faced Bungle', who were planning to wipe all smiles off the face of the earth. Geoffrey did an excellent job, grinning maniacally in his purple suit and painted white face – in fact, the director had to tell him to tone down his performance or it might scare the children at home.

It wasn't long before *Rainbow* left this planet altogether, shooting into space in an episode penned by Freddy called 'Outer Space'. Bungle and Geoffrey – dressed in *Star Trek*-inspired costumes, complete with silver boots – were seen exploring a lunar-style landscape strewn with giant inflatables, inadvisably leaving George and Zippy in charge of their spaceship (the *Rainbow* kitchen with additional knobs and whistles). Rod, Jane and Freddy were beamed down to sing a song about the loneliness of leaving planet Earth behind, while jumping around and tossing cushions about in slow-motion, giving the effect of a moonwalk.

Back on earth, *Rainbow* was even engaging with street culture, when Zippy's cousin Zippo appeared as a rap star, operated by my old friend Nigel Plaskitt from the EPA. Poor Roy found himself struggling to rap in an American accent, something he had never anticipated himself doing when he signed up for *Rainbow*. The rhythms didn't come naturally to him, but fortunately he had teenage daughters to help him practise such choice lines as:

Different I look but different I'm not,
It's just that now I'm really hot.
I wear these clothes like a hip man should,
They're real cool man, don't you think they're good?

('No,' retorted Zippy. 'You look like a deckchair.')

As the storylines got more and more wacky, so too did the outfits. The long-suffering costume department, used to fitting out humans, now had to learn the trickier art of tailoring puppets. Often they would simply buy children's costumes and modify them a bit, which meant they didn't fit properly. Being a 'Unique', Zippy's body shape was very peculiar, tapering outwards, so his clothes had to be fastened at the back with Velcro, while his rugby-ball head wasn't well suited to hats, which had to be stuffed with newspaper to stop them flopping about then stuck in place with wig pins. Comedy facial hair couldn't be stuck on with double-sided tape as it would whip off the puppets' fur when it was removed, so various other means had to be found. The episode 'Who Done It' was a logistical nightmare, with Zippy playing a detective in a stringy beard, trilby, dark glasses and trench coat, and George sporting a beret, a mini moustache and a French accent. We would often arrive in the studio and get quite a shock when we saw how the puppets were dressed – a prince in full Regency regalia or an alien king with antennae and a Ming the Merciless-style collar.

As my work life was growing increasingly surreal, my personal life also took an unexpected turn. I was back at Stockwell Gardens visiting my mother one day when the postman arrived with a letter. 'Look, Ronnie,' Mum said, bringing it into the living room. 'It's addressed to your father.'

I was a little taken aback. It was many years since Dad had died. Surely everyone who knew him would have found out by now. 'I suppose we'd better open it,' I replied.

Mum and I couldn't possibly have imagined what we would find inside. It was a long, handwritten letter from a woman called Penny, claiming to be the daughter of Leslie Le Drew. I checked the date of birth she had given and realised that it matched up perfectly with the year that Dad had gone AWOL when I was a kid.

I couldn't believe it – I had a half-sister out there somewhere!

Mum was very quiet. 'What do you think we should do, Ronnie?' she asked.

I put my arm around her. 'It's up to you, Mum,' I said. Secretly I was rather hoping that we could make contact with this woman and find out more about what Dad had been up to, but for Mum the letter had been quite a blow. I wondered if Dad had ever spoken to her about what happened during the year he was absent. He clearly hadn't ever mentioned a baby.

'I think we'll write and inform her that your father died a long time ago,' Mum said quietly. 'And that we're sorry but we can't be of any more help to her.'

I nodded. I was disappointed, but I felt it was Mum's decision. Together we composed what we thought was a kind but not overly friendly letter, wishing Dad's daughter all the best in her life but gently making it clear that we didn't want to take things further.

As I took the letter down to the post box, I wavered for a moment, aware of a connection that might have been, of a link that might now be severed forever. Of course it was terrible for Mum what Dad had done, but I felt sad that there was another part of him out there somewhere that I was turning my back on. I wondered whether I would ever have the chance to get to know my half-sister.

Chapter 9: Love and marriage

I was now well into my thirties and firmly established as a puppeteer, but when I stood back and looked at my life I could see that I had put all my energy into only one thing: my career. I had spent so many years feeling like that fifteen-year-old boy desperately trying to prove himself, while the storm cloud of the 'proper job' threatened on the horizon, that my love life had come a poor second.

This was partly because, aside from my demanding work schedule, much of my spare time was taken up with sitting on various puppetry committees. I was now vice-chairman of the Educational Puppetry Association – the organisation that had given me my first leg up all those years ago. To be honest, the role didn't require much input, which suited me fine since I was still juggling *Rainbow* and the Little Angel, but one day I got a call to say that the chairman, David Currell, couldn't make a meeting and asking if I would take his place.

Reluctantly, I turned up at the EPA that evening, tired and unshaven. A talk was being given by a woman from Yorkshire who had written a book about using puppetry to help disabled children, and it was up to me to kick off the question-and-answer session afterwards. Anticipating a less than riveting evening, I wearily looked up when a colleague announced, 'Ronnie, meet Caroline Astell-Burt, our speaker for tonight.' My eyes landed on a striking young woman with a profusion of red curls and a smile that made me feel suddenly very wide awake – and more than a little self-conscious about my scruffy appearance. As she stood to give her talk, enthusing about the life-changing power of puppetry and her experience as a house-mother for sick children at Dr Barnardo's, I felt moved but also somehow inadequate. What must this earnest young woman think of me, someone who had made a career out of playing with puppets merely for entertainment?

When she finished her speech, I wracked my brain to think of an incisive and weighty comment that displayed my deep understanding of the subject matter. 'Erm... Puppets,' I said. 'I suppose they're something you see, aren't they? So can you still use them with blind kids?'

While I kicked myself for this clumsily worded remark, Caroline, to her credit, revealed nothing more than a faint flicker of amusement before she delivered a comprehensive answer that somehow made my foolish comment appear to tap into an area of serious academic debate.

When the meeting was over I scurried away in embarrassment, and afterwards tried to put the pretty woman with the curly red hair out of my mind. The world of puppetry is a small one, however, and before long our shared interest brought us together again. This time, I was on a panel judging candidates for a new Arts Council bursary. We had held a long series of interviews and I was flagging by the time our last hopeful applicant knocked on the door. But once again my ennui evaporated immediately as Caroline bounced into the room, proceeding to mesmerise the judges with an impromptu performance of singing glove puppets that floored the competition and won her the grant. I was very flattered when she wrote to me shortly afterwards asking me to be her mentor for the project, and I suggested we discuss it over tea at the suitably grandiose setting of the British Museum next time she came to town.

On the appointed day, we arrived at the museum café only to find that it had just closed, so I offered her tea at my flat near Caledonian Road instead.

'Why don't we walk?' I suggested, thinking it would give me the perfect opportunity to rescue my reputation by expounding on my views about puppetry. So engaged was I in my subject that, as usual, I forgot to notice what was going on around me and the fact that poor Caroline, who was wearing high-heeled sandals, was hobbling along with blisters forming on her feet.

I had promised to make her something to eat when we got in, but I think when she saw the state of my bachelor pad she decided not to risk it.

'Why don't you just take a seat and let *me* make something,' she offered.

Despite the pain in her feet, Caroline managed to whip up a delicious pasta dish while I continued to witter away about my favourite subject. The food was amazing, but when I went into the kitchen afterwards I was astonished by the amount of mess it had produced. Living on pot noodles, I wasn't accustomed to this level of creativity, and it resulted in a heated row about who should do the washing up – hardly the most romantic conclusion to our first meal together.

Luckily, my chance to make amends soon came, when I heard that Caroline had been invited to teach a course at the Puppet Centre in Battersea. Since her own home was up in Yorkshire she needed a place to stay in London, and I immediately suggested she lodge with me. My offer was a reasonably innocent one – at this point I was just vaguely aware that I enjoyed the company of this young woman and felt compelled to try and impress her, but I was a little too stuck in my ways to contemplate making room for her in my life.

Over the course of the week in which she stayed, however, Caroline quietly cast a spell over me. Whenever I walked into my flat I was hit by the homely smell of baking, and on entering the kitchen I found plates piled high with scrumptious cakes and biscuits still hot from the oven. Delicious, home-cooked meals awaited me every evening, beautifully laid out on my old wooden table, which had miraculously acquired a tablecloth and a little flickering candle.

When the time came for Caroline to go, both my heart and my stomach felt pangs of loss. Coming home at night, there was now no one waiting for me and no inviting baking smells coming from the kitchen – just my pot noodle at the cold, hard table.

Back in Yorkshire, Caroline waited patiently for the spell to work. Slowly, slowly, the cogs of my brain started turning and I belatedly arrived at the conclusion that I rather wanted this woman to return. I wrote to Caroline, trying to gauge her feelings towards me, but her responses were too subtle for my comprehension and I didn't trust myself not to mess things up. In despair, I decided to seek the advice of the oracle: my old friend Vivien Trant.

Over tea at her house opposite the Little Angel, Vivien studied Caroline's letters before decoding them for me. 'She's waiting for you to make a move, silly!' she told me. 'Don't let this one get away!'

Several months passed before Caroline came back down to London, and this time I was determined not to miss my opportunity. Once again, I invited her to stay at my place, but this time it had been conscientiously cleaned and tidied ahead of her arrival, and rather than waiting for her to cook me dinners, I planned nights out that I hoped she would enjoy – to the cinema, theatre and ballet. It was after one of these trips to the theatre that I went down on one knee and proposed.

Caroline said yes immediately, but I had a feeling that her family were going to be harder to convince. From what I'd gathered, she came from rather more salubrious stock than I did – her father had studied chemistry at Oxford and was a successful businessman, and her mother had been a bilingual secretary in Switzerland. What would they make of a professional dolly-waggler from a council estate? The thought of visiting them to ask for their blessing filled me with dread.

It turned out my worries were well founded. On our arrival in Yorkshire, Caroline's father, Tony, gave me a terrifyingly manly handshake. 'Hello, Ronald,' he said. 'I think you and I should take the dogs for a walk.'

I tried hard to dispel the image of myself running across the countryside in terror as he set the hounds on me. 'I'd love to,' I replied.

As soon as we waved goodbye to Caroline and her mother, Angela, Tony got down to father-in-law business. 'So,' he said. 'Another puppeteer. How are you going to earn enough money to keep my daughter?'

I began to anxiously expound on my telly career, plans to buy a house and general trustworthiness, rambling on and on until poor Tony probably wished he'd never asked the question. By the time we returned, I think he was as relieved as I was that the walk was over. With our manly chat out of the way, we were both able to relax and enjoy the meal that Caroline's mother had prepared.

We stayed overnight with Caroline's parents and by the morning I felt a little more confident about my prospects as a son-in-law. As we were about to go downstairs for breakfast, I asked Caroline, 'Do you think I can risk calling your parents by their first names now?'

'I'm sure they would be delighted,' she replied.

When the moment came to say goodbye, I shook Tony's hand respectfully, and then turned to kiss his wife on both cheeks. 'Thank you so much for having us,' I said. 'Can I call you Audrey?'

'You could, if that was her name!' replied Tony, as he and Angela roared with laughter.

Our engagement was brief and the wedding was set for 26 January 1983 in St Mary's Church, next door to the Little Angel – John and Lyndie Wright had kindly offered to host the reception in the theatre. The night before, I set off home from Teddington, planning to subject myself to a last evening of loneliness as a reminder of what I would be missing. (Caroline was staying with friends nearby.) But when I got in, the phone rang.

It was John Wright. 'What are you doing for your stag

party?' he demanded. The answer, unsurprisingly, was nothing – I had been so focused on the week's filming that I hadn't even thought about it.

'Lyndie's going to be out,' John announced. 'Come and meet me at the theatre.'

When I arrived, John had cooked us a big fry-up – presumably the blokiest gesture he thought I would be able to stomach – and he poured me a stiff drink. The two of us sat down to this simple meal together – a reminder that, even though my own father wouldn't be witnessing my marriage, someone just as important to me would be there.

When I returned to my flat I was feeling rather philosophical about the big change that was about to take place in my life. I took the two little wedding rings Caroline and I had bought out of their boxes, put them on the mantelpiece and stood back to admire them. Here they were, I told myself: symbols that I had finally grown up.

Just then the phone rang. It was my best man, Peter, a teacher friend I had met a couple of years before through the EPA. I had chosen him for the role because he was a very organised type. Knowing my anxious and absent-minded disposition, he had called to check that I wasn't a complete nervous wreck.

'Now remember, you have to be at the church by 1 p.m.,' he said. 'And don't forget the rings!'

'Don't worry,' I assured him, with my new-found sense of maturity. 'I'm on top of everything.'

The next morning I awoke in a cold sweat, momentarily gripped by the conviction that I was due on stage somewhere or other and had forgotten my lines. For the first time in many years, I was experiencing a bad case of stage fright. I got dressed hurriedly, grabbed the ring boxes and rushed to the church, inevitably getting there far too early.

When he arrived, Peter found me pacing up and down outside. 'Don't worry,' he said, 'it'll all be fine. Have you got the rings?'

'Of course I have!' I snorted, handing him the little boxes. At least I'd got something right.

Peter opened first one, then the other. 'Er, Ronnie,' he said, 'I don't want to scare you, but there are no rings in these boxes.'

'What?'

Instantly the image flashed into my head: two gold rings, looking ever so grown-up, resting on top of the mantelpiece.

By now the guests were arriving and there was no time to go back to the house. Graham, our lovely vicar, did his best to assure me that all was not lost, and promised he would sort something out.

When Caroline arrived on her father's arm, Graham greeted them with some inauspicious words. 'The good news is Ronnie's here,' he said. 'The bad news is he's forgotten the rings.'

Tony's jaw dropped. 'Dad, it's alright,' Caroline said, patting his arm.

'The important thing,' Graham continued, 'is that whatever ring Ronnie offers you in the ceremony, you just accept it.'

Meanwhile, inside the church, the search was on for plausible replacements. In the end it was Sooty who saved my marriage – or, at least, his pal Matthew Corbett. When Matthew heard my plight, he burst out laughing. 'Trust you, Ronnie!' he said as he kindly lent me a large signet ring to act as a stand-in for Caroline's wedding band. Peter produced another ring, for me.

When the moment came, I slid the signet ring onto Caroline's finger. I could see she was trying not to giggle as she held the over-sized piece of jewellery in place with her other hand to stop it falling off. Then she slid Peter's ring onto my finger.

Once I had made it through the ceremony, my nerves fell away and I found the ring fiasco provided me with the perfect anecdote for my groom's speech over at the Little Angel. Everyone thought it was hilarious – apart from my superstitious mother, who was convinced it was a bad omen and anxiously asked me if it meant that Caroline and I weren't really married.

By the autumn Caroline was pregnant. We moved to a house in Highbury and busied ourselves preparing it for the baby's arrival.

I was at the Little Angel one day when John Wright

took me aside and asked me if I would be interested in helping him perform *The Little Mermaid* at a big festival at the University of Michigan which was being organised by the Puppeteers of America. It would be the first time John had taken one of the theatre's shows to the United States and I was honoured that he wanted me to come too.

The only problem was that the festival was scheduled for early June. With the baby due to arrive later the same month it seemed too much of a risk to take the trip, so I reluctantly declined. The next thing I knew, Lyndie came knocking on our door. As I let her in, I knew something was afoot; the Wrights would turn up unexpectedly at our house only if something very serious had happened. Lyndie explained that she couldn't accompany John on the America trip because their son Joe had his eleven-plus exams coming up and this had left John distraught at the prospect of taking the show to such an important event without his 'two best puppeteers'. John was adamant it should be the finest performance the Little Angel had ever given, since this would be its US debut.

I was torn: my mentor, and the man who had been almost a surrogate father to me, needed my support, but I was terrified that if I went on the trip I might miss the birth of my first child. How could I justify that to Caroline, especially when Lyndie was staying at home for the sake of Joe? I ummed and ahhed for weeks, putting off the decision for as long as possible.

Eventually, just a week before the trip, there was another intervention from Lyndie. The phone rang, and when I answered it, she said immediately, 'I'm going to go. Will that help you make your decision?' I realised then how important this trip must be, not just for John but the whole Wright family – and therefore for me as well. John assured me that we would be back in good time for the baby's due date, and Caroline, who was as buoyant and independent a spirit as ever, told me she would be fine.

As soon as I got to America, I felt sure I had made the right decision. The festival was incredible, and *The Little Mermaid* went down a storm. Rather than using microphones we performed the show to a tape that contained all the dialogue and music – Joyce had recorded her dual roles of the mermaid and the Sea Witch, John had lent his voice to the King, and Christopher Leith acted the Prince. Even after twenty years, I still found the show just as magical as I had when I first saw it as a teenager, and the Americans seemed to be equally enchanted.

One evening I was eating with some of the American puppeteers in the university's huge dining room when suddenly a very loud announcement came over the tannoy. 'Ronnie Le Drew from the Little Angel Theatre just became a father!' it boomed, to everyone within earshot. 'Isn't that *great*?'

The other diners erupted into ecstatic applause and cheers, while all I could think was, *Caroline is going to kill me!*

I raced to the nearest phone and asked to be put through to the Whittington Hospital in London, England. 'I need to speak to my wife,' I told the operator. 'I've just become a father!'

'Congratulations, sir, you can have the call for free,' the woman replied. These Americans really seemed to like babies.

There was an agonising wait while the call was put through to the right place, and then finally Caroline came on the phone. I was in a state of nerves, but she said, 'It's OK, darling, everything is fine. We've got a little baby boy.'

'What happened? Who took you to the hospital?' I asked, filled with guilt.

'Oh, no one,' she said, breezily. 'I just hopped on the bus.'

Not only that, but the bus stop was at the bottom of the hill before the hospital. Caroline had resolutely marched all the way up it, passing our vicar on the way. 'I'm just having a baby, Graham,' she had told him, not stopping to chat.

I always knew that my flame-haired wife was a special woman, but she had surpassed herself this time.

On the plane on the way back, I started thinking about the little person waiting to meet me at the other end. After years of entertaining other people's children, not to mention babysitting for the Wrights, I'd received many comments about how I would make a great dad one day.

But I started to worry that all I knew how to do was to make kids laugh. Would I actually know how to be a father?

When we touched down at Heathrow, Caroline stood waiting for me, cradling a little pink thing in a blue Babygro and a white cap. As I drew closer, his face came into focus and I was filled with a mixture of love and protectiveness. 'Go on, go to Daddy,' Caroline said, handing me the baby. I already knew what his name should be: John.

Eight months later, when Caroline fell pregnant with our second child, the first thing she said to me was, 'I'm having a home birth – and you're going to be here.' I didn't argue. The following November she gave birth with me by her side, and this time we were blessed with a beautiful little girl, whom we named Elizabeth.

As it turned out, Caroline wasn't the only pregnant puppeteer at that time – The Lovely Valerie had recently married one of the *Rainbow* boom operators, Pete, and the happy couple were also expecting a baby. As her bump got bigger Valerie realised that she would have to go on leave, since sitting scrunched up under the table trying to operate a pink hippo was not exactly compatible with the advanced stages of pregnancy. I called in as many puppet favours as I could to cover for her, bringing in old friends like Christopher Leith from the Little Angel and my old EPA pal, Nigel Plaskitt. When no one else was available,

John Thirtle, who was still making us replacement puppets every couple of years, took time out from *Button Moon* to operate George.

While Valerie was off on leave, we heard some worrying news from Pete, who was still recording our sound in Studio Three: Valerie had discovered a cyst on her neck and the doctors believed it was malignant. Everyone was terribly concerned, but by the time Valerie returned to work at the end of her leave she had been given the all-clear and the relief in the *Rainbow* house was palpable.

It was great to have Valerie back in the fold, but before too long she was expecting another baby. This time she announced that her absence would be permanent – she had decided to devote herself fully to the much more challenging role of being a mum. I recommended a new puppeteer to take over as George full-time – Malcolm Lord, who I had seen in some productions by Violet Philpott's company, the Cap and Bells Puppet Theatre. Valerie would return now and then for a brief cameo as Zippo or Georgina (George's cousin), but we missed her as a regular cast member. She had always been our rock, steady and stable amidst the madness of the *Rainbow* house.

Unfortunately, the cancer that we had all hoped was gone for good soon returned, and this time its progress was swift. Pete kept us informed of Valerie's condition, and when he took time off work to be with her, his colleagues in the sound department would fill us in on his behalf. As time went on the prognosis got worse, and before long, in one of the breaks between series of *Rainbow*, I received a letter from Pete saying that Valerie had died.

I read the words on the page over and over again in a kind of daze. The news wasn't completely unexpected but somehow I couldn't get my head around it. It was hard to imagine that someone so full of life, and so devoted to her two little boys, could just be gone. It seemed unfathomable that I would never see Valerie again, and more than anything my thoughts kept turning to Pete and the kids. How would they cope without her?

The funeral was held at the parish church in St Margaret's, close to Valerie's home, and all of the *Rainbow* team were invited. During the service I stood at the back with Geoffrey, Roy, Rod, Jane and Freddy, but we couldn't bring ourselves to look at one another, knowing that we would burst into tears if we caught each other's eye. In the front pew, poor Pete was doing his best to comfort the boys, with the help of Valerie's sister and mother. Despite the vicar's kind words, everyone was in a total state of shock. It seemed unbelievable that such a young woman, and one as kind and sweet as Valerie, could have been taken in such a cruel way. I thought of how Valerie had been the first girl to capture my heart when she arrived at the Little Angel all those years ago. During our time spent under the counter together at *Rainbow* we had formed a close bond, and I knew that working on the show would never be the same without her beside me.

Roy, too, had formed a particularly close friendship with Valerie, treating her almost like a daughter. He thought her an extremely talented puppeteer, and the two of them had talked about going on to make their own TV show together. That day he was a totally different man – pale-faced, withdrawn, hardly able to speak to anyone. As we left, he grasped my arm. 'Oh God, Ronnie,' he said. 'How could this have happened?' Silently I put my arm around him as he struggled to hold back his tears.

When we all went back to work again after the long summer break, nothing felt the same. Although we had got used to Valerie's replacement, Malcolm, operating George, it was impossible to come to terms with the fact that, this time, she would never return.

Chapter 10: Lost in the Labyrinth

As time went on, my work on *Rainbow* began to open other doors for me. One week I was demonstrating puppets on Timmy Mallett's *Utterly Brilliant*, the next I was working with Roy Hudd on a Channel 4 drama about the travelling puppeteer Walter Wilkinson. Thanks to a puppetry friend of mine called David Claridge – who called me in as 'Left Paw' on his *Roland Rat* show – I even found myself rubbing shoulders with Frankie Howerd, one of my favourite comedians from childhood.

I was soon working with another comedy legend, Tommy Cooper, who needed some assistance with a magic trick for his TV show. Standing behind Tommy, dressed from head to toe in bright-blue chroma-key Lycra (so I could be edited out later), I was tasked with moving a little silver orb through the air on a stick so it appeared that he was using the power of his mind to send it from one hand to the other. There was only one problem: Tommy had me in such fits of giggles that every time the silver ball began its ascent it soon started jiggling violently, hardly the precise movement he probably expected of a professional puppeteer.

My biggest break, though, came in the summer of 1985, during the long holiday from *Rainbow*. Flicking through a puppetry newsletter one lazy afternoon, my eye was caught by an advertisement from the Jim Henson Company. As the creators of *Sesame Street* and *The Muppet Show*, the Hensons were international puppetry superstars, so I almost fell out of my deckchair when I read that they were looking for some Brits to help out on a major new movie called *Labyrinth*, which was being shot in the UK.

Rock god David Bowie had bravely agreed to share his billing with a cast of puppets, and while most of these were to be operated by the Hensons' American regulars, extra hands were needed for the ensemble parts. I didn't care if I was controlling the hair on Bowie's head – the thought of nonchalantly telling my *Rainbow* pals that I had been working on a feature film next time we swapped summer holidays stories was irresistible.

I'd never been to a proper audition before, having always got work through people I knew. When Caroline asked if I wanted to run though a piece with her as preparation, I scoffed, 'Oh, don't worry, I'll just make something up on the spot.' After all, how hard could it be to score a job as a background puppeteer? I slung my most Muppet-like puppet in my bag (a beaver that had been given to me by a devoted Zippy fan) and set off, certain that the casting would be a mere formality.

When I arrived at the church hall in Hampstead where the auditions were taking place, I quickly began to curse my breezy self-confidence. The place was packed with puppeteers, most of them much younger than me, and nearly all of them Muppet obsessives. There was no private casting suite – you simply queued up, put your name down on a list and waited to take your turn performing with one of the Muppet stalwarts, with all the other hopefuls looking on behind you.

As the other puppeteers began being called up to the front, I could see the familiarity with which these youngsters greeted the *Muppet Show* characters – they were on first-name terms with every single puppet and clearly star-struck to be working alongside them.

I was already beginning to suffer a case of incipient stage fright when Richard Hunt, the only one of the Henson regulars whom I had met before, spotted me across the hall and shouted, 'Hey, Zippy, how ya doin'?' The throng of young rivals turned their heads and shot daggers at me, while the chap next to me obligingly explained: 'They're just worried, mate. If Zippy's here, what chance do they have?'

177

Great – now I had the pressure of expectation, as well as my lack of preparation, to contend with.

Somehow I managed to keep my cool as one by one my rivals performed their impeccably rehearsed audition pieces. I clapped politely at the end of each, until I found myself at the top of the list. 'Ronnie Le Drew...' boomed a young African-American man, Kevin Clash, who was holding the furry red monster he operated on *Sesame Street*, which one of the pipsqueaks informed me was called Elmo.

Tentatively I stepped up to the table where Jim Henson and his team were sitting. Jim was a quiet, thoughtful soul, with the bushy brown beard of a sea captain. He sat very still throughout my improvised performance, watching carefully while Kevin put me through my paces. My little beaver was introduced to Elmo and the two of them got to know each other while the panel of puppeteers made notes on bits of paper, evaluating my puppetry skills like a group of farmers grading eggs. I could feel the eyes of everyone in the room burning into my back, and by the time Kevin finally set down his puppet and turned to whisper something to Jim I was in a cold sweat. I was convinced I had made a terrible fool of myself, rambling away in a squawky cod-American accent (I had reasoned that beavers came from America but forgotten I was performing to genuine Yanks) with no prepared audition piece and no idea which of their wretched Muppets was which.

'Thanks, Ronnie,' drawled Jim eventually, 'we'll be in touch.' A round of applause echoed through the hall, but I couldn't bring myself to turn and see if it was genuine or mere politeness, so I grabbed the beaver puppet and shot out the door.

Once back on the street and away from the stares of the embryonic Muppeteers, I felt the pressure of my embarrassing ordeal surging up inside me. I filled my lungs to the full and let rip with the biggest scream I had ever uttered, frightening an elderly passer-by half to death. I immediately felt guilty – but also unquestionably better about flunking the audition.

A few days later I was astonished to get a call from the Hensons asking me to work on their movie. I suspected I had been bottom of the heap but I couldn't care less – I was over the moon to have scored a job on a feature film. I immediately rang my friend David Claridge (aka Roland Rat), to let slip in passing that I was about to start work with David Bowie. I knew my pal would be insanely jealous – he was such a Bowie obsessive that when *The Man Who Fell to Earth* had come out he had driven all the way down to London from Birmingham in a Ziggy Stardust outfit to stand by the red carpet at the premiere.

My over-inflated ego was soon punctured, however, when I discovered that half the British puppetry world seemed to have been offered a job on *Labyrinth*. Among the numerous friends and acquaintances of mine who had also been called in were Christopher Leith, Nigel Plaskitt, Sue Dacre (a very proficient puppeteer who had designed for the Little Angel) and Gillie Robic (a friend of Caroline's who had recently stood in as George on *Rainbow*). The five of us arranged to meet at St Pancras and take the train to Elstree Studios en masse for the first morning of shooting.

When we arrived, I was giddy with excitement. I had never been to a film studio before and the sheer scale of it took my breath away. We were led through a doorway, past some technical types wheeling along a giant robot, into Stage Nine – a 700 square-metre space that looked like a giant aircraft hangar. Inside, the Goblin King's throne room was being constructed in the style of a medieval castle, with scaffolding rigged up behind it for the puppeteers to sit on. Workmen were cutting round holes in the set walls to accommodate our arms; by the time they had finished it looked like an oversized Swiss cheese that might crumble into pieces at any moment.

There were no scripts available for the likes of us background puppeteers, so we had only the sketchiest notion of the story: the Goblin King (Bowie) had stolen a baby and the child's sister was trying to get it back. Our first scene was a musical number, 'Magic Dance', in which Bowie sang to the baby boy while hordes of goblin minions gathered around to gawp. (The baby – a cute little tyke who actually belonged to the film's designer Brian Froud – was dressed in a red-and-white striped romper suit, and at the end of filming, when the crew learned that my wife had recently given birth, they very kindly offered me the outfit as a memento.) I could see the puppets lined up ready for action not far from the stage. They came in all shapes and sizes, from flying marionettes to lumpen, troll-like glove puppets. I did a quick mental calculation and worked out there must be more than fifty of them – but surely they couldn't have hired that many puppeteers? They had – and before long the hangar was thronging with them, bustling around excitedly, all waiting to be told what to do. I cringed as I spotted some of the young zealots from my horrific audition.

Once the rabble had gathered itself into some kind of order, we were surprised to see Jim Henson arriving on an old bicycle. 'Welcome to *Labyrinth*!' he called out. Jim introduced us to his team from America, who would be operating the lead puppets, and explained that, if any close-up shots were needed of our puppets, they might need to come in and take over – we were strictly 'background artists' and were required only for the wide shots. There were a few muffled *humphs* from the throng – after all, we saw ourselves as the cream of the British puppet crop – but no one dared to contradict the director.

Next, Jim called out our names from a register, assigning a puppet to each of us as he went along. They all had bizarre goblin names – Quilk, Pilch, Spurgus, Weech – and one by one the puppeteers went over to find their charges. We then consulted a chart which had been helpfully pinned up telling us which holes in the cheese our puppets were supposed to be stuck through, before beginning the perilous ascent up the scaffold.

When Jim called out the name of my assigned goblin, there was a great belly laugh from his colleagues. I took this as encouragement, feeling chuffed that the puppet had made such a positive impression before I had even got my hand in. It was only when I saw it for myself that I realised the true cause of their humour: it was the heaviest, most unwieldy puppet of the lot; an ugly, thuggish creature that also turned out to be a nightmare to operate. Reminding myself that only a bad workman blames his tools, I decided to befriend my new puppet partner, and after consulting the chart to find out where the two of us were supposed to be positioned, I clambered up amongst the poles and platforms until we found our designated nook. It was cramped and uncomfortable, the sawdust from the armhole soon ruined my trousers (it wasn't every day I went to work on a movie so I had bought a new pair especially) and I had to share a monitor with the chap on the next platform, but I tried hard to make the best of it.

When the puppets were all slotted through their appropriate holes, Jim came back on set and called up to his assembled goblin horde: 'I'd like you to meet Cheryl McFadden. She'll be choreographing the puppets throughout the movie.'

A young woman with red hair stepped forward beside him, waving up at the wall of her fidgeting goblin charges. 'Hi, guys,' she called out in a cheery American accent. 'The most important thing in this scene is just to keep your puppet moving – it might look tiny on your monitor, but when the movie's screening in theatres every one of your little guys will be on show.' As it turned out, she had nothing to worry about on that count – the more common problem was that, squinting at our tiny black-and-white screens and barely able to see our puppets at all, we would wildly overact, flailing the puppets' arms about just so that we could see what they were doing. Ever so politely, Jim or Cheryl would have to send a message telling us to calm down.

Cheryl was an absolute darling, and took great care to ensure that every shot was composed just how Jim wanted it. All the British puppeteers loved her, and we were amazed that such a talented choreographer was also so comfortable with puppets. As it turned out, these were the least of her talents – a few years later, tuning in to catch the launch of *Star Trek: The Next Generation* on BBC Two, I saw a familiar face manning the *Enterprise* sickbay. It was Cheryl, now going by her stage name Gates McFadden, as the ship's doctor Beverly Crusher.

In the Goblin Kingdom, however, there was only one space-faring celebrity we were interested in seeing, and when he finally came on set mid-afternoon, the mood up on the scaffold was euphoric. To add to the unreality of the experience, we never actually got to see Bowie in the flesh during the filming of the scene; although we were told to react to his every move, the only glimpse we had was on our tiny black-and-white monitors. Even so, his tight leather trousers and outrageous hair made quite an impression.

Ironically, the Starman turned out to be extremely down to earth, quietly walking through his moves with his own choreographer, a hip guy with a background in street dance (I think Cheryl was considered a little too traditional for throwing rock-star moves). Once he was satisfied that he had got to grips with the routine, we were ready to start shooting.

The 'Magic Dance' song had been recorded in a studio, so Bowie was miming throughout, but he had his work more than cut out for him. For a start, the set was perilous for all involved. Great chunks had been removed from the floor to accommodate the lead puppeteers, whose goblins were in the foreground with Bowie, and if he wasn't stumbling into these pits mid-song then he was knocking into one of the little people strung on bungees who intermittently bounced up and down during the routine.

In total there were about a dozen little people on the film, playing the larger goblin characters, including Kenny

184

Baker (better known as R2-D2) and a teenage Warwick Davies, who had been the Ewok Wicket in *Return of the Jedi* and was now playing a goblin called Bumpot. They always seemed relentlessly positive on set, but I didn't envy them their job. One day Kenny's hair caught light and the fire-safety officer had to leap on him with a blanket, while another time Warwick got knocked unconscious by a stampede of galloping puppets. The most challenging job, though, went to Shari Weiser, who was performing the role of Hoggle, the friendly goblin who assists the film's heroine Sarah (played by Jennifer Connelly) in her quest. Shari had to wear an extremely heavy animatronic mask that was operated by Jim Henson's son, Brian, along with three other puppeteers. With eighteen separate motors and servos rattling away just millimetres from her eyes, it looked like something from Room 101. Her hands, meanwhile, were encased in giant mechanical goblin gloves, with each gnarly finger operated individually by remote control.

I was fascinated by all the technology that the Americans had brought with them. Working on *Labyrinth* was a bit like visiting a mad professor's workshop. I had heard of animatronics but never seen them, and the set was stocked with wonders such as a radio-controlled plant with independently blinking eyes on the end of each stalk and mechanical creatures varying in size from a two-inch worm to the fifteen-foot-tall robot, Humongous. It was a completely different world from the low-tech British puppetry scene.

In our lunch breaks all distinctions of nationality were forgotten, and we Brits soon became friends with the American puppeteers – in particular Brian Henson, who acted as a kind of bridge between the two groups. Once the Yanks realised how talented and experienced a lot of us 'background artists' were, they were astonished that we didn't push ourselves forward more. The Americans had a very different approach to their art – while even our most revered master puppeteers tended to hide behind their creations, avoiding the limelight, these guys would push themselves into any photo opportunity alongside their puppets, as if to say, 'Don't forget there's a human being down here!' If you found yourself with one of them in a lift, he'd suddenly turn to you with a blindingly bright smile and say, 'Hi, my name's Bob, I'm forty-three and I'm a fantastic puppeteer!' No wonder they found us Brits so shy and retiring.

Oddly enough, the actors on the movie were more diffident – Jennifer Connelly, then just fifteen years old, had none of the typical brattish behaviour of the child star about her. She was charming, polite and totally focused on the job, as well as being a natural at interacting with puppets, which is not as easy as it looks.

David Bowie, too, was extremely easy-going and affable. One lunchtime, Nigel Plaskitt and I bumped into him having a fag round the back of the set.

'Alright, guys?' he said as we froze in our tracks, astonished at seeing the Goblin King in the flesh, rather than just a centimetre tall on our monitors.

I was so star-struck that I momentarily fell dumb, just standing there with my mouth agape, staring – and I wasn't even a Bowie fan.

Nigel fared slightly better: 'Yeah, not bad,' he said, and we went on our way to the canteen.

As we rounded the corner I grabbed Nigel's arm and practically screamed, 'I can't believe we just spoke to David Bowie!'

He looked at me for a moment, one eyebrow raised. 'Well, I did,' he replied. 'You just stood there, Ronnie.'

It was quite true, but by the time I returned to work for the next term of *Rainbow* I had worked the story up to my advantage, determined to give Roy a run for his money in the name-dropping stakes. 'Oh, David and I had a long chat,' I told my colleagues. 'You know, he's such a lovely guy.'

Although we Brits were supposed to stay in the background on *Labyrinth*, I did briefly manage to claw my way into the limelight. It was in the final battle scene of the movie, which took place in an incredible medieval-style village, with puppets of every shape and size firing canons and machine guns at each other, and huge rolling boulders threatening to flatten everything in sight.

The boulders were operated by remote control, but despite everyone's best efforts to choreograph the chaotic scene – Cheryl directing the little people which way to scarper, Brian instructing his team on the precise trajectory of each rock – things never seemed to go according to plan. Usually it was the little people who got unintentionally flattened, but on one occasion my own goblin puppet, who was supposed to dive out of the way at the last minute, found himself quite literally stuck between a rock and a hard place, and there was nothing I could do to save him. I decided it was best to improvise, so I let him take the full force of the impact (it was minimal really, since the boulders were made of foam) and then threw every fibre of my being into the most dramatic death scene I could muster as he took his last gasp.

When the cast and crew gathered to watch the rushes the following morning, a huge laugh went around the room at my puppet's dramatic death, which I took to be a very good sign – it was usually enough in itself to persuade Jim to use a particular take. But it turned out that I had broken the cardinal rule of Henson puppetry. 'I'm sorry, guys,' Jim said, 'but my puppets don't die.'

It was true that throughout the rest of the battle, even after a puppet had suffered the most comprehensive injuries, Jim would always insist on seeing a foot wiggle or hearing a squawked 'I'm alright' to confirm to children watching that each and every one of them had pulled through. My moment in the spotlight had contravened this unbreakable edict, and was consigned to the cutting-room floor.

I first saw the finished film at a crew screening not long before the official premiere, sitting next to Nigel and Christopher at 10.15 one morning in the Odeon Leicester Square. To be honest, I was so focused on trying to spot my own goblin puppet in the background that I barely took in the story. Even only half concentrating, though, I was impressed by how good the movie looked, and Jim was clearly delighted with it. When it went on general release, however, the film turned out to be a box-office flop, making back only half its budget. For Jim it was a crushing disappointment, but in the long run he was proved right. Following its release on VHS, and later DVD, *Labyrinth* gradually garnered a cult following, and these days Jim's bold experiment of mixing humans and puppets is regarded by many as a classic.

The Hensons were a lovely company to work for, and they kept me on their Christmas card list after the movie. I wasn't optimistic about their chances of making another film, given *Labyrinth*'s poor ticket sales, but not long after, when I was back happily ensconced in the *Rainbow* house, I received a call inviting me to another audition. This time, it was for Jim's old friend Frank Oz, aka Miss Piggy, who was directing a film adaptation of the musical *Little Shop of Horrors*.

This audition was very different from the last one. There was no hall full of excited Muppet fans, no huge panel of puppeteers to impress – just Frank and his assistant, sitting in a little office, with a clipboard and looking like they were conducting a driving test. I found Frank to be cheerful and good humoured and much more outgoing than Jim. He explained to me that the film was a musical comedy-horror about a man-eating plant, adapted from an off-Broadway show of the same name. He had been called in due to his experience with puppets, since the centrepiece of the film was to be an unprecedentedly complex puppet plant.

I had brought a simple marionette with me to the audition, and Frank was delighted to see something other than a glove puppet, following the slew of Muppet fans who had previously traipsed through the door. After pronouncing favourably on my string technique, he gave me a Muppet he had brought with him to operate, while he interacted with it using just his hand as a mouth. It was a quick audition but I felt confident that I had made a good impression and I was glad to receive the call a few days later asking what dates I was free to work on the film.

Unfortunately my commitment to *Rainbow* meant my availability was quite limited so I missed out on some of the early ensemble work with the plant. But before long I found myself at Pinewood Studios ready for a two-week period of training. My mentor was head plant-wrangler

Lyle Conway, a burly American with a string of four-letter words at his disposal. Lyle taught me to work the levers that controlled one of the many huge vines sprawling from under the plant, Audrey II. These were metal poles that you yanked this way and that, rather like the sticks that a railway signalman pulls on, attached to cabling which ran under the sound stage and up into the bowels of the plant. It was very hard to master, so I was glad I had plenty of time to practise.

Working at Pinewood was like a dream come true. I had grown up obsessed with the *Carry On...* movies, which had all been filmed there, and wandering around the complex in my lunch breaks I kept stumbling upon sights familiar to me from my childhood. One day I took a sneaky detour to check out the *007* sound stage, a gigantic aircraft hangar the size of a dozen football pitches. It was empty at the time, but the sheer scale of it was enough to take my breath away.

The *Little Shop* set was very impressive in its own right. The production team had constructed an entire neighbourhood of downtown shops and apartments – a grimy, sordid environment that felt remarkably real, until you looked behind the flats and saw only weights and poles. The whole thing was built on top of one of Pinewood's many swimming pools, which had been drained of water to accommodate the puppeteers who were working right underneath the rest of the cast and crew.

When I first arrived on set, the others were in the

middle of one of Audrey II's musical numbers, 'Feed Me', playing the music at half speed because that was as fast as the puppeteers could get the plant to move. It was a weirdly surreal experience hearing this distorted music and watching the freaky plant moving in slow motion – and even harder for Rick Moranis, who was playing Seymour, the hapless young man who had adopted it, since he had to move and speak at half speed as well. I stood and watched them filming for a few minutes, until Frank called 'Cut!' on the scene. Audrey II's mouth opened again, wider this time, and I started as I spotted a man inside, dressed head to toe in green Lycra, operating the plant's capacious jaws. 'Hey, Ronnie, how's it going?' he called, and I realised that it was Jim Henson's son, Brian.

Although I wasn't supposed to begin working on set until my two-week training period was complete, Lyle could see that I was fast growing frustrated with merely practising, and began finding little jobs for me to do. These weren't strictly what I had been hired for, but I was delighted to be able to help out, carting gory, blood-spattered limbs away after a take or helping to keep the plant's mouth lubricated with KY Jelly.

My first piece of real puppeteer work on the film was to wiggle the prosthetic legs of Mr Mushnik, the shop proprietor, as Audrey II gobbled him up. I made such a good impression that I was chosen for a very special task of my own: a close-up of a single vine as it dialled a number on the telephone. For this, I knelt just out of shot and used a specially constructed precision mechanism. I suppose Frank figured that my marionette skills would come in handy for such a fiddly manoeuvre. Nonetheless, he left nothing to chance, directing me through the procedure moment by moment as he squinted at his monitor: 'Come up here... along there... down... now point... straight in, and...' – I dialled the first number – '...now let it go round... again...' and so on. I had no idea what number I was dialling – it was as much as I could cope with just trying to keep the vine moving while paying attention to Frank's extremely detailed instructions.

Other than this brief moment in the spotlight, I mostly worked under the soundstage alongside all the other puppeteers, a whole team of us pulling on our various levers like slaves in a galley ship and hoping that the plant above looked as though it was moving with one mind. It was a truly collaborative process – very different from operating a glove puppet, where you have complete control of its every movement; but my work at the Little Angel had prepared me for this kind of egoless performance, where your own contribution was just a small part of a far more important whole. Sometimes Frank would have to call 'Cut!' because one vine seemed to have a mind of its own, but generally I think we puppeteers did remarkably well as a kind of collective consciousness. The cast up above us were very complimentary about what we were doing, and Rick Moranis told us he felt like Audrey II was real – whenever lunch was called and the puppeteers let go of their levers, the giant plant would droop forlornly and he'd say he felt as if his co-star had died.

The collaborative ethos extended further than just the vines of the plant – overall, it was the friendliest and most easy-going film set I have ever worked on. Frank even took time out of his lunch breaks to play table tennis with the cast and crew, and everyone ate and mingled together, with no distinctions of rank or status. Rick and Ellen Greene, who played Seymour's love interest, Audrey, were a really lovely pair and hugely supportive of the puppeteers. If Rick ever made a mistake during a take, he would kneel down and shout 'Sorry, guys!' to all of us working below. Ellen, meanwhile, was always game for a laugh, which was just as well because she bore the brunt of the plant's worst behaviour, with vines always trying to tickle her or pinch her bottom. She was probably used to it – as the only cast member to have transferred from the musical straight into the film, she had been working with various versions of that naughty plant for years. The one thing we did have to be careful of, however, was Ellen's huge blonde wig: if we accidentally knocked it off her head, Frank would be forced to call 'Cut!' and we would have to do the whole take again.

However, the most common cause of lost takes in puppetry scenes were purely technical and not the fault of us puppeteers. The technology behind the plant was extremely advanced – it had been designed with the help of the Atomic Energy Authority at Harwell and involved more than eleven miles of cabling – but on occasion it would fail, usually mid-song, leaving Audrey II with a severe case of lockjaw. Everyone saw the funny side of this, and cast and crew would fall about laughing – everyone, that is, apart from head plant-wrangler Lyle, who would storm onto the set in a frenzy, effing and blinding, and desperately try to resuscitate the temporarily immobilised plant.

It was a really wonderful working experience, and I was just sad that I couldn't be there for longer. But inevitably *Rainbow* beckoned, and when Frank Oz came into the green room one day and asked who would be prepared to do a few weeks' extra time beyond the end of our contracts, I was the only puppeteer unable to put up their hand.

As a result, I also missed out on a controversial part of the film's development: the shooting of a totally different ending to the one in the script. Originally the film was to follow the plot of the musical, concluding with the plant eating all the other characters and taking over the world. An entire, separate crew had been working on an elaborate model sequence in which a giant Audrey II rampages through New York, in a kind of homage to *Godzilla* and *King Kong*. This remarkable ending had cost more than $5 million – a sixth of the budget for the entire movie – yet when it was screened to test audiences the feeling was that it simply didn't work. Seymour and Audrey had made too strong an impression by that point, and the film's romantic subplot had set the audience up for a happy-ever-after ending; watching their hero and heroine end up as plant food was not at all what they wanted. Both Frank and Rick were very unhappy about tacking a happy ending onto the movie, but in the end the powers that be prevailed and the two lovers ended the story in married bliss, with only a smiling baby plant at the bottom of their garden hinting at the possible devastation to come.

I was excited to see the fruits of my labours, and I was not disappointed when the finished film, with its revised ending, was finally screened to crew and puppeteers at a cinema in Leicester Square. I fell in love with the film immediately and when it was released I dragged all my friends along to see it. I felt the new ending actually rounded it off rather well, and no one I went with realised that it had been a last-minute addition. The music was a revelation, too – it was the first time I had heard any of it played full speed, and the catchy songs had me tapping my feet in the aisle. Audrey II felt like a real creature, and all its limbs appeared to move in unison. But most satisfying of all, my personal triumph with the telephone made it through to the final cut, and for a few short seconds I could rest assured that my work was holding the attention of millions of people around the world. It was the closest a puppeteer could get to feeling like a genuine movie star.

Chapter 11: End of the Rainbow

Back in the *Rainbow* house, Valerie was very much missed, but her successor, Malcolm, had settled in well. He was a charming, cheeky chap who liked a good prank as much as the rest of us.

One day, Roy came up with a plan to disrupt the camera rehearsal for one of Rod, Jane and Freddy's songs, which they were filming in a country garden set.

'I think we should turn the garden into a nudist camp,' he declared. 'Who's with me?'

I rolled my eyes, but Malcolm enthusiastically agreed. He probably had no idea that Roy was actually a practising nudist.

They had soon roped Stanley into their scheme, but I demurred.

'Too coarse for you, are we Ronald?' laughed Roy.

In the green room, the three of them set about making a large sign that read 'Nudist camp', snickering all the time like naughty children. The set featured a privet hedge, and the idea was to take their shirts off and jump around behind it with the sign, apparently in the buff.

When filming began, Rod, Jane and Freddy danced into the country garden through a gate at the side, smiling away and looking very wholesome against the backdrop of rolling hills. '*Make up your mind, make up your mind,*' they sang, clicking their fingers. Then, behind them, up popped the nudist camp sign. Completely oblivious, the singers carried on, past the privet hedge where the 'naked' Malcolm and Stanley were gaily throwing a balloon back and forth.

The crew by this point were trying hard to hide their guffaws, but clearly enjoying the spectacle so much that they didn't want to let on to Rod, Jane and Freddy what was happening. I saw a slight look of confusion cross Rod's face, but he continued to sing, doing his best to hold his fixed grin.

Then suddenly Roy appeared at the gate, waving enthusiastically and wielding a guitar. He had his back to the camera, but it was abundantly clear that he not only had no shirt on, as per the plan, he had no trousers or pants on, either. Luckily for the rest of us one of the slats in the gate concealed his bottom from view, but as he turned to face Malcolm and Stanley then joined them behind the privet bush, the two of them got the shock of their lives.

The next time we were together in a garden set was, thankfully, a much more family-friendly affair. *Rainbow* had reached its thousandth episode – no small achievement in the world of preschool programming – and a group of children were invited on to the show to celebrate with us. To accommodate them, we were bumped up to Studio Two, which had been festooned with bunting and dressed like a fabulous garden party. The rows of little tykes were all wearing *Rainbow* badges and stuffing their faces with jelly, crisps and biscuits.

Matthew Corbett and Sooty were invited as our special guests, and a big cake with a rainbow on it was brought in while everyone sang 'Happy Birthday'. Zippy and George were seated slightly away from the general merrymaking so that none of the children would be surprised by the sight of a grown man crouching under a table with his hand up their favourite puppet. The producers were so determined not to spoil the illusion for our small guests – lest word spread amongst the country's preschoolers that the *Rainbow* characters weren't real – that Stanley was forced to swelter inside his Bungle head all day long without reprieve.

Nevertheless, it was a wonderful feeling to have reached such a milestone, and we were thrilled to learn that the higher-ups at Thames intended to present each of us with a token of their appreciation. Anticipating a gold watch or something similar, we excitedly went to collect our presents, but my face fell when I saw what they had got us: we each received a rather modest earthenware butter dish.

Fortunately, we were provided with more meaningful mementos courtesy of Jane, who had very sweetly paid out of her own pocket for a set of champagne glasses – one for each of us – which had been engraved with an anniversary message. Once the children had left the studio, we all went out for a proper celebratory meal, this time with alcohol included.

Not long after, I had a landmark birthday of my own: my fortieth. On the big day, I went to work as usual, but as I was mounting the stairs of the yacht club I was suddenly accosted by Joan, one of our stage managers. 'Ronnie,' she said urgently, 'I have to talk to you about something.' She dragged me straight into the kitchen and fumbled in her pocket for a pair of spectacles, which she handed to me. 'Um, I thought you could use these as a prop,' she said, looking flustered.

The glasses were tiny – they would surely look ridiculous perched on Zippy's over-stretched head.

'I can't work with these, Joan!' I told her.

'Right you are. I'll just go and get you a replacement,' she replied. 'You wait here.' She scuttled off, leaving me wondering why she was behaving so strangely.

After a few minutes I got sick of waiting and left the kitchen. I walked into the rehearsal room, where I was met with a loud, 'Surprise!' from the entire *Rainbow* team. They had dispatched Joan to stall my entrance while bubbly and presents were being hurriedly organised for a little party. I was incredibly touched, and it was a reminder that they had become as much a second family to me as those at the Little Angel.

Rainbow continued past its thousandth episode in rude health, with Zippy, George and Bungle at risk of becoming seriously big-headed, having achieved a level of fame almost unprecedented amongst their rivals in children's television. Their latest public engagement was on a new Channel 4 chat show, *The Last Resort*, hosted by a then-unknown presenter called Jonathan Ross. 'Wossy' was then a skinny lad in his late twenties, with bouffant hair and a cheap suit, nervous as hell at the prospect of hosting his own show. All his questions were written out on little cards, which he clutched nervously throughout rehearsals.

We had been hired to perform a skit that fittingly skewered the *Rainbow* team's growing celebrity, featuring Zippy writing a tell-all memoir and gleefully rubbing his hands about how much money he was going to make from cashing in on his story. (I made a note to self!)

Ever the worrier, George was concerned that someone might try and stop the book being published when they realised all the naughty stories Zippy had included about his famous friends. 'Read the chapter about you and Sooty,' he advised Bungle.

Bungle opened the book and a look of horror spread across his face as he read the words: 'The zip flies open...'

The rest of the skit concerned Geoffrey's advice on the best chat show for Zippy to go on to promote his book – *Aspell & Company*, *Wogan* or even *The Dame Edna Experience*. 'Just as long as I don't have to appear on *The Last Resort!*' sneered Zippy, by way of a punchline.

As the house band struck up the *Rainbow* theme, Ross sidled over for a brief unscripted exchange. 'What is the reading age of this one, by the way?' he asked Geoffrey, gesturing towards poor George. 'He's a bit on the slow side, isn't he?'

Roy wasn't going to let a jibe like that go by. 'Is he mocking me because he can't say his wubble-yous?' George retorted innocently.

Slightly ruffled, Ross turned his attention to Zippy instead, leaning over the counter to where I was crouched, and remarking, 'There's a man down there with his hand right up Zippy's backside!'

As the crowd roared with laughter, I clung on to the puppet for dear life, terrified that the rookie presenter was about to rip him from my hands and unmask me on live television. Fortunately Ross quickly moved on to his next studio guest, and Zippy and George escaped the encounter with their fur ruffled but their dignity intact.

With *Rainbow*'s wider fame mounting, Thames began to realise it was sitting on a potentially very lucrative brand. The need to protect it was brought into sharp focus, strangely enough, by a visit from comedian Bobby Davro. Bobby appeared in an episode called 'Guess Who I Am', which began with Zippy, George and Bungle impersonating Rod, Jane and Freddy. While Zippy and George flailed around with banjos as Rod and Freddy, Bungle really went to town as Jane, draping his head in yellow wool for hair and squeezing his bear bottom into an alarmingly short skirt. Their efforts were put to shame by Bobby, however, who then launched into scarily accurate impressions of the entire *Rainbow* gang, mincing around the studio as Bungle, singing 'I'm a Little Teapot' in an even Zippier voice than Zippy and doing a pitch-perfect impersonation of George.

We were amazed at Bobby's performance, but it turned out that he'd had quite a bit of practice. He had been performing Zippy and George in his own show for quite a while by then and had even ordered his own set of puppets, which he proudly showed us. They were much simpler than John Thirtle's 'real' Zippy and George, but for knock-offs they were pretty good.

News of Bobby's puppets filtered upstairs, and before long the powers that be had issued a new edict: Zippy and George were to be copyrighted forthwith, to prevent any further unauthorised appearances. Such is the stringency of this embargo on unofficial activities that although I have my own retired Zippy and George at home, to this day I am not allowed to bring them out in public without written permission.

Thames quickly began to find new ways of capitalising on *Rainbow*'s marketing potential. We had always offered badges and annuals, but now merchandising went into overdrive, with lunchboxes, cuddly toys, posters, T-shirts and videos all hitting the shelves. The linchpin of this campaign for control over pint-sized purse strings was the *Rainbow* comic. The dream was that millions of children would pester their parents for one of these every week, and to ensure that this happened the comic was relentlessly trailed in episodes of the show, with Bungle and George, in particular, frequently buried in the latest edition. The writers' objections counted for nothing – this cash cow was going to be milked for all it was worth.

Inevitably, the idea of a live *Rainbow* roadshow was mooted. Thames granted the rights for the theatre version to Ridley Productions and a very pushy booking agent tried his damnedest to get the whole cast on board. Personally I didn't like or trust him one bit, and Rod, Jane, Freddy and Stanley joined me in trying to explain why we thought the television show wouldn't translate well to the stage. For my part, I was worried that the sightlines in the theatres wouldn't work and kids at the back would be able to spot me operating Zippy.

'Don't worry, we'll give you an orange T-shirt,' was the less-than-reassuring response.

Roy had written the script for the theatre version and Geoffrey in particular felt we all had a duty to be involved. 'You're letting the side down,' he told me when I refused to have anything to do with it. I think in the end a stage manager was drafted in to operate Zippy, while a friend of Malcolm's from drama school, Tony Holtham, took on George. Malcolm himself bravely stepped into the Bungle suit. The costume hadn't been altered for him and he had to hobble around in Stanley's shoes, which were four sizes too small. At least the suit had been dry cleaned to remove the odour of its previous occupant's sweat, though. Malcolm had to get used to the restricted vision inside the bear-head while on tour, and like his predecessor he found this tricky: he once ran at full-pelt into the proscenium arch and was almost concussed.

Overall, it was a pretty tough gig for Malcolm. Just before curtain-up in Liverpool he realised he was coming down with food poisoning, but with no understudies he had to simply soldier on. He got through his first scene alright and then staggered away, ripped the Bungle head off and threw up in the wings. 'I'm sorry, guys, I can't do anymore,' he croaked. 'I'll be sick inside the bloody bear suit.' The company manager had a brainwave – he ordered the wardrobe girl to step inside the suit and gave Malcolm a microphone so he could do his lines from the wings, bucket between his legs. The poor girl had no idea what she was doing onstage, but Malcolm did his best to help her, ad-libbing little clues like, 'Maybe I'll have a look out of the window...' Staggering around half-blind in a suit several sizes too big for her that was already smelling slightly of sick can't have been a career highlight for the poor young woman.

Of course, in time the theatre show settled down, and when I heard it was playing in London I took my little son John Phillip to see it. The experience vindicated my decision not to get involved. The storyline included a villain – something that the television programme would never have done – and the tone seemed much more aggressive to me than in the real *Rainbow*. After John Phillip had burst into tears in the first half, I and a fellow *Rainbow* employee, whose son had been equally terrified, left in the interval. When the cast later asked why they hadn't seen me after the show, I did my best to be diplomatic.

The roadshow ran for several years, but Geoffrey and the others came to regret their involvement with Ridley Productions after the company scrapped their tour dates at short notice without paying them. 'NO POT OF GOLD FOR RAINBOW!' was the inevitable newspaper headline, once the press got hold of the story.

When the touring troupe returned to the *Rainbow* house after their first summer excursion, Malcolm was told that he could stay in the bear suit for good – Stanley had decided to part company with Bungle, though he would continue to contribute to *Rainbow* as a scriptwriter. Over the years various urban myths developed to explain Stanley's departure – in one, he was fired after shouting at a child fan, in another he hurled himself off a building in full Bungle get-up. The truth is much more mundane: Stanley had simply had enough of sweating away, day after day, in the suit. He moved to the countryside and set up an antiques business – a welcome change from the daily grind at Studio Three.

We were sad to see Stanley go, but with Malcolm taking on the mantle we were confident Bungle was in good hands. We never discussed our individual salaries at *Rainbow*, but I assumed Malcolm also got a decent pay rise out of it, since actors were always paid more than puppeteers. Tony Holtham was the obvious choice to take over George for the TV show and I found him to be a precise and thoughtful puppeteer.

Malcolm's Bungle was much more physical and energetic than Stanley's, despite the gruelling rigours of the bear suit. His naughty, cheeky personality dissolved any tension when Geoffrey fluffed a line or dried up – Malcolm had seen how difficult the relationship between Geoffrey and Stanley had been and was determined to avoid a similar dynamic.

While Stanley had been quite strict about not wearing

the bear suit any more than was absolutely necessary, Malcolm was quite happy to keep it on all day. But Stanley put his successor's dedication to the test at one point, penning an episode for us in which Bungle performed a ballet routine. After pirouetting around the studio in a shiny blue tutu to the 'Dance of the Sugar Plum Fairy' for hours, even Malcolm needed a lie-down.

Bit by bit, the *Rainbow* family that I had grown up with was beginning to splinter. Stanley's departure was quickly followed by that of Rod, Jane and Freddy. This time the motivation was financial rather than creative: with the country heading for recession, Thames needed to cut costs on the programme, and slashing three salaries at once was the simplest option. In any case, the musicians now had their own spin-off show so there was no danger of them starving. They devoted their extra time to live performances, touring to major theatres all over the UK – something they continued to do for many years. In 1995 they won the British Academy of Composers, Songwriters and Authors Gold Badge Award for their outstanding contribution to the music industry: over two decades, they had written an incredible 2,000 songs.

After we waved farewell to Rod, Jane and Freddy, we had to rely on various guest stars to provide our musical interludes. Children's presenter and writer Christopher Lillicrap, who had previously written episodes of *Rainbow*, came in with his guitar a few times, and Dawn Bowden, who had supposedly moved into Rod, Jane and Freddy's place next door to the *Rainbow* house, became a semi-regular on the show, providing a much-needed female presence in the now all-male line-up. Extra characters also came and went: *Carry On...* star Patsy Rowlands was 'Auntie' for a while, and an Asian couple moved into the neighbourhood for a bit then inexplicably disappeared.

We were further unsettled when the *Rainbow* house itself was uprooted from the relative luxury of Teddington Studios to a basement room at Thames's Euston Road headquarters. This prompted much moaning from Roy and Geoffrey, who now had a proper commute into work, while I was quietly happy that my own travelling time had been cut. Nevertheless, I couldn't help feeling that the move heralded the end of an era.

Returning to the Little Angel to work on their Christmas show that year, I felt a sense of relief. Here, at least, was one place that seemed to remain forever unchanged. Despite being in his eighties by now, John Wright was still running the theatre with as much enthusiasm as ever. I noticed that rehearsals seemed to tire him out a little more quickly than they once did, but surely that was to be expected.

My complacency was short-lived. Arriving at the theatre one day, I was met with the news that John had suffered a stroke and had been taken to the Whittington Hospital.

I was anxious to see him, and as soon as he was up to having visitors, I hurried over. When I got there, the sight of John in a hospital bed made me feel unspeakably sad, but he was as determined as ever, demanding to know how the theatre was getting on and whether tickets for the Christmas season were selling well.

When he finally came home, it was in a wheelchair – but, worse than that, he could no longer operate his beloved marionettes. A revival of *The Little Mermaid* had been planned, and we all knew that John always played the title role – it seemed wrong even to contemplate going ahead without him. But he called me to one side, insisting, 'I want you to play the mermaid now. She's yours.' I felt incredibly touched that he had given me his signature part, and inwardly vowed to give a performance that John himself would have been proud of. As we rehearsed the production, I realised for the first time what a high level of precision it required to capture the movement of the gliding mermaid quite as exquisitely as John had done.

On opening night, as the familiar music started, I felt a pang knowing that this time my mentor was in the audience merely watching. A part of me was transported to my fifteen-year-old self again, desperately trying to impress him, as I struggled to make the strange role-reversal feel tolerable.

As soon as the show had finished I rushed up to John and anxiously asked if I had done alright. 'Yes,' he said, with a little smile. 'You're doing a lovely job. Just try to relax a bit.'

Me and Bonnie (aged 3) on the boat to England

Dad holding us on deck

Me (aged 10) outside the Stockwell
Gardens estate

Our school photo (aged 8)

(L to R) John Wright, Lyndie Wright, Christopher Leith, me, Joyce Wren and Mary Kenny outside the Little Angel (1964)

Me blowing smoke down a rubber tube for the sea witch's cauldron

Me outside the Little Angel

The Little Angel company in front
of the marionette stage

Me up on the bridge

John, Lyndie and me on the bridge,
with puppets from *Rapunzel*

John Blundall, Ann Hogarth, Jan Bussell, Richard Bradshaw and me
outside the Hogarth Puppets caravan in Kensington Gardens (1965)

Backstage with Muffin the Mule

The audience waits for the start of the performance

The caravan parked up for the night. (Notice the egg stain!)

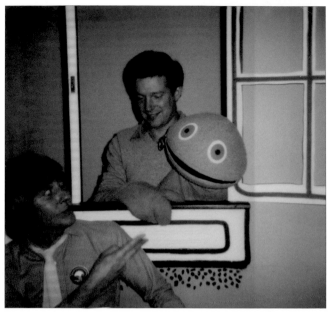

Geoffrey Hayes, Zippy and me on the *Rainbow* set (1973)

On the set with Zippy and George

Me and Zippy some time
in the 1980s

Performing with Snitch and Dodo at a local library

A school visit with Zippy

Zippy and me (1991)

Visiting a local school fete

Valerie Heberden

Roy Skelton in his 'hole' on the *Rainbow* set

Malcolm Lord operating George. (I'm under the counter.)

EP. 4 I/LINK

□= waistcoat closed & sunglasses

EP. 12 "HOLIDAY"
I /LINK

closing
strip of belly
showing
Re-set
BEFORE

Continuity pictures made for Tetra Films,
showing puppeteer Craig Crane and
myself (1994)

Mathew Corbett, with me and Harry under the table operating Sooty and Soo

On location with Sooty and Sweep. I'm at the bottom, operating the puppets. Daphne Shadwell (with script) is directing. Matthew looks on from above.

On the road with Sooty, Sweep and Soo

Me and my goblin on the set of *Labyrinth*

Sitting on Jareth's throne with another goblin puppet

(L to R) Glyn Edwards, Richard Bradshaw, Charleen Agnew, John Blundall and me, with Panto and Violet seated in front of us (1964)

Vivien Trant

Me and John Thirtle, some time in the 1960s

My wedding to Caroline,
26 January 1983

My mother, me and Bonnie, some time in the 1980s

With my grandchildren Olive, Felix,
Daisy and Theo (2018)

Felix

Daisy

Theo

Olive

Not long after John had his stroke, I was shocked to see on the news that Jim Henson had died, at the age of just fifty-three, from a sudden attack of pneumonia. The funeral was held in New York, but a month or so later the Hensons laid on a spectacular memorial service at St Paul's Cathedral, to which many puppet luminaries were invited. Naturally, John Wright was on the guest list, and since Lyndie knew that I had worked with Jim on *Labyrinth*, she suggested that I take her place in escorting her husband to the service in his wheelchair.

It was a truly spectacular event. Readings were given by Jim's son Brian, Frank Oz, and other friends and family, and Big Bird and the whole family of Muppeteers and their puppets sang Kermit's famous song, 'It's Not Easy Being Green', in memory of Jim, to a standing ovation from the congregation. On Jim's strict instructions, no one present – including the puppets – wore black.

Back at the Little Angel, John was trying to do as much as he could despite his physical deterioration. He couldn't operate any puppets but he kept himself busy in the workshop carving new ones, and the cottage next to the theatre, where he and Lyndie lived, was modified to accommodate the wheelchair. But a year or so later a second stroke made far more of an impact – John became much quieter and more fragile, as though the wind had suddenly gone out of his sails.

Lyndie kept things ticking over with the theatre so that John could rest. When I visited him he would often fall asleep mid-sentence and I would always be terrified that he might have died, but a few hours later he would wake again for a brief, but perfectly lucid, conversation. 'Ronnie,' he said one time, 'I know I'm dying. I want you to take over the theatre after I'm gone.' I was speechless. It meant so much to me to know, after all these years, how highly John rated me as a puppeteer. I don't think I'd ever realised until that moment how much faith he must have had in me. The thought that he would entrust me with his most precious possession – the theatre that had been his life's work – was overwhelming. But the idea of the Little Angel without John was one I couldn't even get my head around.

The fourth of March 1991 was Caroline's fortieth birthday and we had invited the Wright family round for dinner. They were seeing Alan Bennett's *The Wind in the Willows* at the National Theatre in the afternoon, so they were going to come over after the show. John and Lyndie, along with their children, Sarah and Joe, who were by now young adults, all enjoyed the production enormously. But in the taxi on their way back John suffered a heart attack, and Lyndie called me from the hospital to say that he had died.

That evening there was a knock on the door. Lyndie and the two children had decided that, rather than cancel our dinner plans, they would join me and Caroline anyway. We were all in a state of shock, but it meant a lot to me that the Wrights chose to spend that evening with us. They had been like a second family to me when I was young, and John dying felt like losing a second father.

The funeral service took place at the Little Angel. I helped carry John's coffin through the auditorium and then sat with Lyndie, Sarah and Joe in the front row. The theatre's blacked-out windows had been thrown open so that daylight filled the space, music from *The Little Mermaid* was playing and puppets had been set up all around. In the midst of such sadness it was an exquisitely beautiful sight, and I thought back to my first time sitting in that auditorium, transfixed by the mermaid's balletic beauty and little knowing that the course of my young life was about to change so dramatically. I recalled the many wonderful years I had spent working at the theatre, and John's formative influence on my career as a puppeteer, and wondered how it could ever be the same without him there.

Despite John's personal wish that I should take over the theatre once he was gone, it turned out that the appointment of a new artistic director would have to go through official channels. I was called in for an interview with the theatre's board, the Potheinos Ltd – named by John after the earliest known puppeteer in Europe. 'Don't worry, Ronnie,' my friend Vivien Trant told me, 'I'm sure it's just a formality.'

I was terribly nervous going in for the interview. The board comprised an imposing group of individuals and I knew that even John had felt intimidated when he used to go and ask them for money. I sat waiting in the theatre workshop, shivering from a mixture of nerves and the cold weather, until I was summoned before them.

The board members asked what I would programme if I was artistic director, and I told them I would continue in the tradition John had established, proposing to revive some of the best productions in the Little Angel's repertoire. They then tried to get a sense of my business skills. Here I felt I had to come clean about my lack of experience, but I suggested that the theatre administrator and I could run things together, with him taking care of the business and me focusing on the artistic side of things. This would also mean that I could honour my existing commitment to *Rainbow*.

Once the board felt satisfied that they had put me through my paces, I was free to go – and to begin the agonising process of worrying if I had made a good enough case to fulfil John's wish that I should succeed him. He had once told me, only half in jest, that I had sold my soul to television when I took the job on *Rainbow* – and I was desperate to prove that it wasn't true.

It was Lyndie who put me out of my misery in the end, coming round to my house personally to inform me of the board's decision. 'Ronnie,' she said gently, 'I'm so sorry, but they've decided to go with someone else.'

I felt crushed, not so much at missing out on the job, but at the thought that I had failed to carry out John's wishes and keep his theatre in a safe pair of hands. 'Who's going to take over?' I asked her.

'Christopher,' Lyndie replied gently.

I breathed a sigh of relief. Christopher Leith had just finished a stint operating puppets for the National Theatre. I knew that he would be a great appointment for the Little Angel, protecting the traditional repertoire while expanding in more innovative directions as well. Lyndie told me about some of his plans, which were far more ambitious than my own – he intended to broaden the ethnic scope of the theatre's productions and provide formal training for apprentice puppeteers. Although I was disappointed to miss out on the top job myself, I felt sure that John would have been happy to see Christopher in charge.

After John's death, with future work at the Little Angel uncertain due to the theatre's new remit, I felt more relieved than ever to have regular employment in the shape of *Rainbow*. But the changes taking place at Thames were making me nervous. Not only were we in a smaller studio with a smaller cast, we were now producing only twenty-four episodes a year – less than half the annual output of our heyday in Teddington. Other shows in the building were shutting down production completely, and the place was beginning to feel a bit like a ghost town.

The year before, Margaret Thatcher's government had passed a law changing the way the ITV franchises were awarded. Many people – including Geoffrey, who followed the story closely in the *Guardian* – saw it as retaliation against Thames for a documentary that had exposed the alleged executions of three IRA suspects by members of the SAS in Gibraltar. Thatcher had attempted, and failed, to block the broadcast, and from then on saw Thames as a personal nemesis. Previously, the franchises had been awarded based on a mixture of good accounting and quality programming, but under the new system they would simply go to the highest bidder in a blind auction. A rival company, Carlton, had attempted a takeover of Thames a few years before and were still desperate to get their hands on the franchise. If they succeeded in wresting it from Thames, there was no knowing which programmes, if any, would survive.

At the time, we weren't privy to the political ins and outs of all this, as they were being discussed at length among the powers that be upstairs, but it was clear that Thames's future hung in the balance and nobody was certain what the outcome of the auction would be. Our priority, as ever, was to keep the quality of the programme high and to try not to worry too much about what might happen next.

The last episode of our twentieth series was a classic *Rainbow* instalment, penned by our regular writer and guest guitarist Christopher Lillicrap. Entitled 'If Only We Hadn't', it featured Zippy and George ransacking the kitchen in an attempt to make a silver toy rocket, which they had read about in one of Geoffrey's books. For once, the two puppets played together nicely, carefully emptying out a tube of washing up liquid for the rocket's fuselage, feeding cornflakes to the birds in the garden so they could make wings from the empty cardboard box, and then wrapping the finished rocket in several sheets of tinfoil. Their creation was a triumph, but when Geoffrey returned from clearing out the shed and offered to make some chocolate cornflake cakes, they realised the mistake they had made. With a dirty baking tray, no tinfoil and the last of their cornflakes fed to the birds, the trio would have to wait for their treat until Geoffrey got back from the shops.

Christopher's script embodied many of *Rainbow*'s best qualities: strong character interplay, a subtle underlying message, and even a bit of the show's trademark cheeky humour – when Geoffrey told the others that he was having a clear-out and asked for suggestions for what to get rid of, Zippy helpfully chimed in, 'You can start with Bungle – we don't need him anymore!'

The episode ended with Geoffrey's usual farewell to camera: 'We've got to go, but we'll see you again soon, I hope. Goodbye!'

Those two words – 'I hope' – rang in my ears as we all went home for the summer.

A couple of months later, I saw on the news that our fears had been realised and Thames had lost their franchise to Carlton. Worse still, the new bosses had announced that only two programmes were expected to survive the chop: *This is Your Life* and *The Bill*. There was no mention of a last-minute reprieve for *Rainbow*.

After nearly twenty years working on the show, I couldn't quite take in what was happening. *Rainbow* had been the most solid, dependable thing throughout most of my adult life. It had always weathered the storms that had buffeted it before: sex scandals, budget cuts and even the cast's bitter script wars. Now it seemed that Mrs Thatcher, not content with stealing milk from millions of schoolchildren, was confiscating their favourite TV show as well.

The news of *Rainbow*'s demise was formally confirmed in a letter from our producer, Charles Warren. He wrote saying he knew that by now we would all have heard the rumours, and that it was his sad duty to confirm that they were true. There would be no more *Rainbow*.

I felt numb with disbelief and fear. For the first time in two decades I had no regular work lined up, and I now had a mortgage and bills to pay, and two young children to take care of. My successful career as a puppeteer had suddenly come crashing down around me, and the only 'proper job' on my CV was a stint of envelope-stuffing some thirty years ago.

I began to wonder whether my father had been right about 'this puppetry lark' all along.

Chapter 12: Christmas with the Muppets

That weekend I ran to the place where I knew I would get sage advice and comfort: Vivien's house opposite the Little Angel. As my friend poured out the tea, I poured out my heart.

'It's all over, Vivien,' I declared. '*Rainbow*'s finished, and so is my telly career. I'll never be able to keep going as a puppeteer now. I'll be penniless.'

Vivien nodded understandingly as she sipped her tea. When I'd finished my prophecy of doom, she cleared her throat.

'Ronnie,' she said, 'did you think that *Rainbow* would last forever?'

'No, of course not,' I began. 'Well… maybe.'

'*Rainbow*'s been a great success for twenty years, and you should be very proud of that,' she told me. 'But there's more to Ronnie Le Drew than Zippy.'

On the way back home to Highbury, I mulled over what

Vivien had said. Perhaps *Rainbow*'s longevity had given me a false sense of security. What right did I have to expect the show to go on forever? I didn't own the programme – I had been no more than a paid employee. I was a jobbing puppeteer and always had been, and now that this job was over I would just have to move on to the next one.

But as I walked along the pavement, unrecognised by the passers-by in the street, the painful reality hit me that it was Zippy who had made himself a star over the past two decades, not me.

The next morning I awoke with a sense of dread in my stomach. I went downstairs and joined Caroline and the kids at breakfast, but when she left to take them to school the house was empty and there I was: just me, alone, with nowhere to go and nothing to do.

I tried to busy myself clearing away the breakfast things, and had half-heartedly begun to do some housework when the phone rang. I dashed to grab the receiver like a drowning man reaching for a lifeline.

'Hello?' I panted.

'Hi Ronnie, it's Pete Coogan.'

I almost dropped the phone. Pete was the production manager for the Hensons and I knew a call from him was bound to bring an exciting opportunity.

'How busy are you at the moment?' he asked.

I looked at the particles of dust I had whipped up

into the air with my broom. 'Oh you know, bits and pieces,' I said.

'Well, Brian's doing a Muppet version of *A Christmas Carol* with Michael Caine as Scrooge, and we're looking for some Brits to help out. There's not as much to do as on *Labyrinth* – probably only a couple of weeks' work and mostly crowd scenes – so I'd understand if you weren't interested...'

'I'll take it!' I cried.

By the time the kids came back from school the entire house had been cleaned in a joyful frenzy from top to bottom and Dad was whistling away as he cooked their tea.

I arrived at Shepperton Studios a few days later, buzzing with excitement. This was where *Gandhi* and *Cry Freedom* had been shot, and here I was, about to star in a film with Michael Caine! (Well, not 'star', I reminded myself – the puppets were the stars!) Inside, the studio looked absolutely enormous. In one corner, part of the set was lit up, and as I drew closer I found it was a not-quite-lifesize version of a Dickensian London scene, all cobbled streets and quaint, wonky houses covered in snow (well, foam) and looking very Christmassy, despite it being the height of summer outside. It was set high off the ground to make room for the pits that the puppeteers would stand in so that their characters could appear to walk at street level.

'Hey, Ronnie, how's it going?' called a familiar voice. I turned to see Brian Henson and rushed over to greet him. It had been only two years since I'd seen him at Jim's funeral, but he looked so much more grown-up somehow. The company was his now, and here he was, about to direct his first Muppet movie without the guiding eye of his father. Before I had a chance to talk to him, however, he was whisked away and drawn into a conversation about lighting. In the past, Brian had always been the bridge between the puppeteers and the director, and between the American puppeteers and us humble Brits. But it was clear he wouldn't be able to play that role any longer.

I was relieved to spot a gaggle of British puppeteers drinking tea at the side of the set. Among them I recognised many old friends: Sue Dacre, Gillie Robic, Christopher Leith, Nigel Plaskitt, John Thirtle and his partner Ian Allen. 'How are you, Ronnie?' Sue asked, as I joined them and was passed a cup of tea.

'Oh, fine,' I replied. I knew they were all probably wondering how I was coping with the loss of *Rainbow*, but I was determined not to go into it.

Luckily it wasn't long before we were put to work filming scenes for the opening number, 'Scrooge'. Sung by a succession of impoverished-looking puppet and human extras milling about the wintry streets, it told of the meanness and cold-heartedness of Scrooge – or 'Mr Humbug', as they called him. Just as in *Labyrinth*, we Brits were to clamber up scaffolding and stick our puppets through holes in the set so they could sing from the windows of the little houses. The Henson company's Creature Shop had obviously been busy creating a whole world of Victorian puppets, and soon it was Muppet mayhem all around. Wizened old crones chucked slops out of their windows, market sellers flogged squawking turkeys that wouldn't stay in their boxes, a horse and cart carried melons that cried out that they were being abducted, a cow mooed as it meandered through the streets, and in amongst it all two real sheep were wandering around, bleating. Meanwhile, the humans had to bustle about in period costume, pretending to look busy while trying their best to keep an eye on where the puppeteers' pits were so they could avoid falling into them.

Into the chaos marched Michael Caine, looking every bit the miser in his black clothes and pointy shoes. All he really had to do was stomp about looking miserable for a few minutes before muttering the word 'humbug' and shutting his front door on us, but the number took days to film, due to the multitude of Muppets involved. I couldn't help wondering how he felt, being surrounded by a cast of puppets, but every time Brian yelled 'Cut!' the miserable grimace he had assumed would melt away and he would be laughing and joking with the lead puppeteers down in the pits. I silently prayed that I would get a chance to appear in a scene with him, rather than staying stuck up on my scaffold, but I knew that it was usually the American puppeteers who tended to get the more prominent roles.

The real star on set wasn't Caine, however. It was someone far more important: Kermit. Before he died, Jim Henson had bequeathed the green amphibian to Steve Whitmire, a lovely young puppeteer from *The Muppet Show*, and all eyes were on Steve as he took on the unenviable task of recreating the character in his first filmic outing since Jim's death. I noticed that Frank Oz, operating Miss Piggy as usual, was being extra encouraging and supportive to the young man. Privately, everyone wondered how Steve would cope with all the emotional baggage that Kermit brought with him, and it was strange seeing someone else operate the good-natured little frog. But Steve seemed to rise to the challenge and did a very competent job – even if, to my mind, it wasn't quite Jim's Kermit anymore.

A few days later, I arrived on set to find that filming had fallen behind and we Brits weren't going to be needed for a while. Some of the others happily busied themselves with tea-drinking and chatting, but I couldn't sit still. Once I'd exhausted all opportunities to roam around and nose about the studio, I and a few of the other minor puppeteers hit on a new vocation – volunteering to hold the star puppets in between takes, in readiness for their American operators.

The likes of Miss Piggy and Kermit were so important that we were required to wear white gloves at all times to protect the puppets from our sweaty hands. I couldn't believe my luck when, having donned the gloves and stood obligingly waiting to receive a Muppet, Kermit himself was placed into my care. After checking that nobody was looking, I seized the moment and slipped my hand into the famous puppet, having a quick work of the head. The cloth was beautifully soft and allowed for plenty of movement, which made it possible to make lots of lovely facial expressions. I was getting rather carried away with making Kermit pull funny faces when one of my friends nudged me and I quickly took my arm out, passing the puppet back to its rightful owner with a respectful gloved hand.

The film ended with another big singing number, 'Thankful Heart', with everyone gathering around the table for the Christmas dinner Scrooge had provided, following his personality change. The table was piled high with food, some of it fake, some of it real – including a turkey that was bigger than most of the puppets. To my delight, somehow the puppet I was operating that day ended up near the top of the table, where Michael Caine was sitting. Brian continually stopped filming to call for more puppets to move up to fill the screen and make it look busier, which meant we puppeteers were squeezed tighter and tighter together. But I didn't mind – I was literally within shoulder-rubbing range of a movie star. This time we unknowns were the ones who he was joking and chatting with in between takes, asking whether our arms were aching and cheekily offering us grapes to eat from the display. I might be contorted under a table, but here I was, starring in a scene with a cinema legend.

After my brief brush with fame on *The Muppet Christmas Carol* it was a bit of a jolt coming back to reality. In order to make ends meet I revived my old *Snitchity Titch* show, with the puppets that Panto and Violet had helped me make at the EPA all those years ago, and toured it around local schools and fetes. Unfortunately, time had not been kind to Snitch, and during one particularly sunny outdoor performance, the glue on his neck melted and his head fell off. I had to hurriedly reaffix it with one hand while stalling for time by means of an improvised Dodo monologue with the other. In my haste I brought Snitch back on stage without realising he had his head on back to front, and again Dodo had to explain this to the audience.

Meanwhile, I kept popping my own head into the Little Angel to remind them that I was available for work. When a revival of *The Little Mermaid* was mooted, I was given the honour of not only performing John Wright's role of the mermaid, but directing the show as well. I imagined him looking down on the production and hoped that, if he was, he would be proud of it.

After the run finished I continued with my solo performances with Snitch and Dodo, and slowly the months began to creep by. The kids who came to see me seemed to be growing rowdier than ever and I privately began to wonder how much longer I could carry on as a one-man band. Luckily, I got a call from a friend, Francis Wright, who urged me to come to an audition for a new BBC show for which he was puppetry coordinator. I was torn, being both excited by the idea of working for the BBC and worried about whether I was up to the job, since I would be required to provide the voices for the puppets I operated; although I'd voiced characters at the Little Angel and in my own one-man shows, on *Rainbow* Roy had always been the voice man. But Caroline gave me the nudge I needed and I turned up to the audition nonetheless.

The show turned out to be an adaptation of the popular *Arabel and Mortimer* books written by Joan Aiken and illustrated by Quentin Blake, about a little girl and her pet raven. The BBC knew it was on to a winner with the idea and had invested a lot of money in the series, commissioning shedloads of beautiful latex puppets – but none of them were there at the audition. It was an experience I was having more and more often now that I was considered an established puppeteer: people no longer wanted me to prove that I could operate a puppet, since they assumed as much from looking at my CV. In this case, they were more interested in hearing what voices I might do for the various characters. Being given a free pass for my puppetry should have bolstered my self-esteem, but in fact it did the opposite.

I was handed a script and asked to read the part of a police inspector. Without a puppet on my hand I felt naked, and as I began speaking I was horrified to hear the most awful cod Cockney accent come out of my mouth as I peppered my lines with ''Ello, 'ello, 'ello'. The director said barely anything, while the producer smiled kindly and asked me to wait outside. I thanked them and took a seat, cursing myself and waiting for the inevitable rejection.

After what seemed like hours, my friend Francis emerged.

'I know, I know, I was terrible,' I said apologetically. 'Thanks for thinking of me, anyway.'

'No, Ronnie, I came out here to tell you you've got the job!' he said.

I was so surprised I nearly fell over, and I thanked him profusely. Francis gave me another piece of good news too: my friend Gillie Robic had been cast as Arabel.

A few weeks later filming began, and by the time it did I had marked up in highlighter pen all the lines for my dreaded police inspector. I had also spent many hours rehearsing a new, more convincing accent and was finally convinced that I'd nailed it.

'Hello, Ronnie,' said the director, as I took a seat at the first read-through. 'We've decided you're not going to be the policeman after all. Can you read the part of the mayor, please?'

My heart sank. 'Oh, yes,' I replied, 'of course.'

As the read-through began, I tried desperately to think what a mayor would sound like before we reached my first line: 'What was Lily on about?'

Somehow, in my nervousness, I found myself saying it in a Scottish accent. 'Whar wus Lily ohn aboot?'

Out of the corner of my eye, I could see the director turn to look at me in surprise.

'Could you try that a little differently?' he asked.

'Wha' were our Lily on abowt, eh?' I pronounced, in an absurd, high-pitched Liverpudlian voice.

Where on earth had that come from?

'Maybe a bit more upper-class,' suggested the director.

'Whot was Lily gewing on about?' I repeated, in what I hoped was a top-drawer accent.

The director let out what sounded like an annoyed sigh and the read-through marched on.

By the time the first day of filming came around, I was still grappling with what on earth to do with my wretched mayor. He was in theory the most high-status person in the little town, but he was a very pathetic character whose secretary had to bolster him up all the time and who didn't exactly inspire confidence. The plummy voice I was planning to do just didn't seem to convey that. Then, suddenly, inspiration came to me – in the form of the prime minister of the day, John Major. When the wretched lines finally came up, I narrowed my throat to impersonate his strained tones. Gillie, who was doubling as the mayor's long-suffering secretary, had to suppress a laugh as this unrehearsed, dweeby new mayor came to life. But the director was, finally, impressed, and John Major stayed with us for the rest of the series.

Once I had mastered the voice, I found there were more practical problems to contend with. Beautiful though it was, with its miniature rows of terraced houses, well-tended gardens and little park, the *Mortimer and Arabel* set had been designed very much with the puppets, not the puppeteers, in mind. This made life very awkward for those of us at the taller end of the spectrum. Everything was so small that to keep out of sight I was required to bend down in some very awkward positions, and I could see that Marie Phillips, who operated Arabel's hysterical mother and who was also on the tall side, was suffering too. But we did our best to take breaks where we could to rest our aching limbs and, as we puppeteers were used to doing, to keep our mouths shut about the problems we faced.

One day, I was crumpled up as usual while operating the mayor, who was having a particularly long whinge at Gillie's secretary, when I suddenly felt a searing pain in my shoulder. I was about to cry out in agony when to my relief the director yelled 'Cut!' and called a ten-minute break. As everyone dispersed, I took myself off into a quiet corner to examine the extent of my injury. Gingerly,

I tried to lift up my right arm and immediately the sharp pain shot up into my shoulder again. Horrified, I quickly dropped it and rubbed it vigorously to try and soothe it. After a few seconds the pain had subsided and I tried once more, but immediately the sharp sensation told me my arm was not going to cooperate.

We were called back onto the set and as I returned to my position I panicked. How was I going to get through the next scene when I couldn't lift my hand to operate the puppet? Gillie must have seen the look of fear on my face because she whispered, 'Ronnie, are you alright?'

I forced a smile. 'Couldn't be better,' I assured her.

Crouching down again, I discovered I could avoid the worst agony by supporting my right arm with my left hand. If I did it when no one was looking, once my arm was in position I could carry on controlling the puppet as usual. Somehow I managed to carry on like that until the end of the day's filming, before rushing off to the chemist to buy a bumper pack of paracetamol.

Back home, I told Caroline what had happened.

'Ronnie, you'll have to call them and tell them you can't go in tomorrow,' she said. 'If you carry on you'll only make it worse.'

I thought of poor Violet, slipping her disc on the set of *Rainbow* and being bedridden for nearly a year because she had been too obliging to speak up. I didn't want to end up like that, but at the same time I was aware that within the puppetry world there was an unspoken code that you didn't complain and you kept your injuries to yourself – because someone fitter and more willing than you was always waiting to replace you under the table.

'Oh, it's not that bad now that I've had the painkillers,' I told Caroline. 'I'm sure it's just a pulled muscle and a hot bath will sort it out.' But the bath did nothing to relieve the pain, and soon I was experiencing hot and cold sensations running up and down my arm.

That night, I found it impossible to sleep lying down, and after many fruitless hours tossing and turning I discovered the only comfortable position was sitting upright in a chair. I spent the rest of the night drifting in and out of consciousness, waking up every couple of hours when the painkillers wore off before gobbling some more and sitting bolt upright, praying for sleep to come.

In the morning I woke with a start, wondering what I was doing in a chair. Then, as I tried to lift my hand to rub my tired eyes, the stab of pain in my shoulder served as a sharp reminder. Caroline begged me not to go in to work but, determined not to let word of my injury get out, I staggered in, feeling distinctly woozy from lack of sleep and all the pills I had popped.

Once again, I made sure no one was looking as I shoved my helpless, injured arm up into position with my good arm, and held it there so it could work the puppet, clenching my teeth to ride out the pain. Each time the director yelled 'cut' I took myself off into a corner to take more painkillers and attempt to rub the pain away, while the other performers gathered round chatting as usual. It was very unlike me to be so antisocial, and soon people were beginning to ask questions. Was something wrong? Had they offended me in some way? I felt increasingly guilty as I evaded their well-meant enquiries.

That night, Caroline once again begged me to tell the BBC that I couldn't carry on with the job, and once again I refused. Nor did I agree to go and see the doctor, since I knew he would probably insist that I stayed off work. After another wretched night in my chair, popping pills at regular intervals, I came downstairs to find poor Caroline on her knees, literally praying that her husband would be delivered from his suffering.

As the week wore on the pain got worse and worse, and it began to feel as though someone had stuck a red-hot poker up my arm and was using it to stoke my nerves and tendons. I noticed the painkillers were becoming less effective and, even when I sat still, the throbbing sensation was overwhelming. I thought back to Harry Corbett's horror when he heard that I hadn't insured my hands, and deeply regretted brushing off the suggestion. He was right – as a puppeteer, they were my livelihood, and if they didn't work, neither could I. These thoughts finally prompted me to go to my GP, desperate to find out what was wrong and to get some relief from my misery. 'I think I've torn a muscle,' I told him.

'No,' he informed me, 'you've trapped a nerve, and I want you to take two weeks off work to give it time to heal.'

'I can't possibly do that,' I said at once. 'I have some very important business on at the moment.'

'And what would that be?'

'I'm, er, operating puppets in a show about a girl and her pet crow.'

'I see.'

Eventually the doctor relented and said he would give me a cortisone injection to relieve the pain. As the liquid sank into my tortured flesh it was as if the frazzled nerve had been doused with cool water, and I was astonished to discover that the effect was so immediate that I could lift my right arm up straight away.

'It's a miracle!' I exclaimed at the displeased doctor, and hurried from the room before his warnings about taking it easy recommenced.

Caroline was delighted that her prayers on my behalf had been answered, and I was able to carry on with the rest of the shoot more or less pain-free. But the horror of seeing my puppet career almost meet its maker remained with me. I was no longer the youngest puppeteer on the block, and it was a stark reminder of just how easily everything I'd worked for could suddenly be snatched away from me.

I had been too busy on *Mortimer and Arabel* to pay much attention to the newspapers, but around that time a campaign had been mounted by the tabloid press – the *Daily Mirror*, in particular – to bring back *Rainbow*. One paper had staged pictures of Geoffrey and Bungle queuing at the job centre, while a petition to reinstate the programme had been signed by thousands of fans.

Following Vivien's advice, I had tried to push my disappointment about *Rainbow*'s demise to the back of my mind, and I had been lucky enough to be distracted by my jobs on *The Muppet Christmas Carol* and *Mortimer and Arabel*. But knowing that so many thousands of people still wanted us on their TV screens reignited my indignation and sadness that the show had been pulled while still at the height of its success. I was contemplating this as I prepared to head over to the Little Angel one day, to rehearse a production I was directing of *Hans The Bell Ringer*, when I got a call from my old friend John Thirtle.

'You'll never guess what I'm doing,' he said excitedly. 'I'm making a set of Zippy and George puppets for a new *Rainbow*!'

'Ha ha, very funny,' I said, wondering how John could possibly think I'd find his wind-up amusing.

'No, I mean it, Ronnie. It's for a different company, Tetra Films. Alan Horrox has bought the rights to the show.'

I felt a rush of hope shoot through me. Alan Horrox had

been the last head of children's programmes at Thames, and, having worked on *Rainbow* as a director in the early days, he had always been a big fan of the programme.

'But I think I should let you know something,' continued John. 'They're casting from scratch. You'd have to audition for the role of Zippy.'

That rush of hope stopped dead in its tracks somewhere near my windpipe. 'I see,' I croaked. Audition – for the same job I'd been doing for two decades? I could barely believe it.

'Well, you might as well go up for it, Ronnie – you've done it for a hundred years,' John said encouragingly. 'Oh, and another thing I heard on the grapevine: they're not going to have a presenter. Or a voice man.'

I winced. Poor Geoffrey would no doubt be upset that he wasn't to be included in the line-up, especially after he had been publicly campaigning for the show to return. But at least he wasn't going to be replaced, which was apparently about to happen to the rest of us if we couldn't convince Tetra that we were capable of doing our old jobs anymore. Most alarming for me, though, was that Roy's considerable talents were considered surplus to requirements, so if I got the job I would face the daunting task of stepping into his shoes.

Despite feeling pretty wounded about having to audition, I was determined that if *Rainbow* was to fly high again, I was going to be up there with it. The return of the show was the best news I'd had all year, and the thought of turning my back on it, only to see someone else operating Zippy the next time I switched on the telly, was too unbearable to contemplate. I duly rang Tetra Films and was given an audition a few days away. Once the moment of truth was set down in my diary, I felt my hurt turn into determination and spent hours on end practising Zippy's voice by watching endless videos of *Rainbow*, repeating the lines back to the TV like a hypnotised preschooler, much to Caroline's irritation. I knew it was paramount that I got it absolutely right, but even after many hours of parroting, I wasn't convinced with the results.

Eventually, I decided to enlist the help of a voice coach – a lovely lady called Janette Nelson. Janette agreed to my bizarre mission and listened patiently as I *arrghh-arrghhed* at her in Zippy's characteristic tones. 'More nasal, more nasal!' was her most frequent advice, and by the end of the session I was practically speaking out of my nose.

The voice lesson made me feel more confident and I arrived at the Tetra offices in Tottenham Court Road a few days later clutching a bag stuffed with my Zippy puppet (one of the old rehearsal models), fully ready to resurrect him. I was surprised to find Tetra's HQ was a tiny little place above a travel agent, and as I was ushered to a seat I realised there were four other people also sitting there expectantly with bulging puppet bags. Two of them were puppeteers I knew from the circuit, who greeted me with a sigh. 'Oh well, if you're here that's us out of the running!' one of them remarked wryly. But I was nowhere near counting my chickens.

After a few minutes the director appeared from behind a door and called me into a room. It was Paul Cole, who I knew had directed John Thirtle and his partner Ian's puppet series *The Spooks of Bottle Bay*.

'Well, we know you anyway, because... you know,' he said.

I tried to ignore the weirdness of the situation, and chirped, 'Actually I've got a Zippy puppet with me here. Would you like to see him?'

'Yeah, that would be great.'

Summoning my whole being up into my nasal cavity, I put my hand inside Zippy and instantly I was in the grip of his naughty character.

'Arrghh-arrghh, well, so you're going to be directing me, are you? Well, I hope you know what you're doing!'

Why on earth had I said that? I was supposed to be making a good impression.

'Now, don't forget,' Zippy continued, 'I don't like it when my friends get more lines than I do. I get on with George, he's alright, but Bungle – arrghh-arrghh – he doesn't have to be in it, does he?'

Zippy rambled on, and I felt I hardly had any control over what he said. Was it funny, or was I making a complete fool of myself? Paul and a colleague who was in the room seemed to be laughing, but I couldn't tell if they were just being polite.

Either way, it was a good five minutes before they seemed to remember that they were the ones in charge of the audition.

'Now the new series is going to be very different,' Paul said, as I hastily returned Zippy to his bag. 'For a start, it's going to be set in a shop.'

'A shop?'

'Yes, a toyshop. Zippy, George and Bungle are going to be running a toyshop.'

'Right, I see,' I said, trying my best to sound positive. Perhaps without Geoffrey around to support them, the furry trio had been forced to enter the world of employment.

'There's no Geoffrey,' Paul said, as if reading my mind. 'But there will be a blue rabbit called Cleo.'

'Great!' So far, so bizarre.

'Well, we'll be in touch,' smiled Paul, and we all said our goodbyes.

They certainly had a different take on *Rainbow*, I thought as I descended the stairs to Tottenham Court Road Tube station. Mainly I was just relieved that the audition was over. It had been an awkward situation and not a little humiliating, having to prove I could do something I had already been doing for twenty years. I crossed my fingers that it wouldn't be long before I got a call offering me my old job back. It would be unspeakably awful to have auditioned and been deemed inferior to someone else who had no experience in the role.

I had rarely been so anxious about the outcome of an audition, and for the next few days I was a bundle of nerves, half feverishly excited at the thought of *Rainbow* coming back into my life, half gripped with terror at the humiliation that would ensue if one of those other puppeteers in the waiting room had trumped me. I realised that a large part of my sense of identity had come from being Zippy for all those years, and even if the programme hadn't been on air for a while, if it returned without me that identity would have been taken away.

For days I sat nervously by the phone, until finally it rang.

Chapter 13: Rainbow rebooted

'Well, Ronnie,' said Paul Cole as I clutched the phone nervously, 'it's obvious you've got the job.'

I felt relief wash over me, followed quickly by excitement at the prospect of returning to what I now realised was the puppet I most cared about in the world. It was more than a year since Zippy and I had worked together (aside from our brief performance in the audition room) and I couldn't wait for us to be reunited. With Roy and Geoffrey out of the picture, it would certainly be a very different experience from what I had grown used to. Would a new team be able to recapture the same magic that had made *Rainbow* so popular for more than two decades?

I hadn't even ventured on set before I began reading about the show in the press. Someone had tipped the media off about the *Rainbow* revamp and before long the details were splashed across the newspapers, mostly under variants of 'ITV admits it bungled'. The *Mirror* had gladly taken credit for prompting an embarrassing U-turn and saving the programme.

Not all the press was positive, however, and much of it focused on the absence of Geoffrey – who, at fifty-one, was seen as a victim of ageist casting – and on the new puppet, Cleo, who was widely believed to have 'replaced' him. At this stage, Cleo had yet to be designed and only the sketchiest of details were available, but what little was known about her was enough to raise the hackles of tabloid journalists. The *News of the World* slammed the show for ditching Geoffrey ('found guilty of being over thirty and of being a man') in favour of 'a pale blue, floppy-eared dog (or bitch) called Cleo'. The paper hadn't even got its facts straight, since the new puppet was actually a rabbit.

Snarky comments from journalists were one thing, but soon interviews with my old friends began appearing as well – and it turned out that they had strong feelings about the new show as well. I had assumed that Roy and Geoffrey, who always seemed to have so many contacts in the business and who were frequently on the phone to their agents, would have heard about the *Rainbow* revival long before I got the call to audition, but it turned out that no one had bothered to inform them. Roy announced in the London *Evening Standard* that he felt 'deeply hurt' when he found out about the show from a friend; poor Geoffrey was 'stunned and shocked', according to the *Sun*, and saw the news as a 'kick in the teeth'. Apparently, the first he had heard about it was from a story in the paper. Bungle and George were equally disillusioned – Malcolm told the *Daily Express* that he had offered to play the hapless bear for Equity's minimum wage, while Tony had called three times to ask if he could audition for George but no one had got back to him.

Poring over the details of my friends' collective disappointment, I began to feel a little guilty for having accepted the job. It was Geoffrey, Roy and Malcolm who had campaigned to have *Rainbow* reinstated and they obviously felt betrayed by Tetra's approach to reviving the programme. Our new producer, Alan Horrox, put out a statement to the effect that Geoffrey had no particular right to a part on *Rainbow* as he hadn't even been with the show since the very beginning – which was patently absurd, since he had been part of the show longer than I had. But there was little else Alan could do to divert the tide of hostility that was already building towards the show – and we hadn't yet shot a single episode. Even the organisers of the Save Rainbow Campaign were beginning to express their anger – as far as they were concerned, without Geoffrey and Roy what we were making just wouldn't be *Rainbow*. I thought back to Rod, Jane and Freddy's infamous 'love triangle' – the last time the programme had made such negative headlines in the press. This time it felt even worse, because I was at the centre of the storm.

It was hardly the best backdrop against which to begin filming, but the first read-through was fast approaching and, as much as I was worrying about my old colleagues, I was keen to get to know my new ones. I gave my friend John Thirtle a ring to get the lowdown on my new castmates.

The first piece of news I wheedled out of him was very encouraging. 'Gillie Robic's agreed to play Cleo,' he told me excitedly.

I couldn't have been more pleased. Having an old friend on board made the whole enterprise seem much less daunting, and I knew Gillie was an excellent puppeteer. She was a seasoned pro as far as lip-sync puppets were concerned, and I was sure that in her hands Cleo would soon win over any hostile viewers.

'I don't know who'll be making the puppet,' John continued. 'I was supposed to be doing it, as well as Zippy and George, but Ian and I have got a lot on with *The Spooks of Bottle Bay* and I haven't been all that well, so I think they'll have to get someone else in. The other two are nearly finished, though, and I've given you some moveable eyes this time.'

'Thanks, John, that sounds great,' I replied a little weakly.

My confidence in Gillie was beginning to be tempered by worry. John's puppets were a big part of *Rainbow*'s magic formula. Would someone else be able to make the new Cleo puppet to his high standard? At least my new

Zippy had been made by the maestro himself, I thought with relief.

'And who's the other puppeteer?' I asked nervously.

'A guy called Craig is taking over George,' John continued. 'He's a lovely young man – very bright and very keen, but he hasn't quite got to grips with when to keep his mouth shut on set, so you might have to give him the odd kick under the table.'

'I can cope with that,' I said, relieved that Craig sounded like a nice enough chap. After all, the George puppeteer was invariably the person I spent the most time with. 'And what about Bungle?' I asked.

'Do you know a guy called Richard Robinson? I worked with him on *Spitting Image*. Quite posh, went to Cambridge, I think.'

'Oh yes, I've met Richard,' I replied. We had worked together briefly on a TV pilot that never made it to air.

'Well, apparently he's been running a community theatre in Covent Garden,' John continued, 'and he worked for years on *The Riddlers* and *Puddle Lane* so he knows his stuff as far as kids' TV goes. I'm sure you'll get on fine, and doing the show without a presenter will give it a different energy.'

'Yes,' I murmured, thinking back guiltily to Geoffrey's angry comments in the press. I knew it must be hard for him, being left behind after so many years with the programme. I felt sure that Malcolm and

Roy would bounce back and find other work – unlike poor Geoffrey, their faces hadn't become synonymous with *Rainbow*, so they had more scope to reinvent themselves.

My anxiety must have shown in my voice.

'Don't worry about all that nonsense in the papers,' John reassured me. 'You'll have forgotten all about it by the time you start filming.'

Rehearsals for the new *Rainbow* were held at a school in Battersea. Arriving at the old, red-brick building for our first read-through one Friday morning, I thought back to my first visit to the Teddington yacht club all those years ago. Compared to the dour, gloomy school in front of me, it had been the height of glamour. But times had changed, and I had to get used to it.

As soon as I entered the rehearsal room, I realised just how different it all felt. Although I still had some of the same first-day nerves I had had all those years ago, back then I had been the youngster trying to slot into an existing group – now, however, I was the old pro to whom everyone else was looking for reassurance.

A tall, skinny man in his twenties wearing little round spectacles bounded up to me. 'You must be Ronnie,' he beamed enthusiastically. 'I can't believe you worked on the original *Rainbow*!'

'Pleased to meet you,' I replied, a little awkwardly.

'I'm Craig,' the young man continued, thrusting a hand towards me.

'Oh yes, I've heard about you,' I said, shaking it warmly.

Craig turned out to be every bit as charming as John had said, and was clearly an accomplished young puppeteer. He had been working a lot with the Hensons – in fact, our paths had almost crossed on *The Muppet Christmas Carol*, where he had been operating some ice-skating penguins – and he was full of ideas of how to bring George up to date. 'I've spent all weekend watching tapes of the old *Rainbow*,' he told me excitedly, 'and I've decided I'm going to make some changes. Kids today are a lot more streetwise, and I don't want George to come across as a sissy. So the voice is going to be a bit stronger and the movements will be faster and more Muppety. The old *Rainbow* was great in its day, but we've got to move with the times, don't you think?'

'Yes, I suppose so,' I replied, a little taken aback. I could see what John meant about this young man having a lot to say. I was also a little worried on my own account. Should I have spent my weekend watching old *Rainbow* episodes and coming up with a new approach to playing Zippy? It hadn't occurred to me that the character could be in for an overhaul – I had just assumed we would pick up where the old show left off and that I would do my best to copy Roy's performance.

I was relieved to spot Gillie across the room and excused myself to go and talk to her. It turned out that she still hadn't seen the Cleo puppet and she was beginning to get a bit worried. 'I know we're only reading today, Ronnie,' she told me, 'but it's hard for me to get a sense of the character without knowing what she's going to look like.'

'Don't worry, you'll be fine,' I told her, doing my best to sound reassuring. 'Just play it sort of... rabbity.'

'Hmm,' Gillie replied, still looking anxious.

We gathered around the table to begin the read-through and Melanie Stokes, the show's researcher, began handing out the scripts. Our director, Paul Cole, sat at one end, and to his right was the new Bungle, Richard Robinson.

'Have you met Richard?' Paul asked, seeing me look in their direction.

'Yes, a while back,' I replied. 'Hello again.'

'Good to see you,' Richard replied, quite formally.

'Alright then, everyone,' Paul said, bringing the room to silence. 'Before we start, I just wanted to talk a bit about the new programme. Now, obviously we're delighted to have Ronnie with us, who as you know has played Zippy for donkey's years' – my cheeks flushed red at this – 'but I want to emphasise that this *Rainbow* is going to be very different. We won't have a presenter, the show is now set in a toyshop, and we have the lovely Gillie Robic performing a brand-new character, Cleo the rabbit.'

Paul turned to speak directly to Gillie. 'Now, I'm afraid we've been having some problems getting your puppet made, darling. Believe me, I'm as keen as you are to get a look at it, but we're having trouble finding someone at such short notice, now that John Thirtle can't do it. Don't worry, as soon as we're done here Melanie is going to be bashing away on the phone in search of another brilliant puppet-maker.'

'Uh huh.' Gillie nodded uncertainly.

Suddenly Richard Robinson leaned forward in his chair and announced, 'I'll do it.'

Paul turned to him. 'What's that, Rich?'

'I can make the puppet,' he said. 'I have quite a lot of experience, actually. Just tell me what you want it to look like and I'll bring it along on Monday.'

'Are you sure about this, Richard?' asked Paul. 'I know you've got your lines to learn as well.'

'Yes, of course,' came the reply. 'It's really not that complicated.'

There was a moment's silence and Gillie caught my eye across the table.

'Well, thanks, Richard. That would be wonderful,' Paul replied, before returning to the speech he had obviously prepared. 'I think the changes that we've made are going to help the show, but I won't lie to you: the motivation behind a lot of them is to save money. There just isn't the same kind of cash around as there was with the old *Rainbow*, so this is going to be a streamlined, back-to-basics show. We've got a lovely little studio in New Malden to record in, but the time there is going to be short so we have to get in, do the best shoot we can and get out again, with a minimum of fuss and faffing.'

There were understanding nods and murmurs of agreement all round. 'Alright then,' Paul said, 'let's get on with the read-through.'

Although I had by now got used to the notion of *Rainbow* being set in a toyshop, and not featuring a presenter, actually reading how the new format played out was still quite a strange experience. After a few minutes of Zippy, George and Bungle bickering together, I kept waiting for Geoffrey or Jane to appear and sort them out, but the show remained stubbornly puppets-only. Cleo was the closest thing to an outsider who ever appeared in the shop, although it wasn't quite clear what her relationship to the other characters was – sometimes she seemed to be a regular customer, sometimes a nosy neighbour, and sometimes a playmate. Gillie read her part a little uncertainly, perhaps unsure how to pitch the new character with no idea what she was going to look like, but she adopted a soft, northern accent, which offered a nice contrast to the hysterics of the rest of us.

In Geoffrey's absence, Bungle appeared to have become the de facto parent-figure, which was somewhat hard for me to get my head around. After all, who would leave a blundering bear in charge of a small business? Richard's Bungle voice was posher than Malcolm's or Stanley's, but otherwise the character himself didn't seem all that different. George, meanwhile, as Craig had promised me, was coming across much stronger – in fact, the little pink hippo was giving as good as he got from Zippy. I had been used to the other two characters being a bit on the weak side compared to my own, but suddenly Zippy seemed to have the lowest status of the trio. Meanwhile, I was so busy concentrating on impersonating Roy that I was struggling to bring my own performance up to match those of my new colleagues.

At least Zippy seemed familiar enough on the page, the only noticeable change to the character being that he had acquired a couple of rather annoying catchphrases: 'Simple, pimple!' and 'Fantasticola!' Well, I thought to myself, I guess that must be moving with the times.

At such an early stage in the process, I was careful to keep my reservations to myself. I didn't want to complain that it 'wasn't like the old days', or that the new writers had completely misunderstood the beloved characters. But not everyone around the table was quite so reticent. Most keen to air his every opinion was Richard, who would frequently break off in the middle of a line to address the director. 'I'm not sure about this, Paul,' he said at one point, squinting at the script. 'It says Bungle puts his foot in a bucket, but I don't think that's really in character.' I did my best to keep my eyes from rolling. Of course it was in Bungle's character – the clue's in his name, after all!

Perhaps Richard had taken Bungle's promotion to parent-figure rather to heart and felt his dignity must be preserved as much as possible. Or perhaps he was just used to a different way of working; after years spent on other stalwart kids' TV shows, Richard had become accustomed to lengthy dissections of the script and characters. 'Can you talk me through Bungle's motivation here?' he would ask several times per episode, or 'What exactly is the purpose of this line?'

Paul was typically diplomatic. 'All right, Rich, let's sort that out later in rehearsals,' he would respond, whenever Richard raised a new query.

Personally, I had found it nerve-wracking enough simply having to learn my lines, without questioning the quality of the writing, and all I wanted to do now was get my hands on the puppet. As soon as I got into the rehearsal room on Monday morning I rushed over to where the new Zippy had been propped up and got my hand inside.

The first thing I noticed was the weight. The blinking eyes that John had mentioned on the phone were controlled by a heavy mechanism in the head, which meant the whole puppet was a much greater load to carry, but the biggest structural change was the arm, which was now of a piece with the body, and as a result my movements felt a little constrained. The neck seemed longer than I was used to as well. I was going to have to adjust to this new version of the creature I thought I knew so well.

Poor Gillie was in a much worse situation. While Richard was busy debating and deconstructing the script with Paul, she had got her hands on the puppet that he had knocked together for her over the weekend, and the results were not encouraging. The Cleo puppet was a lurid blue colour, with broad, angular features and small, goggly eyes. It looked more like a dog than a rabbit, and a pretty mangy one at that.

'Ronnie, what am I supposed to do with this?' Gillie whispered, bringing the lumpen creature over to the side of the room, where I was playing around with my new Zippy.

'Oh, it's not too bad, Gillie,' I lied. 'It'll just take a bit of getting used to.'

'It's not the look I'm worried about,' Gillie replied. 'Just try having a work of it.'

I set Zippy down on a chair and took hold of Cleo. 'Oh dear,' I murmured, without thinking. I could barely even get my hand through to the mouth.

After a few moments playing around with Cleo, I could understand why Gillie wasn't happy. The puppet was stiff and unyielding, as awkward to manipulate as it was uncomfortable to look at.

'I just don't know what I can do with that thing,' she told me. 'I feel like I've been given a toy violin when everyone else has a Stradivarius.'

'Maybe you should say something,' I suggested.

'Well, ordinarily I would,' she replied. 'But we've got to work with Richard, haven't we? I don't want to get off on the wrong foot with him.'

I nodded, handing the bright-blue rabbit back to Gillie, who carried it away listlessly under her arm. Neither she nor her puppet looked much like a happy bunny that morning.

I settled down behind a table with Craig, ready to begin the first scene in the toyshop. I had obsessively committed Zippy's lines to memory but pinned my script up just in case, as I had in the past. Crouched down with my arm in Zippy once again, I was suddenly hit with a wave of nostalgia for the old days. In a way it felt just the same as ever, but then I looked around the room and saw a whole new group of people surrounding me for whom this was a new and untested experience. I thought, too, of my old *Rainbow* friends who had so wanted to be a part of it and hadn't been asked back.

So lost was I in my thoughts that when it came time for Zippy to speak I almost missed my cue, momentarily forgetting that there was no Roy in the corner to say the lines. I coughed and blustered my way into them, doing my best to get Zippy's voice right and trusting that the puppetry would take care of itself. But working with Craig's new, improved George was a bit of a distraction – the character suddenly had so much more energy than I was used to, and to begin with it really threw me.

I couldn't possibly blame the puppeteer, though. At the end of each scene Craig would whisper, 'Was that alright?' or 'Is there anything you think I should do differently?'

For me and Craig, the rehearsal went reasonably smoothly, but Richard and Gillie seemed to find it much more difficult. Gillie was was still struggling to get the Cleo puppet to move in the way she wanted it to and was so focused on physically forcing it to bend to her will that the characterisation slightly went out of the window. Richard's Bungle costume was more teddy-bearish than ever before, and his performance was even more camp than the previous Bungles had been. 'Oh, won't somebody help me? *Pleeease?*' he squealed after a box fell on top of him. Every few minutes the head would come off and Richard would address a new query or problem to our increasingly frustrated director.

'Best we don't get involved,' I muttered to Craig, grabbing at his jumper when I could see he was about to stand up and offer his own solution.

'OK,' he agreed, crouching back down again and waiting patiently for Richard and Paul to rectify the problem.

Somehow we got through the first week's rehearsals and a wave of relief washed over me. Perhaps this new *Rainbow* wasn't such a mad idea after all, I thought to myself. It seemed like it was actually possible.

On the way home, a sobering thought hit me: would Roy be watching the new *Rainbow* when it aired? And what about Geoffrey, Malcolm and Tony? I knew they were unhappy about the whole business of the show coming back without them, but that didn't mean they wouldn't be curious. What if they decided my performance as Zippy wasn't up to their standards? I could cope with sour grapes because they hadn't got the gig, but I didn't like the thought of them judging me.

That evening I barely slept, tossing and turning all night long as I waited for our first day of filming to begin.

When I arrived at the studio the next morning, it felt almost like coming home. The three permanent sets (shop front, kitchen and basement) were each smaller than the one I had been used to on the old *Rainbow* but they felt like a part of the same world I had inhabited for so many years.

There was a kind of nervous buzz among the cast and crew, however, and everyone was on edge. Gillie was still deeply unhappy with the puppet Richard had made for her; Richard, meanwhile, had a number of script points he wanted clarified; and Craig had to be stopped from making a new suggestion every five minutes – each one perfectly valid in its own right, but capable of adding considerably to the demands of the day. 'Why don't we have the puppets walking into shot here?' he would ask, or 'I think we need a few more props in this scene – can we get some of the toys off the shelves for Zippy and George to play with?'

'Easy, Craig,' I whispered anxiously. 'This is only episode one. Let's not try running before we can walk!'

We already had greater physical challenges than on the old *Rainbow*. In the past, Geoffrey could always be called on to help with practical matters, but without any human characters this now fell to either Richard – who with his bear paws on wasn't much use – or me and Craig. I was worried enough at the prospect of remembering my lines and doing the right voice, without also having to make a spaceship out of cardboard boxes and sticky tape.

As director, Paul's approach to the new series was ambitious despite the smaller budget. Like Craig, he was keen to see the puppets moving around as much as possible rather than always stuck behind a counter, so we would be wheeled about on movable trolleys below the frame – sending my ingenious scheme of carefully pinning up my lines straight out the window.

As the cameras began to roll for the first episode I was relieved that the words did not desert me, but with so many different things to concentrate on the whole thing went by in a bit of a blur. I barely registered that Zippy's behaviour in the story was wildly out of character, telling George that it was important they let Bungle go to a party he had been invited to, even if it messed up their own plans. I scarcely noticed Richard stopping proceedings for the umpteenth time to complain about an awkward line or bit of slapstick comedy he felt didn't suit Bungle's personality. To be honest, I was quite grateful for the constant pauses as they gave me the chance to mentally go over my lines and get my thoughts together.

I think Gillie found Richard harder to deal with than Craig and I did, since, having made her puppet for her, he frequently stopped to give her tips on how to operate it. 'Oh, I wouldn't do it like that,' he would tell her as soon as the director called 'Cut'. 'Why don't you try it this way?' Gillie would do her best to smile sweetly, but I could tell she wasn't having a good time.

All in all, it wasn't the nicest working environment, and with so many new things to concentrate on, it hardly felt like slipping back into a comfortable old role. The actual puppetry of Zippy I could do in my sleep, which was just as well because it was the last thing on my mind. Still, I kept telling myself, at least I've got a job again – and I'm sure things will settle down soon enough. After all, even the old *Rainbow* had a few false starts before it became so beloved. We were probably doing a decent enough job on the new one, and in time we would get better and better.

When we watched the first episode back, however, my complacency quickly faded. There were Zippy, George and Bungle on the screen, and yet somehow it just wasn't *Rainbow*. My Zippy voice grated terribly, and I dreaded to think what Roy would make of it. Gillie's puppet Cleo looked as awful on screen as off, and her vocal performance seemed a little uncertain too. I quite liked what Craig had managed to do with George, but I didn't feel that my Zippy had been able to match his new-found energy. As for Bungle, the character simply didn't make sense: one minute he seemed to be the responsible adult in charge, making wisecracks about the others refusing to tidy their rooms, like a long-suffering parent; the next he was tripping over and flailing about on the floor like the blithering idiot of old. The basic premise of the show just didn't work, and with no human figure around there was no straight man for the other characters to play off. And anyway, who in the world would leave this bunch in charge of a toyshop (even if it only ever had one customer)?

A kind of creeping dread began to settle in my stomach as I realised what the playback had reminded me of: that afternoon, two decades earlier, when I had tuned in to see my friend Violet's new show *Rainbow* – the disaster that I felt sure would be cancelled in a matter of weeks. In the many years I had spent with the programme, I had almost forgotten how badly it could go wrong.

Paul was grinning encouragingly as the closing credits rolled. 'Well done, everyone!' he said, offering hugs all round. Was he really not aware of what a turkey we had just made? Or did he simply not care, as long as we got the job done on time and on budget? Looking around at my castmates' faces, I was sure Gillie and Richard felt the same way I did, but Craig seemed relaxed and cheerful so I couldn't bring myself to say anything negative. 'Well done, everyone,' I echoed, as enthusiastically as I could.

The next day, we all went back to work and pressed on with filming the next episode – after all, what was the point of giving vent to private anxieties? Over the ensuing weeks I would just have to knuckle down and get on with it.

But while I tried to keep quiet about my misgivings, others were decidedly more forthright. Before long, the first reviews began appearing in the press. 'Oh dear, oh dear,' concluded the one-star review in the *Daily Mail*, while a full-page spread in the *Colchester Evening News* was headed 'Look What They've Done to *Rainbow*!' Worst of all, a lot of the negative attention focused on Zippy and George's voices, claiming the much-loved characters had been 'replaced by imposters', which was particularly galling for me. The letters page of the *TV Times* offered the thoughts of disappointed parents, while even our young viewers seemed bitter about the new programme. In one piece, an eleven-year-old fan described how the new show made her 'feel sick'. Elsewhere, a disillusioned thirty-five-year-old *Rainbow* addict described it as like 'discovering the truth about Santa Claus', branding the show 'an outrage' and 'a fake'. I pictured Geoffrey and Roy sitting down to their breakfast and poring over the reviews. What would they make of the critical slating we had received?

It was hard dragging myself back to Battersea to rehearse the next batch of episodes, but somehow we all managed to slog through it. The mood on set was a little muted, but Richard seemed to have lost none of his perfectionism. In fact, if anything the poor reviews had only fed his zeal for constant improvement. To be fair to him, he was saddled with a rather confused character and all he wanted was a bit of logic to hang on to as he tried to play him. Simply 'bungling' through each ropey script clearly wasn't an option as far as he was concerned.

However, as time went on, Richard's obsessive attention to detail began to grate more and more, until finally things came to a head. We were shooting the last episode of the series and Glyn Edwards was in the director's chair, Paul having decided that he needed to share the load out a little. Perhaps the script was worse than usual but, for whatever reason, the frequent breaks to question Bungle's motivation, and debate every prop and action seemed almost incessant.

'Look, I'm sorry, Richard, but we just can't keep going on about what Bungle would or wouldn't do,' Glyn snapped, after several hours of being bombarded with questions.

Richard went rather quiet and we got on with the next few scenes mercifully quickly. But soon a new problem arose and Richard was demanding that Glyn address it again, whipping off his bear-head and announcing, 'I'm just not sure that Bungle would open the box before the others get there.'

Poor Glyn had had enough. 'For God's sake, can't you just do what it says in the script?' he bellowed, cracking his pencil in two for emphasis. 'I've had enough of this!'

The whole studio fell silent and you could have cut the atmosphere with a knife. Richard had a horrified look on his face, but Glyn wasn't about to back down and apologise. Blimey, I thought to myself, crouched down behind the counter. What's going to happen next?

Suddenly I saw Craig rising to his feet beside me, about to offer his own two pennies' worth. I grabbed at his T-shirt and yanked as hard as I could. 'Craig!' I hissed. 'Not now!'

'Perhaps you're right,' he laughed nervously. 'We should stay out of this one.'

The two of us huddled behind the counter in silence for a while, before peeking out to get a look. Richard had the bear-head back on and Glyn seemed to be busy muttering something to one of the cameramen. Before long, 'action' was called and we pressed on with the scene. Bungle seemed a bit less animated than usual, but there were no more interruptions to query the script and we got through to the end of the show in record time.

'Thanks, everyone, that's a wrap,' called Glyn, making for the door. I stood up and looked around the studio, but Richard was already gone.

I found him slumped in a chair in the dressing room, sitting in the body of his costume with the bear-head resting forlornly in his lap. There was sweat dripping from his brow and a look of abject misery on his face.

'Hello, Ronnie,' he muttered quietly, as I shut the door behind me.

'Are you alright, Richard?' I asked, drawing up a seat beside him.

I thought perhaps he was about to cry, but somehow he marshalled his feelings and managed a weak smile. 'I'm alright,' he replied. 'I'm sorry if I've been difficult to work with. I'm just not used to doing everything this quickly, and with so little care. You must know what it's like – you've worked on shows that were so much better.'

I nodded. I completely understood where he was coming from. Like me, Richard had worked for years on some of the cream of the crop of kids' television and had grown used to colleagues who expected perfection. The programme we were making now couldn't possibly match those standards.

'I just want it to be as good as we can make it,' he said quietly. 'I don't want my work to look naff.'

'I know, Richard, none of us do,' I told him. 'But you have to accept that things are different now. It's not like the old days, when we had time to take things slowly. This isn't one of your old shows, and it isn't my old *Rainbow* either. We've known from day one that the mantra here is quick and cheap – it might not be how we'd like it to be, but for now that's what we've signed up for.'

It was only in saying it out loud that I realised how disillusioned I myself had become. But the difference was that ultimately I had accepted it. This wasn't *Rainbow* as I knew it, and it never would be, but perhaps if I could only let go of the past and embrace what was here in the present, it needn't be so awful after all. Besides, who knew whether we'd be invited back for another series, especially after the reviews we had received. At that moment I was just relieved that filming was at an end and I could go home.

But at the back of my mind another thought still niggled. I might have come to terms with the show we were now churning out, but would my old friends ever forgive me for what we had done to *Rainbow*?

Chapter 14: More Muppet mayhem

My son John Phillip was fast approaching secondary-school age and Caroline and I had spent many months worrying about which of our local schools in London looked the least terrifying. Suddenly, she hit upon a bold idea. 'Why don't we move up to Yorkshire, near my parents?' she said. 'The schools are much nicer up there, and houses are a lot cheaper than in London.'

'But what about my work?' I replied anxiously. I still received fairly regular employment from the Little Angel, and there was always the hope that I'd be called back for another series of the new *Rainbow*, as dubious a pleasure as that might be. Surely I couldn't just up sticks to the country?

Caroline had the perfect solution: 'You can keep the London house as a bolthole for when you're working and get some lodgers in to cover the mortgage.'

I could see that my wife was determined, and her plan really did seem the best possible option. So it was that we packed up and moved the family to a lovely house in Grassington in the Yorkshire Dales.

The move up north also allowed Caroline to realise a long-held dream, thanks in part to a grant from Jim Henson Productions. For the past few years she had been running short summer courses under the name London School of Puppetry, but up in Yorkshire there was scope to expand, and soon residential students were coming up to study. I helped out with classes on marionette and glove-puppet operating but I steered clear of the puppet-making side of things, since I knew it wasn't my forte. Teaching had always been Caroline's passion, and over the course of the first few years up in Yorkshire we were able to grow the school into a serious enterprise offering a professional diploma.

I was coming down to breakfast in our new house one morning when Caroline waved me over to the phone.

'Ronnie, there's someone on the line who wants you to be a rabbit,' she said, matter-of-factly.

My career being what it was, she was used to communicating such information without batting an eyelid.

The call was from an animation company in London who had been asked to provide footage for an advert and wanted someone who could do a decent rabbit shadow puppet with their hand. I hastily got a book out of the library on hand shadow puppets and spent the rest of the day madly practising rabbity gestures in front of a lamp in the living room – two fingers raised like little ears, with the rest of my hand squeezed into what might passably be mistaken for a head.

'Dad, what on earth are you doing?' John Phillip asked me when he arrived home from school.

'Working,' I replied. He rolled his eyes.

By the time I arrived at the little company's offices in Great Portland Street a couple of days later, I was quite proud of my rabbit, which could even twitch its nose pretty convincingly.

'So what have you got?' they asked.

I duly stood behind a screen with a big light shining onto it and performed my heavily rehearsed shadow rabbit while they scrutinised it from the other side.

'Ooh, he's good,' I heard one of them say.

'What we're going to do is make a film of your hand then create a computerised copy of it,' they informed me when I emerged from behind the screen.

'OK. So what's this for again?' I asked absent-mindedly while they set up.

'Something big,' the technician whispered to me excitedly.

'Oh,' I said. 'OK.'

The filming took about twenty minutes, and just as I was about to leave, one of the men said, 'We really, really like your hands. I don't suppose you could do a few finger points for us while you're here?'

'Sure,' I said, beginning to think these people had a bit of a hand fetish but not wanting to be rude. I didn't mind – after all, I had thought I'd be there all day, but at this rate I'd be out in less than half an hour. I duly pointed my finger a few times while they filmed away. On my way out I was handed an envelope with £50 inside – not bad, I thought, for such a little job.

A while later I switched on the telly and caught an advert for the new National Lottery, which had recently been given the go-ahead by the government. There was my little rabbit, twitching its ears, only now it was in the moon and a little girl was looking up at it, awestruck. Then my hand appeared at the window of a house, tapping on it and pointing at a dorky-looking man inside as a booming voice told him, 'It's you...' So that was the 'something big' the footage had been intended for! No wonder the guys at the little animation company had been so excited. Caroline and I had a good giggle about how I was probably the most famous hand in Britain, and then we forgot all about it.

A few weeks later, we were at home in Grassington having lunch with the vicar, when the phone rang. Caroline went to get it. 'Ronnie,' she called, in a rather embarrassed voice, 'it's the *Sun* for you.'

The vicar looked at me quizzically. 'Terribly sorry. Won't be a moment,' I said, rushing into the hall.

Would the vicar think I was caught up in some kind of

tabloid scandal? As I took the phone, I was aware that she and Caroline were completely quiet, listening intently to find out what the phone call was all about.

'You're Ronnie Le Drew, right – the bloke who used to be in *Rainbow*?' a gruff male voice asked me on the other end of the line.

'Um, yes.'

'And you were the "It Could Be You" hand?'

'Yes.'

'So you must be really angry – I mean, really, really furious – that the advert is being shown every day and the Lottery's making millions of pounds but I understand you've been paid a pittance?'

I was stunned. How on earth had the *Sun* got hold of the story? Perhaps my hand really was a celebrity now, and it would be hounded constantly by the red tops.

'To be honest with you,' I said, trying my best to sound disinterested, 'I didn't know when I did the job that it was for the National Lottery.'

'But what about your agent?' the man said. 'Aren't they angry?'

'I don't have one,' I replied. 'Someone must have just passed my name on and they rang me up out of the blue.'

Despite my efforts to insist that I wasn't furious in the least, the reporter kept on and on like a dog with a bone and seemed convinced that there was a story there. He asked if they could send a photographer round the next day, and – more to get him off the phone than anything else – I agreed.

'What was all that about?' Caroline asked when I came back into the room.

'Oh, nothing,' I smiled. 'More tea, vicar?'

That evening, Caroline and I were out having a Chinese and wondering how the *Sun* could possibly have got hold of the information about my £50 pay packet, when I bit into a spare rib and heard a crack. To my horror, a crown on one of my front teeth had broken off, and I now had a ghastly, gap-toothed grin, with what was left of the original tooth hanging down like a fang.

'What am I going to do?' I wailed. 'The photographer's coming tomorrow!' Then I had a thought that made me smile so much Caroline had to shield her eyes from the unpalatable sight. 'This could be the perfect excuse to wriggle out of the photograph!'

First thing in the morning, I phoned the *Sun* and explained that I couldn't possibly have my picture taken, after all. 'You wouldn't want a photo of me at the moment,' I said happily. 'I look terrible.'

The woman on the end of the phone sounded about as convinced by my unlikely tale as a teacher hearing that the dog had eaten my homework. 'It doesn't matter, we can touch it up,' she said, and hung up before I had time to protest.

I had just hours now before the photographer was due to arrive and my fang would be shown to the world. I rang the dentist but couldn't get an appointment. Seeing my evident panic, Caroline piped up, 'I know! I'll get a bit of cardboard and make you a tooth.'

'I'm not one of your puppets, you know,' I called after her, as she hurried off to find the right materials.

After suffering her amateur dental work for the next half hour, I decided I was better off just facing the photographer with my fang and pleading with him to be kind.

'Don't worry about the tooth,' he said, when I met him at the door with my tale of woe. 'Just smile and do that pointing thing with your hand. Now do it again, but look like you're really miserable.'

'I'll be really cross if you use "Fangs for nothing" as the headline,' I said, as the camera clicked away.

The next day I rushed to the newsagent full of dread, so worried about the fang that I had almost forgotten the reason for the story in the first place. There it was, a little article a few pages in, describing my anguish over being paid just £50 by Camelot and how they should be ashamed of themselves.

In fact, it wasn't Camelot who had paid me, and the quotes which peppered the article bore little relation to anything I had said. But I didn't care: I was just relieved that the grumpy woman on the phone had been true to her word, and my fang had been carefully erased from history.

Living from job to job with no regular income, I had begun to keep one eye constantly on the telephone whenever I was inside the house. Like one of Pavlov's dogs, I had become programmed to respond to the sound of the ringer – as soon as it went off my heart rate shot through the roof and I raced over and grabbed the receiver, praying that the call would bring deliverance. However many times I felt the bitter pangs of disappointment, I never lost the conviction that the next time it rang, there might be work at the other end.

Now and again I turned out to be right. One morning I grabbed the receiver to find a lady on the other end of the line who wanted to book me for some work on a Wrigley's chewing gum advert that was going to be shown on French television. They needed a puppeteer to operate a flame-breathing dragon puppet, and somehow my name had risen to the top of their list. It was only a couple of days' work, rehearsing that Friday afternoon before filming the following Monday, but to me it was a respite from sitting around at home on my own, with only the odd performance of *Snitchity Titch* to keep me occupied

Unfortunately, jobs, like buses, have a tendency to arrive all at once, and before long the phone was ringing a second time. 'Hi, Ronnie,' came the distinctive voice of Pete Coogan, the Hensons' production manager.

'Hi Pete, how are you?' I asked, trying not to let the excitement show in my voice.

'I'm good, Ronnie. I'm calling because Brian's making

another movie, over at Shepperton. It's going to be *Treasure Island* this time. We've got Tim Curry, Jennifer Saunders and Billy Connolly playing the human parts and we were hoping you'd like to help out with the background puppetry again.'

I couldn't believe it – another Muppet movie! I was itching to scream 'Yes!' down the phone, but Pete was still talking. 'It'll be a couple of months, on and off, if you can spare the time.'

'Hmm...' I murmured, flicking through my well-worn imaginary diary.

'John Thirtle's going to be working on it – and Sue Dacre, Gillie Robic, Nigel Plaskitt – so you'll have plenty of friends around.'

It was sounding better and better by the second. I knew by now that any movie I worked on would involve a lot of hanging around waiting, so having old friends to catch up with would be an excellent way to pass the time. I was particularly keen to have a proper chat with John Thirtle about the *Rainbow* reboot fiasco. Since filming began, I hadn't had a chance to discuss it with him.

'I'd love to do it!' I blurted out, forgetting that I was supposed to be keeping my cool.

'That's great, Ronnie, I knew you would,' Pete chuckled. 'We'll see you at 8 a.m. on Monday.'

'OK, great,' I replied without thinking. 'I'll see you— oh, hang on...' Monday morning... What was it about

Monday morning? Of course – the wretched dragon commercial! I was about to double-book myself.

'I'm really sorry, Pete,' I said, 'but I'm actually working on Monday. I can come first thing on Tuesday, though, if that's alright.'

There was a pause at the other end of the line and I waited anxiously to hear the reply. 'Yeah, sure, Ronnie. That's fine,' Pete replied eventually. 'We can find a way to cover for you on Monday. See you soon!'

Phew, I thought to myself as I hung up the phone, already beginning to wish I had said no to the flame-breathing dragon.

As it turned out, my regrets were only multiplied when I started work on the commercial. At first it seemed like quite a nice gig. I spent a good few hours that Friday at a workshop in London, going over the movement with the craftsman who had made the dragon puppet, while the director, a short, cockney bloke in a leather jacket, sat quietly in the corner, nodding and grunting now and then. The dragon wasn't finished yet – it had yet to be painted and the fire-breathing mechanism added – but it was near enough done to get a sense of how it would move, and I developed quite a nice, snakey movement for the long neck.

I spent the weekend at the house in Islington and arrived on Monday morning with my mind already on the following day – on seeing my old friends Gillie, Sue, Nigel and John, and working once again on a Muppet movie. I was silently praying that the commercial shoot would be quick so I could have plenty of time to relax that evening before a cripplingly early start the next day. (The journey to Shepperton was nothing compared to what it would have been from Yorkshire, but even so, getting to the studios in time for an 8 a.m. call wasn't something I relished.)

Unfortunately, the Wrigley's shoot didn't go smoothly. The finished dragon puppet looked absolutely stunning, resplendent with green scales, giant wings and huge flames issuing from its mouth every few seconds. But when I got my hands on the puppet I realised that all the extra weight made it impossible to manipulate the neck properly. I could just about force the puppet to move in the right direction, but it felt like manoeuvring an oil tanker, and even after the crew hung the neck on a bungee to take some of the weight, all the grace I had developed the previous Friday was gone. Everyone sat around looking meaningfully at their watches as I tried to get my head around the new set-up.

As we began to shoot the scene, it was clear that the director wasn't getting what he wanted. After dozens of disappointing takes, he finally came up to me. 'What's the problem, mate?' he asked. 'You were alright in the rehearsal.'

'I'm sorry,' I replied, 'but this thing is a lot heavier than it was before. In the rehearsal it was a much better puppet.'

'Well,' he huffed, 'maybe we need a better puppeteer!'

In the end, the make-up team were persuaded to come in as unofficial weight-bearers and we managed to get the commercial in the can, though not until the early hours of the following morning – by which time the cockney bloke had become so annoying that I was beginning to wish I could breathe fire myself.

I got home at about 2:30 a.m., just in time for a few hours' sleep before I had to be up again and on my way to Shepperton, wondering how much fun with my old friends I'd missed out on for the sake of a day being hectored.

I arrived at the studios tired but excited and keen to catch up with everyone. I found my way to the background puppeteers' green room (in reality a conservatory attached to the old stately home at the heart of the studio complex), where we were to wait until we were called for a scene. As I entered the conservatory, I was met by a sea of friendly faces, including many old comrades. There was Sue, Nigel, and Gillie – looking rather happier than I had seen her last, on the set of the revamped *Rainbow*. But my dear old friend and former flatmate, John Thirtle, was nowhere to be seen.

'What's happened to John?' I asked.

'He was here yesterday,' Sue told me, 'but he wasn't feeling well so they took him into hospital.'

'Hospital?' I asked, confused. 'Is he alright?'

'He didn't look well, Ronnie,' Sue said. 'They've said it's pneumonia but I think really it could be something else.'

It took a few moments for the penny to drop. This was the

mid-nineties, and by now the spectre of AIDS was something that had become increasingly familiar. I knew a little about the horrible disease, but only from more distant friends and acquaintances – not from anyone as close to me as John.

'Can we visit him?' I asked anxiously.

'Better talk to Ian, I guess,' was the reply.

As it turned out, Ian was very protective of his partner's rest time in the hospital. Ever the workaholic, John was insisting on reading through the scripts for the latest series of *The Spooks of Bottle Bay*, even with an oxygen mask attached to his face, so perhaps it was just as well he wasn't overrun by visitors. But as the days went by and he remained in hospital, I grew increasingly sad that I wasn't able to see him and find out first-hand how he was doing. If only I hadn't done that stupid dragon commercial, I thought.

In the meantime, there were Muppets to worry about. I was chatting with my old friends when one of the American Muppeteers, Kevin Clash – alias Elmo on *Sesame Street* – barrelled into the conservatory and approached our little huddle. As always happened when one of the principals approached, a flurry of excitement went through our little band and everyone began to shuffle forwards slightly in the hope of attracting Kevin's attention and being picked for a bit of actual puppetry.

'It's alright, guys,' Kevin said. 'I just want to talk to Ronnie, if you don't mind.'

I had just started to take a step back to clear Kevin's path through the throng when I realised what he'd said. Talk to me? Why on earth would he want to talk to me? I was quite pleasantly surprised that he even remembered which one of the assembled horde I was, given that half the British puppetry community was hanging out in that green room waiting for their chance to glimmer faintly in the background.

'Yes, Kevin?' I said. 'Can I help you?'

'You do all that string stuff, don't you, Ronnie?' Kevin asked. 'You know – marionettes.'

My eyes lit up. This was a topic I could talk about for hours. 'Yes, I do,' I replied. But this was a Muppet film – what could they possibly want to know about marionettes?

'The thing is, we have this scene coming up in which the pirate Muppets jump off the ship,' Kevin continued, 'and Brian wants to do it in a wide shot. We've made some legs to go on the regular puppets and the workshop team are stringing them up right now.'

Stringing the Muppets? A load of rod-and-glove puppets? I tried not to let my scepticism show.

'It won't be anything like what you're used to, Ronnie – no fancy controls or whatever. But we figured you'd be the best man for the job. We'll rig up a gantry on the ship set so you can operate the strings from up above.' He leaned in close to whisper in my ear. 'I need you to get together a team who you think can make this work. Pick whichever of these guys has the most string experience.' He glanced meaningfully around the room. 'That OK, Ronnie?'

'Yes, of course, Kevin!' I gushed, scarcely believing my ears. Only twelve hours ago I had been told I was hopeless at manipulating a simple latex dragon, and now one of the chief Muppeteers had selected me personally for one of the most demanding scenes of the shoot. I scanned the room, mentally taking account of who was there that had a background in marionette work – and then picked a group mainly composed of my oldest and best friends, who were all equally excited to have been chosen. My only regret was that John was not around to join in the fun.

When we arrived on the deck of the pirate ship a couple of hours later, I almost fell into the water myself, I was so awestruck by the scale of it all. A near-life-size replica galleon, the HMS *Hispaniola*, was floating in a giant tank in one of the Shepperton sound stages. Several of the Muppet villains of the story, Long John Silver's band of pirates – who by this stage had taken over the ship – had been rapidly doctored by the production team; where their control rods would normally have protruded from their heads and arms, clear nylon had been attached instead. I winced slightly to look at it. Kevin had been right – this was not the kind of string work I was used to, and I knew that nylon was notoriously bad for stringing puppets.

My motley team clambered up to the top of the rickety gantry that had been built just out of shot for us to operate the puppets from. The camera was locked on a static shot which showed one side of the ship but cropped out the water below, where a team wading in the tank were ready to catch the puppets as they were thrown overboard, and throw splashes of water up into the frame to make it look like they had actually hit the water. To add to the mayhem, there were a handful of human pirates on board as well, who also had to hurl themselves off the side of the ship, taking care to avoid any puppets or puppeteers.

Remarkably, the shoot went reasonably smoothly. It was very hard to have any control over the puppets, given the nylon stringing, but all that was really required was one fluid jump, and then they fell out of shot. After a couple of takes, we had it in the bag – and then the gantry was moved to the other side of the ship so we could film a reverse shot from there. Again it went very smoothly and the company broke early for lunch, to rapturous applause from all present.

I was already beginning to feel rather chuffed with myself and my little band of British string experts, but the crowning glory came in the canteen, when Steve Whitmire, the mild-mannered chap who had taken over Kermit after Jim Henson's death, came up to me and said, 'Well done, that was a very funny,' Dave Goelz, who operated The Great Gonzo, shouted 'Nice set!' to me across the room. My cheeks were flushing red, and after the awful experience of the advert the previous day it was nice to feel that my skills were so much appreciated.

Not everything on the *Treasure Island* shoot went quite so well, however. Another big scene I was involved with was the grand entrance of the captain of the *Hispaniola*, Abraham Smollett. The character had been built up in the dialogue as a 'raging volcano … tormented by demons' and his arrival was choreographed to match. The plan was that a grand carriage pulled by two real horses would storm through a busy cobbled street towards the harbour, Muppet extras scrambling to dodge the wheels, before it suddenly halted. A bugler would announce the captain's arrival, the door to the carriage would be thrown open – and out would step the diminutive green figure of Kermit the Frog. It was a great visual gag, but for it to really work the build-up to Kermit's reveal had to be as overblown and dramatic as possible.

My role was a small but important one, especially for a so-called background puppeteer, since my puppet was the bugler whose parping would announce the captain's grand entrance. I was chuffed to be asked to perform such a vital part and wondered why one of the main Muppeteers hadn't bagsied it – until I found out exactly what it entailed. Steve Whitmire, as Kermit, was nowhere to be seen – he would come in only for the close-up, when the carriage door opened. This meant that for the treacherous race through the cobbled streets to the waterfront I was alone inside the carriage, with my hand through a hole in its ceiling to operate my bugler, who was sitting next to the man driving the horses.

As we sped along the cobbles, the other puppeteers did their best to whisk their puppets out of the way before they were crushed under the thundering wheels. Inside the cab I felt a little removed from the mayhem outside but I could hear enough to imagine what a nightmare the scene must be to film; I was struggling just to focus on the little monitor at my feet so I could see how the shot was taking shape. With every jiggle of the carriage the monitor would jerk this way and that, and to make matters worse the radio signal would frequently fizzle out, so the image jumped all over the place. It was all I could do to focus on the puppetry during the numerous takes while doing my best not to feel sick.

On one run-through the ride seemed even rougher than ever, and as I clenched the monitor between my knees I suddenly heard a neigh from the horses. The carriage seemed to rear up, and then suddenly lurch to one side. There was a splash, followed by shouts all round, Brian's 'Cut!' being the least of them.

'Are the horses OK?' I heard someone yell, as the splashing and whinnying continued. Suddenly it dawned on me – one of the animals had fallen into the tank of water that was supposed to be the sea. 'Oh my God,' I heard someone cry, 'think of the insurance if they die!'

I clambered out of the carriage, two wheels of which were now partly submerged in the tank. The poor horse was flailing around in the water while its handler tried to calm it down. Thankfully it was only about a metre deep.

Four strong guys managed to get the carriage upright again, and it was carefully checked over to make sure nothing had been permanently damaged. The horse was declared unharmed too, but it was a pretty traumatic incident for all concerned.

'Oh, Ronnie,' someone called, noticing me standing at the side. 'Are you alright?'

'Yes, yes, I'm fine,' I replied, dusting myself down. A valued string puppeteer I might be, but clearly livestock and props took priority.

Most days were much less eventful than that one, however; in fact, the task I was required to do more than any other on *Muppet Treasure Island* was to wait around in the conservatory, doing nothing. On the whole, we background puppeteers were being paid to sit about chatting and drinking tea – or occasionally to nip over to the bar for a cheeky Pimm's if we thought there was little chance of being called to work. As the days went by, the boredom began to grow and our little band of layabouts grew increasingly frustrated. My friend Sue tried to keep the ennui at bay by suggesting we play a game of

Consequences, but being short of paper we had to use her laptop instead, carefully scrolling down a line at a time as we passed it around the room. After several days cooped up with hardly any puppet work to do, the game had grown into almost an entire novel – a crime thriller about a murder, with as many incomprehensible twists and turns as you would expect for something written blind by committee.

We soon began branching out into other parlour games, the favourite of which was Wink Murder. Frustrated by the lack of performing opportunities on the film we were being paid to work on, we grew increasingly excited at the prospect of letting out dramatic death wails as we were surreptitiously winked to death. Unfortunately, in one particular session, one of our number was a puppeteer by the name of Geoff who had a kind of facial tick. This meant his eye would flicker of its own accord, leading to unintentional massacres. When we finally realised that it was just a tick, and that Geoff was not the real murderer in our midst, few of us could restrain ourselves, and the death rattles were soon accompanied by snorts and guffaws of laughter as we rolled around on the floor, beside ourselves with hysterics.

As the pitch of laughter and screaming reached its zenith, the door to the conservatory was thrown open and a very angry-looking figure stood at the threshold.

'What are you, a bunch of children?' he bellowed.

'Some of us have to work here, you know!'

He stormed back out of the room, slamming the door behind him, and we all did our best to suppress another round of laughter, panting and wheezing on the floor as we tried to calm ourselves.

'You know who that was, don't you?' said one of our number, gasping for air between giggles. 'It was only Kenneth Branagh!'

It turned out the great thesp had set up his offices next to the conservatory while he worked on his magnum opus, *Hamlet*, which was being shot at Shepperton. He had obviously not counted on sharing a workplace with a gaggle of hysterical puppeteers while he tried to get inside the Dane's tortured mind.

The next day, we were politely informed that we would have to vacate the conservatory for the rest of the shoot and hang out in a less salubrious green room instead. Apparently, the Prince of Denmark had booted us out of his kingdom.

As the days and weeks rolled on, with little more to do on the film itself, my mind began to wander to other things, foremost among them my friend John Thirtle, who was still in hospital and whom I had still been unable to visit. I waited anxiously for news that he was feeling better, but such happy tidings never arrived.

One day, when I walked into the green room, Sue Dacre looked up quickly. 'Oh, Ronnie, can I have a word with you?' she asked.

We stepped outside and she put her arm around me. 'I'm so sorry to tell you this, but John's died,' she said.

I felt as if I'd been punched in the stomach. I couldn't even bring myself to reply.

'Oh, Ronnie, this must be so hard for you,' Sue said. 'Come on, let's go for a walk.'

We wandered around the set together, Sue doing her best to comfort me while holding back her own tears. My mind went back to those early years when John and I had been flatmates, spending our evenings together surrounded by sawdust from his puppet-making. After my lonely years at school he had been my first real friend – the person I had leaned on when I left home – and we had remained close ever since. He had, of course, also given me my big break in television by asking me to puppeteer Zippy. My life would have been so much poorer if he had not been in it.

When I finally felt ready, Sue and I returned to the green room. All the British puppeteers working on the film were shocked to hear the news, and the atmosphere in the room was suddenly much more sombre. John had many friends among the group, and for the rest of the day, whenever we weren't needed, we passed the time sharing our stories and memories of him. But nothing could stop the feeling of utter bleakness I felt at his loss, and I was very grateful when we finished early and I was able to run home to be alone.

With so many of John's friends among the British puppet cast, the Henson team were kind enough to give us all the day off for his funeral, which was held at the Little Angel. Lyndie had painted the coffin with characters from children's stories and commedia dell'arte, and the beautiful ceremony included speeches and poetry readings. John's partner, Ian, with his typical sense of humour despite the circumstances, had hired a traditional Routemaster bus to ferry friends and family to the crematorium. It was as joyous an occasion as was possible, given the shock and grief we were all feeling.

Back at work the next day, the Muppeteers were very respectful of the loss their British colleagues had suffered, and letters came down to us from the very top, remarking on how tragic it was that John had died. But there was nothing they could do to relieve the sense of gloom that had settled on the green room. The rest of the shoot was far less joyous than it had been, and the work seemed increasingly difficult and unpleasant. We spent quite a lot of time up to our waists in the tank of water, carefully holding up our puppets so that they could 'swim' without actually getting wet, while the camera glided by on a kind of floating raft. The water was filthy by this point, and the wetsuits we were given grew increasingly clammy and disgusting. I was relieved when my final day's work on the film was complete and I was able to head home.

Despite the dark cloud that John's death had cast over the entire experience, I was excited a few months later when the film was finally finished – and delighted to see that my sequence of the pirates jumping overboard and my frantic bugler had both made it through to the final cut. However, when the credits rolled at the end of the film, I was shocked to see my name had not been included. 'Sorry, Ronnie,' I was told when I asked what had happened. 'There just wasn't room for all the background puppeteers.'

At least John Thirtle had been given a credit, but seeing his name scrolling up as I sat in the darkened cinema, and realising that it would never be up there again, I missed my dear old friend more than ever.

Chapter 15: Hard times

John Thirtle's death hit me hard, and not long afterwards I found myself faced with another piece of devastating news. I was at the house in London one rainy October afternoon when the phone rang. I rushed to answer it as frantically as ever, but something about the silence on the other end of the line made me hesitate, even as I asked who was calling.

'It's Lyndie, Ronnie.' Her voice sounded choked. 'I think you ought to sit down, darling.'

Obediently I dragged the phone over to the kitchen table and sat down, coiling the wire anxiously around my finger. 'What's happened, Lyndie?' I asked.

My mind was racing as I waited for her to answer. Had one of her kids had an accident? Could the theatre have burnt down?

'There's no easy way to tell you this Ronnie. It's Vivien Trant.'

'Vivien?' I had spoken to my old friend, my 'oracle' who lived across from the Little Angel, only yesterday.

'She's been murdered, Ronnie.' I heard Lyndie catch her breath. 'I'm so sorry.'

I could scarcely believe what I was hearing. Stupidly I said, 'How do you know?'

'The police are all over the square,' Lyndie replied. 'They've taped up the door to the house and they're calling it a crime scene.'

Hearing that my friend had died was almost more than I could take, but the full story was even more horrific. Vivien's daughter, Sophie, had married a man from Morocco, but recently the pair had been forced to separate – this much I knew, although I hadn't ever heard the full story. Apparently, the cause of the split was her husband's traditional Islamic views, and following a recent holiday to Morocco he had come back more stringent than ever, increasingly dissatisfied with his Western wife, who had never converted to Islam. The couple had a baby daughter together, and when Sophie had refused to have her brought up as a Muslim her husband had hit the roof. Sophie had left their marital home and moved back in with her parents, Vivien and John, where she had received a number of threatening phone calls from her increasingly enraged husband. 'Have you got your throat ready?' he had shouted down the line on one occasion. 'Because I am going to cut it.'

Vivien and John had been desperately worried for Sophie and her daughter, but as long as she was with them they felt she was safe. Then Sophie's husband had arrived on their doorstep with a knife and forced his way into the house. Stabbing his poor wife to death wasn't enough for him – he didn't stop until he had murdered his own baby daughter and her doting grandparents too. The police had arrived at the house to find the four dead bodies, having been summoned by a 999 call which consisted of nothing but screams.

As Lyndie told me, step by step, what had happened, I listened, frozen. I felt totally numb, unable to move from my chair. When she finished, there was a long pause while she waited for me to say something. But I couldn't get any words out.

'Ronnie?' Lyndie asked gently after a while. 'Do you want me to come round? I'd invite you here to the cottage but it's so busy outside.'

Finally, I managed to rouse myself from my stupor. 'No, it's alright, Lyndie,' I replied. 'I think I ought to drive up to Yorkshire and tell Caroline what's happened.' Somehow the thought of explaining it all over the phone felt unbearable. I thanked Lyndie for calling me so quickly, grabbed my coat from the hook in the hall and hit the road.

Once on the motorway, I drove like a man possessed, the tears streaming down my face as rain pelted the windscreen in front of me. A horrible thought crossed my mind. If there were so many police outside Vivien's house, it was only a matter of time before the press got there too. In my mind's eye I could see Caroline sitting down with her dinner in front of the telly, idly switching on the news – and the tray of food crashing to the floor. I was determined to get to her before the story got out. Caroline had become a close friend of Vivien as well, and it was only right that she should hear what had happened from me – not from some stranger in a television studio.

About half an hour from home, I realised I was about to run out of petrol. I pulled off the M1 into a service station to fill up and dashed into the little shop to buy some tissues. There on a TV screen behind the counter was Vivien's front door, criss-crossed with police tape just as Lyndie had described it.

'Can you turn the volume up please?' I begged the woman at the till. She glared at me for a moment, no doubt thinking me a difficult customer. Part of me wanted to scream at her, *That's my friend's house! My friend has just been murdered!*' But even in my frenzied state I cringed at the thought of causing a scene.

The woman adjusted the volume. A reporter was standing in the pokey square that divided the Little Angel from Vivien's tall Victorian house, thrusting a microphone into the face of a woman I had never seen before. The words 'FAMILY FRIEND' flashed up on the screen as the stranger explained how shocked and traumatised she felt. I hadn't thought it was possible for me to feel any worse about what had happened, but the sight of this woman, who I was sure didn't know Vivien from Adam, harping on about the tragedy the family had suffered was enough to make my blood boil. As the camera cut back to a newsreader in the studio and the focus switched to a new story, I dashed back to the car and set off again, hoping against hope that Caroline hadn't seen the bulletin.

When I arrived at the house, it turned out that she was blissfully ignorant. It felt strange to be glad of such a small mercy amid such unimaginable horrors, but I suppose I was clutching at straws.

'Ronnie, what are you doing here?' Caroline asked as I raced through the door.

'I think you'd better sit down,' I told her, putting my arm around her and guiding her towards the sofa. 'I'm afraid I've got to tell you some bad news.'

Caroline sat in stunned silence as I talked her through the whole horrible story. I recognised the expression on her face – it was exactly how I had felt when I was on the phone to Lyndie. By the time I got to the end, I realised that sharing what had happened had left me feeling slightly calmer.

There was a long, sad silence. Then, with her typical bold positivity, Caroline somehow broke through it.

'Why don't we go for a walk?' she suggested briskly. 'It's not quite dark yet.'

As the sun began to set in the distance, the two of

us walked together through the woods and I clutched Caroline's hand tightly in mine.

After the terrible press for the toyshop reboot of *Rainbow*, I was not at all confident about Zippy's chances of ever finding employment again, so it came as quite a surprise when I answered the phone one day to an invitation to shoot another series of the show.

'We're changing the format again,' I was told by Melanie Stokes, formerly our researcher and now the producer in overall charge. 'It's going to be called *Rainbow Days* this time. The episodes are only ten minutes each, and we're going back to a house set-up instead of the toyshop.'

Thank God for that, I thought to myself.

'There'll be some changes in personnel, too,' she continued. 'Craig will be back as George, and the two of you will still be voicing the puppets, but Richard won't be joining us as Bungle this time.' (This was not exactly a surprise to me!) 'We've got a lovely man called Paul Cullinan who's going to take over the role,' Melanie explained.

'Oh, right,' I said. 'What about Gillie?'

She hesitated for a moment. 'I'm afraid Gillie won't be returning either – we just felt Cleo never really took off and we wanted to pare things down, with just the original characters that made *Rainbow* such a hit before.'

'Of course,' I murmured. Again, the news wasn't exactly

shocking – the writing had been on the wall for Cleo before we even shot our first episode. I did feel sorry for Gillie, though, and hoped she wouldn't take it too badly.

Then another thought drifted into my mind. 'You said the original characters? You mean...'

'Well, Zippy, George and Bungle obviously...' Her voice trailed off and she hesitated for a moment. 'Plus we've decided to bring back a presenter.'

So Geoffrey's campaign to resurrect *Rainbow* had finally got him his job back!

Melanie soon put me right. 'It won't be Geoffrey, I'm afraid. We felt he was a bit too... well, not what we're after this time. There's a lovely young black guy called Dale Superville who's going to take on the role. He's just out of drama school and he's really keen to work on the show.'

'He sounds great,' I told Melanie, privately wondering what poor Geoffrey would make of it.

'There are going to be some changes backstage too,' she continued. 'Budgets are even tighter than before, so we're going to shoot single-camera and we'll be working back at the school in Battersea.'

'Is that for rehearsals again?' I asked her.

'Well, yes,' she replied briskly, 'but we're going to shoot the show there as well this time. It'll be much quicker than filming in a proper studio – and we won't have to move everything back and forth.'

Hmm. That didn't bode well. But could it possibly turn out any worse than last time?

'I'd love to do it,' I replied. After all, work was work – and by now I had learned not to be too sniffy when any came along.

Pulling up outside the old red-brick building, I realised that I no longer felt any nerves at the prospect of beginning again. There might be a new class for the new year, but I was an old hand. I just hoped that didn't make me the dunce who never graduated.

The new additions to the *Rainbow* family all turned out to be charming. Melanie had us all sit in a circle on the floor as if we really were a nursery class, and we went round introducing ourselves one by one. Paul Cullinan, the new Bungle, was an easy-going bloke from Liverpool, while our presenter, Dale, was as engaging and enthusiastic as I had been led to expect. It can't have been easy for Dale, because Geoffrey was something of an elephant in the room. No one wanted to bring up his name, and in the end it was Dale himself who acknowledged the issue. 'I'm not sure I can live up to what Geoffrey did,' he whispered to me, knowing that I was the grey-haired relic that had been with *Rainbow* since the dawn of time – or at least since Dale had been the right age to watch it.

'You'll be great,' I replied. 'Don't worry about Geoffrey. You just be Dale.'

In fact, Dale was a natural as the show's presenter. There was no need to raise his spirits or boost his energy – his own good humour was infectious and soon came across on screen. And Melanie, who was also directing, quickly won the trust of all involved.

Paul, meanwhile, fitted the role of Bungle perfectly. There was no preciousness about him, no fussiness – he was quite prepared to make a fool of himself, falling over and becoming the butt of every joke if it made the show funnier. He gave Bungle a new, squeakier voice than his predecessors had done, but once I got used to that I found I really liked his take on the character.

As we began to walk through the first episode on the new set – a stripped-down living room, with the puppets mostly popping up behind the sofa – I realised my initial misgivings about this second reboot were fading. Perhaps it will work out after all, I thought hopefully. The scripts made much more sense now that there was a human presenter at the heart of them, and Dale did some lovely *Jackanory*-style poetry readings, as well as the odd song on his guitar, which gave the show more of the old Variety feel that we had in the days of Rod, Jane and Freddy. Zippy and George's bickering relationship seemed to hit just the right note, and they got regular little vignettes together, looking out of the window – harking back, it seemed, to the old Moony and Sunshine interludes of the very early *Rainbow* series, only much sharper and wittier.

Even the single-camera filming turned out to be a blessing in disguise. It meant we had to pay more attention to continuity, but we could really get into our stride as we went through a scene – there was much less stopping and starting than in the old days. Under the new budgetary constraints, it was important that we whizzed through the shooting as quickly as possible, and it seemed hardly any time at all before the first few episodes were in the can.

Nervously, I sat and watched the first show played back, aware that last time my optimism had soon turned to horrified disillusionment. But this time I felt convinced that we had done a decent job. There was no escaping the reality that the show was a cheaper version of the original *Rainbow*; there were no fancy song-and-dance routines, no wild flights of fancy in the scriptwriting, or outings to the seaside or the jungle. But for what it was – an amusing, entertaining and educational show for preschoolers – I felt we had hit the nail on the head. It felt good to be proud of *Rainbow* once again. And for me, personally, it was an important milestone – after a horrible few years of physical pain, personal tragedies and professional frustrations, I finally felt I was back on top.

But of course it was too good to be true. Despite the best efforts of all involved, it was not long before I received the crushing news that *Rainbow* had been cancelled yet again. The latest reboot had been nice, apparently, but it wasn't what audiences wanted anymore, and a final decision had now been taken: there was no scope whatsoever for the show to come back a third time. We had tried our best, but ultimately we had failed.

I felt gutted when I heard this news – worse, almost, than when *Rainbow* had been cancelled the first time, five years earlier. We had all worked so hard to bring the show back from the brink – changing with the times and adapting to the penny-pinching of our bosses – but it hadn't been enough. It seemed Zippy and I would now be parting company forever.

I was still reeling from the sound of the final nail being hammered into *Rainbow*'s coffin when I chanced across a listing in the *Radio Times* for a new children's show called *Mole in the Hole*. There in the cast list were a number of very familiar names: Geoffrey Hayes, Roy Skelton and Malcolm Lord, along with a pair of puppeteers I had vaguely heard of. So, the old *Rainbow* gang had managed to get back on the telly after all! I felt pleased for them, but a little hurt that they hadn't asked me to be involved. Perhaps Geoffrey was still angry about the *Rainbow* reboot going ahead without him and resented me for taking the job. Still, at least he had finally moved on from *Rainbow*'s cancellation, dusting himself down and moving on to something else.

I tuned in with interest to catch the show, but what I saw was like some kind of bad dream. I felt like I was watching

Rainbow in a parallel universe, with Geoffrey playing the same role as the man of the house, Malcolm channelling Bungle, only in a moleskin instead of a bear suit, and Roy providing the voices for a pair of puppets who bore an uncanny resemblance to Zippy and George: a cranky, harsh-voiced dog and a dopey, effeminate cat.

The whole thing was excruciating to watch – especially for me, having just had my own *Rainbow* show ripped away from me. Melanie had worked hard to reinvent the programme, to take the old, beloved characters and move them in new directions; to produce something, within limited means, that captured the spirit of the original – and it had been cancelled. Yet here was this dire programme being proudly beamed across the airwaves. I felt depressed, in an odd way almost betrayed – and utterly disillusioned.

Chapter 16: Doctor's orders

With the second *Rainbow* revival now consigned to the dustbin of history, I finally had to lay to rest any hopes that the show would come back into my life. The first failed revamp had been bad enough with its poor reviews, but having tried again and created what I genuinely thought was a great show, only to have it cancelled, was somehow even more painful. Perhaps, after all, *Rainbow* should have died with Thames, I mused, going out in its prime so that people would remember it at its best.

I realised that, for me, the revivals had been a poisoned chalice. After a wobbly day or two, I had managed to accept *Rainbow* being cancelled the first time around, especially with the distraction of *The Muppet Christmas Carol* and Vivien's sound advice that there was more to life than Zippy. But each time the programme was resurrected, it stirred up my hopes again, making it harder to let go when it was then axed.

At one point I heard that the Hensons were working on

a new movie – *Muppets from Space* – but this time I didn't receive a call to work on it. And now there was no Vivien to turn to for tea and sympathy. So many of the people I had loved and looked up to had been taken from me over the past few years, and their loss seemed to cast a long shadow over my life.

With my television work all but dried up, I had fewer and fewer reasons to be in the house in London, and was now more or less in Yorkshire full-time. I tried to resurrect my *Snitchity Titch* show again, and got a few children's party bookings, but there wasn't as much call for puppetry 'oop north' as there had been in leafy Islington. Caroline did her best to involve me in the running of the puppetry school, but much of what she was teaching the students was concerned with making puppets rather than performing them, and I had never been much of a maker.

More and more I found myself with nothing but housework to occupy me all day, until I gladly rushed to the school gates to pick up the kids. They were the only thing that gave me a semblance of routine: getting them up in the morning, making their breakfast, taking them to school and then looking after them in the afternoon until Caroline finished her lessons. I could see that the country life was better for the children – more space to run around, and undoubtedly better schooling – so I told myself I must persevere and make the best of things. But

I hadn't counted on just how isolated I would feel up in Yorkshire, and I was becoming increasingly depressed.

All my life I had been running – running from the threat of unemployment and the terror of admitting that my father might have been right: puppetry was not a 'proper job'. I had pushed and pushed myself, working at the Little Angel at weekends and during breaks from *Rainbow*, never daring to take a single family holiday and keeping quiet about my injuries on *Mortimer and Arabel* rather than risk being fired. But now, despite my best efforts, rest was being forced upon me – far more of it than I had ever had before. Luckily my telly years had allowed me to build up some savings, which covered the mortgage, and Caroline was bringing in enough from the puppetry school to keep us going if we tightened our belts a bit. But in those long, lonely afternoons in Yorkshire, I was forced to face my ultimate fear: that my days as a puppeteer were over. And what was Ronnie Le Drew, if he wasn't a puppeteer?

As Caroline and the children flourished, I became more and more withdrawn, hardly leaving the house for days at a time. All my puppetry friends were based in London, and up in Yorkshire I felt totally cut off from the rest of the world. A kind of hollow loneliness added to my sense of professional failure. When the Labour government won their landslide victory in 1997, I watched it on television with a feeling of complete detachment, as if it didn't apply at all to the reality I lived in. When Princess Diana died, I knew that I would have been among the crowds bringing flowers to Kensington Palace – but up in Yorkshire I felt shut out from the national mourning that I read about in the papers.

The year 1997 rolled into 1998 then 1999, and still my career was on ice and my life growing smaller and smaller. It's strange but, apart from one or two particularly bleak moments, I can recall almost nothing of those years. A conscientious diary-keeper, my entries from that time have either been lost or were never made. I seem to have unconsciously blocked out any memories of that period, perhaps because they were just too painful. It seems almost indulgent to describe a lean period in this way – particularly as I wasn't queuing at the dole office or losing my home – but, to me, for whom puppetry had been everything, it was worse than losing all my worldly possessions. Without my family to keep me going, I don't know what I would have done.

It was due to my increasingly low spirits that when my old friend Nigel Plaskitt invited me to go to London to see a new musical he was working on as puppet director, I initially refused. The production was a stage version of *Doctor Dolittle*, with puppets from Jim Henson's Creature Shop and featuring the voice of Julie Andrews as the parrot Polynesia. It was right up my street, and normally I'd have been itching to go, but I just couldn't summon the enthusiasm to make the trip. 'I'd love to, but thirty quid for a ticket is just too much for me right now,' I lied.

Nigel was not to be deterred, however, and he soon called back to say he had got me a comp ticket and wouldn't take no for an answer. Somehow I managed to summon the energy to get on a train to London, and soon I was standing, rather shakily, among the crowds outside the Hammersmith Apollo. Catching sight of Julie Andrews' name screaming out in large letters from the poster, I felt a small stirring of excitement – an emotion I hadn't known for a long time.

Nigel greeted me warmly and we went in. The title role was being played by Phillip Schofield, who had made his name in the 'Broom Cupboard' at Children's BBC, accompanied by a puppet called Gordon the Gopher. Perhaps that was why he had agreed to share the stage with an assortment of puppet creatures, I thought.

Soon after the lights went up, Phillip performed a duet with Polynesia, a beautiful yellow-and-blue macaw with the heavenly singing voice of Julie Andrews, which had been pre-recorded. There were other puppets, too, such as Dr Dolittle's dog Jip and his greedy pig Gub-Gub, while human actors played Chee-Chee the monkey, who had escaped from an Italian organ grinder, and the Pushmi-pullyu (push-me, pull-you), a lama with a head at each end of its body. But the majority of the enormous cast of animals, from Dab-Dab the housekeeping duck to Too-

Too the owl accountant, were animatronic. I couldn't help feeling their robotic movements rather spoiled the show, and wished that the director had felt able to rely on the skill of the puppeteers instead of turning to technology. The pig got the biggest reaction of the night and that was because, being a puppet rather than a machine, it could immediately respond to what was happening.

'So what do you think, Ronnie?' asked Nigel after the show. I could see he was extremely proud of the production.

What could I say? 'It's fantastic,' I told him.

'I was hoping you'd say that,' he said, 'because they're looking for someone to take over Polynesia the Parrot. We're going on tour in January for three months, and the woman playing her at the moment can't come. I said you'd be great for the role.'

Here was one of my oldest friends offering me the chance to break my dry spell and take a leading role in a high-profile musical. The show might have its flaws, but it was a big-budget production, and this was going to be a tour of the UK's major theatres.

So what did I say?

'Oh no, Nigel – that's very kind of you, but I couldn't possibly.'

'Ronnie, it won't be like normal puppet touring – you'll be a principal!' Nigel insisted. 'You won't have to move sets or anything.'

'Oh, I really couldn't leave the family for that long,'

I said, and to Nigel's astonishment I got back on the train to Yorkshire.

The truth was that, after my years spent in the narrow life of home and family, I had become nervous of going out into the world again.

Caroline soon sorted me out. 'You've always wanted to do a musical, Ronnie. You can't pass this opportunity up.'

'But the kids...'

'They'll be fine.'

So it was that I found myself in a Kennington warehouse on a cold January day at the beginning of the new millennium, waiting for rehearsals to begin. Usually I would have been as excited as a kid at Christmas about starting work on a new show, but my confidence was so low that this time I felt nothing but nerves. Having been used to puppet shows where the cast rarely numbered as many as eight, being surrounded by a musical theatre cast of nearly forty, not to mention about a dozen musicians, was completely overwhelming.

The building looked like it had been taken over by a hoard of lunatics – the pig puppeteer, Andy Heath, was crawling along the floor oinking; the Pushmi-pullyu actors were rehearsing their strange double act without costumes, looking to the untrained eye like a couple of co-dependent, hobbling, old women; and a man was scampering along on all fours barking. I was particularly confused about the latter, until someone explained that this actor had replaced the puppet Jip, since the poor puppeteer had been suffering terrible cramps trying to perform him. Elsewhere it was evident that the producers had learned their lesson, and massages were being given to some of the other puppeteers to soothe their aching limbs. Meanwhile, a young blond man in his twenties seemed to be intent on lovingly grooming the animatronic animals with a hairbrush, as if they were real pets. (I later learned that the performances tended to ruffle up the animals' fur, and that this chap – Robert – was tasked with brushing them down each night to make them look pristine again.)

As well as a puppet Polynesia, there was also an animatronic version of the character, controlled from offstage using a pair of joysticks. I was relieved to discover that the person sharing operating duties with me on this was Sarah Burgess, a puppeteer I knew from the Little Angel. I was less happy to learn that we were pretty much the only newbies on the touring production – most of the others had come straight from the West End show and already knew their parts backwards. The thought of walking in and taking the lead puppetry role was intimidating to say the least.

Unlike the other animals in the production, who communicated with grunts, squeaks, quacks and oinks, Polynesia had more than 700 lines pre-recorded by Julie Andrews that I had to learn to sync with. Most challenging of all were those sung in the opening number, 'Talk to the Animals', in which Polynesia perches on Dr Dolittle's chair and duets with him.

The first day Phillip and I rehearsed together, he strode into rehearsals smiling warmly and looking as much like Mr Nice Guy as he did on telly, which was both a relief and a surprise, since I had assumed no one could be quite that likeable in real life. However, he clearly wasn't feeling too comfortable about our duet, either. It required impeccable timing on the part of the sound technician, who had to press the button to make sure the recording of Julie Andrews kicked in at the right moment, and if Phillip went a little too fast it could throw the whole thing out.

Phillip's solution to the difficulties of working with a pre-recorded co-star seemed to be to gradually erode Polynesia's lines. 'This bit goes on a bit, doesn't it?' he would say. 'Why don't we just cut it a little...' The director, though, seemed to have other ideas, frequently adding in new lines that Julie had just recorded in New York. 'That's boring,' Phillip would protest. 'I'm the one who's actually here!' The constant toing and froing was a nightmare for me. Every time I mastered one version of the song, I would be told it was changing again. The poor sound technician, too, was slowly going bananas. At last, though, the song was finalised – and as a result of the long-winded rehearsal process, Phillip and I had got to know each other a bit better, which made me feel more at home among the cast. That was just as well, because before long we were headed far away to Edinburgh for our opening run. Going to London had been difficult enough after my years of exile in Yorkshire, but in Scotland I'd know no one apart from the cast, so I decided to share some digs with a couple of the actors.

On our first night, Phillip again lived up to his Nice Guy reputation, sending everyone in the show a personal good-luck card. As the auditorium filled up, I waited backstage, dressed head to toe in black, with an earpiece in place so I could hear Julie Andrews' pre-recorded lines whether or not I was on stage. I was wracked with nerves and beginning to wish I had followed my gut instinct and stayed safely at home. But when, over the tannoy, I heard the words 'Mr Schofield and Mr Le Drew, please come to the stage' I was suddenly beside myself with excitement. The thrill of hearing my name called out in a proper theatre, along with that of the lead actor, was almost overwhelming. I could hear the buzz of anticipation in the audience before the curtain went up, the lovely sound of the overture played by a live orchestra, and the applause when Phillip walked onto the stage. I might have worked in theatre all my life, but a musical has a very different energy to anything I had done before.

Our opening night went off without a hitch, much to my relief. No one, though, could have been more relieved than Phillip, who on the London press night had suffered the embarrassment of his animatronic friends going haywire on him as the radio signal used to control them suddenly cut out. The reviews had praised his fortitude and improvisation skills, but it was something he dreaded having to go through again.

Unfortunately for Phillip, however, such glitches turned out to be a recurring problem. I soon discovered for myself that the animatronic devices were susceptible to technical problems, and Polynesia appeared to be particularly prone to them. On numerous occasions the wretched bird stopped responding to her controls and just sat there, beak open, staring out into the darkness as if possessed. One time when this happened, Phillip had just said the line, 'What do you think, Polynesia?' when, to my horror, she went into one of her trances. I saw Phillip turn upstage and say again in a strained voice, 'What do you think, Polynesia?' while looking at me in the wings with a beseeching, desperate expression on his face. 'Oh God, the battery's gone flat,' a technician told me, and I tried frantically to mime the bad news to Phillip. Like a true pro, he covered up for the parrot's failings and made it through the scene, and Polly's batteries were hastily replaced in the next scene change.

Another recurring problem was with the servomotors, whose failure would cause the parrot to go into so-called automatic mode. This meant that she suddenly started performing repetitive robotic movements completely out of my control, like some kind of avian breakdancer. The horrified human actors on stage would try to turn their performance up to eleven to distract attention from their gyrating co-star for as long as it took for the techies to regain control over her.

As we travelled around from city to city – Bristol, Birmingham, Liverpool, Manchester and more – our biggest fear was not empty houses (we always seemed to be full, and the audiences couldn't get enough of Phillip and his menagerie), but whether there were any taxi companies unwittingly using the same radio frequency as our animatronics team. A clash meant that every time a particular cab drove past the theatre, it would interrupt the signal to an owl or a goat and cause them to jerk unpredictably or freeze up in a most unnatural way. Knowing how many children there were in the audience, the last thing we wanted was to create mass hysteria by giving the impression that any of the animals had just suffered a stroke and died, so the long-suffering sound man would be tasked with ringing round the taxi firms and begging them to change to a different frequency.

Unfortunately the animals were stuffed full of machinery so they couldn't even be manipulated by an actor if they stopped working, though Phillip became increasingly adept at catching the duck's head whenever it suddenly 'died', holding the lifeless machine while it continued to deliver its dialogue. Though Phillip must have known the dangers of working with children and animals – animatronic or otherwise – even he had his limits when the technical hitches seemed to come one after the other. He would wait until a convenient scene change, when he wasn't required for a while, then march backstage and demand, 'Bloody hell, what on earth was going on out there?'

That's not to say Phillip didn't have a sense of humour – he had quite a mischievous one, as it turned out – and having bonded with him in the role of his trusty parrot sidekick, I witnessed it more than most. Many was the time that Phillip would turn upstage while singing and, out of sight of the audience, pull the most ridiculous face, knowing full well that it would leave me struggling not to corpse behind my parrot. His favourite game was to see how late in the overture we could leave it to get into our places before the show began. I am sure a few children must have spotted the puppeteer with a black beanie on his head diving behind Dr Dolittle's chair as the lights went up.

Phillip might have been Mr Nice Guy, but he was certainly not Mr Boring. While we were on tour it became clear that he liked to gamble if there was a classy casino around; he also loved his wine – a passion that got him into trouble one day when he went to a wine-tasting event. The session was in the afternoon, so he must have thought he would have plenty of time to get back to the theatre for that evening's performance. We were quite relaxed about it because, while the idea of some stars spending the afternoon on the bottle would have caused a few nervous raised eyebrows, we all knew Phillip was too much of a wine connoisseur to do anything but taste and spit. So we were surprised when, as the clock backstage crept towards 7 p.m., there was still no sign of him. Our production manager, a white-haired man who had been in the business for years and was always turned out in an impeccably smart black shirt and trousers, was pacing up and down, asking where our lead had got to. I was terrified for Phillip because I knew the man was a stickler for rules and if the clock struck the hour then officially the understudy, a young actor waiting nervously in the wings, would have to go on in his place.

Phillip dashed in moments after 7 p.m., apologising profusely, having been caught in traffic; sure enough, he was stone-cold sober. We all breathed a huge sigh of relief – but then the production manager piped up. 'Sorry, Mr Schofield, but Equity rules clearly state that if a principal arrives less than half an hour before the show, the understudy has to go on,' he said, marking down the decision in his little logbook.

Phillip was not at all happy – there he was, ready to go on, yet now the audience would have to be told that the star of the show was 'indisposed'. Meanwhile we knew that the kids would be disappointed – many of them had come especially to see their favourite telly presenter. I and a few other members of the company made sure that we were chatting away to the young understudy while the announcement was made so that he wouldn't hear the inevitable groans from the auditorium, and assured him that we were all looking forward to doing the show with him. The understudy proved to be brilliant, and Phillip made sure never to irk the production manager by being late again.

Working on *Doctor Dolittle* brought me a rare opportunity to perform on stage without a puppet, when Nigel Plaskitt mentioned that they needed someone to be a huntsman for the final scene before the interval. There were no lines, but it was a chance to get dressed up in a costume and appear in my own right. 'I'll do it!' I said.

'But, Ronnie,' Nigel warned, 'it would mean you'd have to get your blacks off and get in costume in a minute and a half, and then spend the interval setting your puppet for the second half...'

Needless to say, I was more than happy to give up my interval for a moment in the limelight, and strode onto the stage in my huntsman's gear with pride. My brief appearance was in a courtroom scene, and I soon discovered it was the perfect opportunity to get to know the rest of the cast better. As it turned out, not having any lines in a scene didn't actually stop you talking, and while the judge was delivering his long monologues the rest of us would be nattering away under our breath. In fact, some of the cast were so busy exchanging cheeky remarks about the front row of the audience that their fake moustaches began to come unstuck.

It seemed there was never a dull moment with musical theatre people, and no end to their furtive romances and one-night stands, all of which would be gossiped about over coffee the next morning. One of the girls was desperately in love with the married musical director and would turn to me for advice. 'You have to put him out of your head, darling – he's taken,' I would tell her. 'I can't!' she would lament. 'I just can't help myself!'

Meanwhile one of the male members of the cast with a boyfriend back home would talk to me about his crush on a co-star. I would urge him not to mess around on tour, but it was no good and soon a secret affair had started.

Phillip might be the Doctor, but it seemed that I was becoming quite the agony uncle on the show. From thinking I would be homesick and lonely on tour, I had begun to feel that I was part of a travelling family, and I rediscovered my love of the special camaraderie that exists in theatre.

One day I was just fixing myself a pre-show cuppa in the green room when I heard a commotion from the sofa in front of the telly. 'Ronnie, look!' one of my castmates called out, pointing to the television. 'It's your old friend Geoffrey.'

I set my cup down and immediately ran over, and

before long quite a lot of the cast had gathered round to watch with me. It was Geoffrey, sure enough, but he seemed to be stacking shelves in a supermarket. 'I wonder what he's up to,' I muttered to myself, thinking it must be a shot for some new show he was presenting.

It turned out I had got the wrong end of the stick entirely. The show was called *After They Were Famous*, and its mission was to catch up with the household names of yesteryear to find out what they were doing now. In Geoffrey's case the answer was worse than I could ever have imagined – after several years spent trying and failing to get *Rainbow* going again, and *Mole in the Hole* not having taken off, he really was stacking shelves at Tesco for a living.

The mood in the green room grew awkward and the other performers went very quiet. Of course, all actors fear their work drying up and having to get a 'proper job'. Geoffrey's plight was a sobering reminder that, however much fun we were having on tour, it wouldn't go on forever.

'I hope they paid him well for the interview,' muttered one of my new friends, as the programme moved on to find out what life was like now for the former Bionic Woman.

'I doubt it,' someone else replied.

I slunk away from the group and busied myself with my tea. Poor Geoffrey, I thought. How humiliating – to be reduced not only to stacking shelves but to going on a programme like that. And I thought I'd had it bad with my own dry spell.

But whatever Geoffrey's troubles, he was resourceful, and he clearly saw in his professional failures a strange kind of asset. Before long I saw him popping up on screen again, this time in an advertisement for Virgin Money as a cautionary reminder to save wisely when the going is good; by this stage he was driving his own minicab, having put shelf-stacking behind him. I was sure Virgin must have paid him a decent appearance fee, but even so my heart still went out to him.

By the autumn, the *Dolittle* cast had become a tight-knit group, and it was a blow for us all when news came that Phillip was going to have to leave the show because of increasing television commitments. His replacement was to be TV comedian Russ Abbot, famed for his madcap characters such as Basildon Bond, Cooperman and C.U. Jimmy a red-headed, tartan-clad Scot who babbled away in such a broad accent that no one could understand a word he said. Some of the company were rather unsure of this casting, to say the least, and bitterly lamented the loss of Phillip. But I couldn't help feeling that, when it came to playing a mad doctor, Russ looked the part more than Phillip, who had to wear sideburns and a wig to turn him into Dr Dolittle.

We all waved a tearful goodbye to Phillip, and Russ had only one complete run-through with the whole cast before he had to step into his predecessor's shoes. The poor man obviously picked up on the negativity in the company, and after a couple of rather lacklustre performances from the rest of the cast he took the brave decision to tackle the issue head-on. When we were all gathered backstage, he cleared his throat and said, 'I know I'm new, and I've heard that some of you are unhappy that I'm not Phillip. But the fact is I'm not. I'll be doing the part my way, and if you've got any problems, come to my dressing room and we'll discuss it. I want to enjoy this experience and I want you to enjoy it too.'

There were a few mutters of disapproval, but his honest words seemed to win the cast over, and soon we were all going out for curries together as if Russ had been one of our number for years. We even learned to put up with his ad libs at the end of the show, when he would respond to particularly enthusiastic applause by going into characters from his TV show – something he was particularly apt to do when we performed up north, where he was very popular. Sometimes the red wig would even go on, as C.U. Jimmy took over the stage from Dr Dolittle.

In fact, Russ stayed with the production for even longer than Phillip had. The show just seemed to run and run, with the tour being constantly extended to take in new cities. I would always rush home to see my family whenever we had a short break, but in what seemed like the blink of an eye, I realised that I had been on the road for almost two years.

Then, while we were playing in Bristol, we were called into a company meeting and told that a possible run in Dublin had not come off, and that this would be the last theatre on our tour. It had been an incredible twenty-one months, and as we all rushed off to call our loved ones and let them know we would at last be coming home, I was struck by how much my life had changed since my nervous first rehearsal at the start of the year 2000. I was no longer a timid homebody who thought his whole career was over just because his days on *Rainbow* were. I had rediscovered my first love – theatre – and proved to myself that, even far away from home and family, I could survive and enjoy life on my own. And for months I hadn't even thought about *Rainbow* at all.

Sometimes it's not until we truly let things go that they finally come back to us. As I was eating breakfast one morning, I got a phone call from Fremantle Media, the global media group that had acquired the rights to *Rainbow* after Thames lost their ITV franchise. They had been contacted by the organisers of School Disco, a retro-themed club night at Hammersmith Palais, who were interested in getting the old *Rainbow* gang on stage to perform for their twenty-something punters. These 'kids' apparently loved nothing better than dancing in school uniform to hits from their eighties childhoods, and would no doubt love the idea of seeing Zippy, George and

Bungle resurrected too. The idea tickled me, and while a year and a half ago I had thought I'd never play Zippy again, I could see this occasion for what it was – a bit of nostalgic fun. 'Why not?' I said.

A few days later, however, I got another phone call – this time from my old friend Malcolm Lord, the last Bungle on the original *Rainbow*. 'Ronnie,' he said, 'it's great that you want to do School Disco. But I think I should warn you – Geoffrey's going to be taking part as well, and he's not too happy with you…'

Chapter 17: Zippy, Superstar DJ

Pulling up outside Hammersmith Palais in a taxi, I was shocked to see a huge queue already snaking around the block. Evidently this retro club night was quite a big deal. A large sign outside the building proclaimed 'School Disco, second anniversary show, with secret special guests.' Well, that's us, I thought, clutching the case in which my old Zippy puppet had been carefully stowed. I gingerly wound down my window to get a better look at the crowd outside.

'Blimey, Ronnie, look at the queue,' said my friend Mark Mander, leaning over to my side of the taxi to get a look at the crowd. Mark was a young puppeteer I had met on a production of *The Secret Garden* at the Little Angel, and when not performing kids' shows he was fast becoming a sensation on the alternative circuit as the immaculately made-up head of a puppet 'living doll' called Clementine.

I had roped Mark in to play George, one of his own childhood puppet heroes. He had spent the better part of the cab ride trying out the voice on me, and his version was probably the campest I'd heard. 'Well, he is pink, you know, darling,' Mark remarked tartly when I pointed this out to him.

As we made our way inside the club, I was struck by the sheer scale of the event. Inside, hundreds of young men and women in school uniforms were gyrating wildly, while a man dressed as a traditional headmaster, complete with mortarboard and gown, invited a few of them at a time to dance on a stage.

We pushed our way through the throng of bodies, me holding my case to my chest for dear life – who knew what this crazy bunch was capable of? – then round the side of the stage to the entrance of a dingy little dressing room. As the door swung open Malcolm came forward to meet us, enveloping me in a warm bear hug (he was Bungle from the neck down already).

'Ronnie, it's great to see you,' he beamed. 'And great to have you on board, Mark,' he added, extending a hand to him.

We stepped into the dressing room and plonked our bags down on the floor. It was only then that I noticed another figure in the corner of the room, hunched over slightly in front of a mirror. Underneath a sky-blue polyester jacket I could see one of those trademark loud shirts.

Geoffrey slowly turned around, looking up and clocking me and Mark. 'Good to meet you, Mark,' he said, smiling, suddenly the cheery presenter.

'Likewise,' Mark replied. 'I'm a long-time fan.'

Geoffrey's gaze flicked back to me and the smile faded. 'Ronnie,' he muttered. 'Glad you're well.'

'Hello, Geoff,' I said quietly. In twenty years of working together, I had grown used to the change in atmosphere that accompanied one of Geoffrey's moods, but I had never been the cause of one before. There was no Pamela here to mollycoddle him now, and no Charles to buy him a manly drink. If we were to get through the show, I realised, somehow I would have to bring him round myself.

I decided to go for the direct approach. 'Now look, I've heard you're not very happy, Geoff…' I started.

'Uh huh,' Geoffrey grunted.

'Is it because I worked on the new *Rainbow*?'

There was a moment's pause before he replied, 'I'm not sure I'd call it that, to be honest.'

I decided to ignore the slight and wait patiently to hear what Geoffrey had to say.

'You let the side down, taking that job,' he continued. 'It wasn't up to our standards and you know it.'

I bit my tongue to avoid launching into a sharp critique of the catalogue of errors that was *Mole in the Hole*, determined that I would be the bigger man.

'Look, Geoffrey, I know you wanted to bring *Rainbow* back how it used to be,' I told him, 'and I'm sorry they didn't ask you to be involved. But it wasn't me who decided to change the format.'

Geoffrey's face was impassive. 'It's not like I was stitching it up behind your backs, you know,' I continued. 'They made me audition for the part. I didn't just waltz in there and get my old job back.'

By now I could see his scowl beginning to soften. 'Geoffrey, I need work as much as you do,' I continued, thinking back to the sad image of him as a taxi driver. 'It was a job. Maybe it wasn't as good as what we all did together in the past, but with the resources we had I'm proud of what we achieved in the end. I'm sorry they didn't call you in as well, but you can't really blame me for that.'

There was a pause as I waited to see what Geoffrey would say. It seemed to last for hours.

'Alright,' he murmured finally, standing up and offering me his hand. 'Let's try and enjoy this, shall we?'

Thank God, I thought. If we were going to face a club of drunken youngsters together, at least we could be a united front.

Half an hour later, Geoffrey was being wheeled on stage inside a giant birthday cake, to the cheers and screams of what sounded like a thousand deranged fans. When he burst out of the cake, the crowd went absolutely wild. Geoffrey and Bungle danced around onstage with a handful of carefully chosen revellers (personal bouncers on stand-by in case they got into any difficulties) while Mark and I – mercifully – performed from a balcony above, gazing down on the proceedings like Statler and Waldorf from *The Muppet Show*. Mark needn't have worried about perfecting his George voice since, over the din, none of us stood a chance of being heard. Hundreds of balloons were released over the heads of the audience, deafening music thumped away, coloured lights whirled around above our heads and the crowd danced on into the early hours of the morning.

Although the youngsters seemed oblivious, to those of us who were stone-cold sober, the heat soon became almost unbearable. Up on our balcony, Mark and I were necking bottles of water, and looking down at Geoffrey I could see the sweat pouring off him. I could scarcely imagine how Malcolm must be feeling in his bear suit, but he and Geoffrey were clearly having the time of their lives, dancing up and down the stage with a gang of energetic young women who looked like wild-eyed extras from *Grange Hill*.

Only then did it hit me: bizarre as it seemed, to these young people we were stars – icons of their childhood – suddenly crossing over into the adult world. Their enthusiasm was infectious. Looking down, I caught Geoffrey's eye for a moment and could see a twinkle in it. I knew what he was feeling: it was good to be wanted again.

As it turned out, the gig at Hammersmith was only the first of many appearances made by the *Rainbow* gang for our legions of newly grown-up fans. A couple of weeks later we were booked to appear on *Night Fever*, a late-night karaoke panel show broadcast on Channel 5 and hosted by Madness frontman Suggs. Once again, a school disco theme was the order of the day, and although we were spared having to dress up ourselves, everyone else – including team captains Darren Day and Leslie Grantham – was in typical grey-and-white school uniform, while Suggs himself was dressed as a headmaster. Our role was to score the woeful singing efforts of both the panellists and audience members, while the likes of Rod Stewart and Lionel Blair dropped in to show them how it was really done.

Somehow, Zippy, George and the rest of the *Rainbow* cohort had become celebrities once again as the kids who had grown up watching the programme were coming of age. While less than a decade earlier, *Rainbow* had seemed gone forever, now suddenly we were very much in demand.

Rainbow was edging into its thirtieth-anniversary year, but it was another long-standing brand that really brought us back to wider public attention. Marmite was celebrating its centenary, and to mark the occasion the company commissioned a series of advertisements that played on people's famous love–hate relationship with it. The ads featured people struggling with the idea of eating Marmite at different moments over the past hundred years – from a freak show in Blackpool c. 1902 (when Marmite started production), in which a man eats it neat out of the jar, to a base camp at Mount Everest in 1950, where desperate climbers decide whether to eat it or starve, to the *Rainbow* kitchen, 'Somewhere in England, 1974', when Zippy refuses to eat his breakfast because he can't face the sticky brown spread. I was delighted to get a call asking me to come in and do the honours, especially since it meant being reunited on set with Roy, and was even more pleased to learn that Zippy was firmly in the 'hate' camp – after years of surviving on paper plates of twiglets at children's parties, I had developed a strong dislike of Marmite myself.

Clearly, Zippy and George were becoming part of a world far bigger than the *Rainbow* house. A few months later, I got a call inviting me to come and work on the pilot episode of a new comedy show for BBC Two, *Dead Ringers*. I had heard Jon Culshaw and Jan Ravens' impressions show on Radio 4 and was keen to see what they had come up with for the *Rainbow* puppets.

The bizarre script didn't disappoint. The sketch was a spoof episode of the reality TV show *Faking It*, in which members of the public are taught a new set of skills and then try to blag their way past a panel of experts.

In this case, Zippy had set his sights on getting to the heart of power by pretending to be Cherie Blair – his improbably broad grin lending him the requisite physical resemblance. As the voice-over put it, 'Zippy has spent his whole life irritating people with his big wide mouth and being a bit of a know-it-all, so it just might work.'

First Zippy kidnapped the real Cherie, then he put on a black wig and pink dress and met Tony for an 'intimate dinner at Number 10', during which he gave an account of his day at the law courts: 'I got loads of slimy foreigners off on technicalities – and I got Bungle deported!'

In the final scene we are told that Zippy 'faces the ultimate test' – convincing Tony that he really is his wife, in the Number 10 bedroom. We hear the prime minister's satisfied noises, and he shouts that he is 'up above the streets and houses' with pleasure. But when he pulls back the sheet next to him, it is not Zippy but George who has been sharing his bed. 'Ooh, the pleasure was all mine, prime minister,' the pink hippo simpers, while Zippy laughs maniacally from the doorway.

The revival of interest in *Rainbow* hadn't gone unnoticed at Fremantle Media, the company that now owned the rights to the show. One morning, I was summoned to a meeting at their offices just off Tottenham Court Road. Sitting around a huge boardroom table were Geoffrey, Malcolm and Mark, plus some corporate big wigs and a young man with slicked-back hair and the unmistakable air of a promoter.

'This is Guy,' one of the suits informed us, 'and he's got an idea we want you to hear.'

'Cheers, mate,' the young man replied, turning to us enthusiastically. 'School Disco was massive, right? It proved there's a huge demand for *Rainbow* out there. So... I want to take you guys on tour all round the country!'

There was a pause while the four of us took in the news. I could see Geoffrey's eyes widening. 'What sort of thing did you have in mind?' he asked, barely containing his excitement.

'We'd be looking to work the university circuit,' Guy replied. 'Maybe throw in some bars and nightclubs as well – like what you did at Hammersmith Palais. I'm thinking we have Zippy and George spinning a few discs, a bit of banter – and we'll call it the Rainbow Disco Roadshow. Kids can't get enough of all this retro stuff at the moment – we'll make a killing.'

Geoffrey was listening carefully. 'So if Zippy and George are doing the records, how would Bungle and I fit in?'

'Well,' Guy replied breezily, 'I'll be straight with you. Some of the gigs we're looking at will be more of a small-scale operation, so we'll just take the two puppets, do a quick set and get out. Others have room for a bit more and can afford to pay for it. Have you ever seen *Play Your Cards Right?*'

'Um, yes,' Geoffrey replied, probably wondering what Bruce Forsyth's eighties' game show could have to do with all this.

'Well, that's where you and Bungle come in – only you'll be Brucie and Bungle'll be flipping the cards over.'

Geoffrey seemed satisfied with that.

'So what d'you reckon?' Guy asked us. 'Shall we give it a whirl?'

We all looked at each other. I knew none of us could resist the idea of resurrecting *Rainbow* for legions of screaming fans.

'Yes!' we replied, as one.

Our first engagement was at the University of East Anglia. Guy had hired a van and a quartet of burly roadies to drive us up there, and we spent much of the journey going through our lines, which he had written in consultation with one of the Fremantle executives. Geoffrey and Malcolm had already learned theirs, while Mark and I had no need to since we would be able to pin up a script beneath our record decks.

The show was an appealing mix of naff jokes and cheesy music, with the odd profanity thrown in to prove that it wasn't actually for preschoolers. We were to open with 'Let Me Entertain You' by Robbie Williams, followed by Queen's 'We Will Rock You'. Then the four of us would introduce ourselves: 'MC Zippy' (complete with baseball cap and laden with bling), 'DJ George', 'Jazz-it-up Geoffrey' and 'Fat Boy Bungle'. George would then offer his best Elvis impression as a way of introducing the next song, 'A Little Less Conversation'. Then came his own 'favourite' song, ABBA's 'Dancing Queen', and the Bee Gees' 'Stayin' Alive', which would prompt Zippy to claim that the Bees Gees used to sing on *Rainbow* too: 'One had a beard, one had very long hair, and the other had a very high-pitched voice.' 'That was Rod, Jane and Freddy!' Bungle corrected him. We would finish off with 'It's Raining Men' (predictably, another of George's favourites), 'YMCA' (complete with audience participation) and 'Hit Me Baby One More Time' (or, as Zippy insisted, 'Zip Me Baby One More Time'). Then in typical *Rainbow* fashion, we would all share a moment recognising the value of teamwork, and finish with 'We Go Together' from *Grease*. All in all, it seemed like a recipe for a fun night.

I was pleasantly surprised by the hotel we were staying in, which was considerably swisher than I'd expected. This tour was no *Doctor Dolittle* but it seemed like we were going to be well taken care of. The dressing room provided by the student union didn't disappoint, either – it was spacious, clean and welcoming, and some kind soul had left a few bottles of wine out for us. When it became clear that we weren't going to drink them – not before our first show, anyway – Guy slyly slipped them into his bag. 'We don't want to leave these behind!' he said.

It soon became clear exactly why we would be needing a room for the night, even though the university was only a few hours' drive from London. The student union was providing a whole evening's worth of entertainment, and we weren't required onstage until well after midnight. By the time our routine started, the students were already legless, and their enthusiasm at the sight of their childhood legends was off the scale. There were cheers and shouts every few seconds, and all in all the show seemed to be going down a storm – with one exception: every time one of the characters swore, a collective gasp went round the room. After one particularly blue exchange, the atmosphere grew appreciably cooler. These kids might be up for a raucous, boozy party in the company of Zippy, George and co., but hearing the beloved puppets (not to mention Geoffrey) swearing was clearly a step too far. 'Tone it down, eh boys?' Guy called from backstage – and for the rest of the night the four of us improvised our way around the scripted swear words.

With the record-spinning part of the evening concluded, it was time for a game of 'Play Your Cards Right'. Geoffrey and Bungle picked a couple of likely-looking contestants out of the audience – a young man and woman who were both looking rather the worse for wear. I had already been surprised at the state of the crowd we had attracted – not having been to university,

I'd always assumed it to be rather dull and serious, but these students were soon to confirm how wrong I was. As Geoffrey and Malcolm tried to begin an innocent game of 'Higher or lower?', some friends of the two young people came up with their own idea to spice up the proceedings. 'Strip poker!' one of them shouted, and before long the suggestion had gained traction. Round after round, the two students shed layers of clothing, until the boy was standing there in just his pants and socks. When the female student began unbuttoning her top, Malcolm improvised anxiously – 'Ooh, careful, you'll embarrass an old bear if you go any further!' In the end, rather than see how far they were willing to go, Geoffrey decided to call off the game and declared the young woman the winner. So this is the ivory tower of academia, I thought to myself as we packed up our things and headed back to the dressing room.

We were just about to pile into the van for the short trip back to the hotel when Guy arrived at the dressing room door with a gaggle of fans, all seeking autographs from their heroes. (Guy had given me and Mark T-shirts with Zippy and George on them so people would know who we were.) One by one, we signed whatever they had brought for us – old *Rainbow* annuals from their childhood, napkins, newspapers, whatever was to hand.

'Can you do me a "Love from Zippy"?' slurred one drunken girl, staggering up to where I was sitting.

'Of course,' I replied, looking under my chair for a biro that had fallen on the floor. It was only when I stood up again that I saw what she intended to be autographed – she had undone her top and was pushing one of her boobs in my direction.

'Oh…' I stammered, not sure how exactly to proceed.

'You might have more luck with a felt-tip, Ronnie,' Mark laughed, chucking me a bigger pen.

'Love… from… Zippy,' I wrote, trying my best to maintain eye contact with the fan rather than focus too much on what I was signing. 'There you go!'

'Cheers!' she replied, happily buttoning her top back up as she left the dressing room.

At least on that first night we had the prospect of a clean bed to return to after we came off stage, but as time went on, and budgets grew tighter, the touring experience became rather less salubrious. Before long, it was just me and Mark on the road for most of the gigs, and even if we finished at two or three in the morning, we would have to get straight back in the van and drive back home to London, sometimes arriving well after sunrise.

My view of universities grew less and less rose-tinted as I saw first-hand what an average student night out comprised – even Oxford, that bastion of the academic establishment, seemed to be little more than a den for riotous drunkards. But amongst the jeering, the sloshing, and even the occasional vomiting, I always felt a genuine warmth and affection from the crowds, and however grotty and sordid the dive, we were always made to feel welcome. We met a few other former legends on the road as well, crossing paths with the likes of Timmy Mallet and Chesney Hawkes, who were both working the retro circuit for all they were worth. Chesney, in particular, turned out to be a lovely guy, not to mention a *Rainbow* devotee himself, having watched the show as a child. And it turned out that the feeling was mutual, since Mark was a big fan of 'The One and Only'.

Before long, the tour was broadened out from student unions to other venues, and Guy booked us on a circuit of Brannigans nightclubs all over the country, not to mention the odd gay bar, where George always went down a storm. There was even talk of a trip to Ibiza, although having diligently watched an episode of *Ibiza Uncovered* for research purposes, I was rather relieved when that particular gig didn't come off.

Generally, the bar and nightclub gigs were not so different from those at the student unions, although the crowds tended to be a little rowdier. Wherever we went we had a team of minders with us: four big guys who shared the duties of driving, heaving our kit about, and generally keeping us out of trouble. I could never understand why a *Rainbow* roadshow required such a lot of muscle, until one gig in Birmingham when the heavies really proved their worth. We were driving around town in an open-top limousine, with Zippy and George looking out and trying to drum up business for that night's show. As we stopped at a set of traffic lights, I felt my puppet ripped out of my hands. Standing up in the vehicle I could see a young guy making off with Zippy in his arms. I was dumbfounded. I had never heard of a drive-by puppet-napping before.

Fortunately, our team of minders had quicker reflexes than me. I had barely taken in what was happening before one of them – who had, apparently, trained with the SAS – was barrelling down the road in hot pursuit. He caught up with his quarry in no time, wrestled the puppet from the startled young man and rushed back to return Zippy to my arms as if he were a precious lost child.

Unfortunately, though, there were some occasions when the minders were too late to intervene. For some reason, when the crowds got really rowdy, poor George always seemed to take the hit. I could never work out what anyone, however drunk, might have against the amiable pink hippo. Perhaps he had awakened some latent issues from childhood – at any rate, more than once he found himself on the receiving end of a punch from a member of the audience.

The first time this happened, Mark fell over and chipped a tooth. The second incident was even more surprising – far from a rowdy student gig, it was a corporate event for Hallmark Cards at the Savoy Hotel. Once again, an angry audience member stormed the stage and took a swipe at the poor hippo. This time Mark was left with nothing more than a sore hand, but he was seriously contemplating legal action. In the end he decided not to prosecute – there was no guarantee that a judge would recognise what had happened as bodily harm, especially since it was directed not at a man but at a fluffy hippo. 'Perhaps I should take it as a tribute to the power of puppetry that George made someone so angry,' Mark consoled himself philosophically,

The real nadir of the tour, though, came with a show booked for the Skegness branch of Butlins. We turned up to find the crowd already paralytic, and soon learned that we had in fact been booked as a warm-up act – for a group of strippers, who were already busily adjusting their tassels backstage. The problem was that the boozy audience only had eyes for the main attraction and viewed our part of the evening as an inconvenient delay. We rushed through our set in record time and hurried back to the dressing room – and for once made it home at a reasonable hour.

After many months on the road Mark and I thought we'd seen it all, but our next gig was to prove the most astounding yet. The School Disco company, who had booked our first appearance at Hammersmith Palais, was staging a retro festival on Clapham Common, hosted by our *Night Fever* 'headmaster' Suggs, and the *Rainbow* gang were to be a key part of the event.

Getting the puppets ready backstage, I could hear the crowd beginning to gather, but it was not until we took our places on the stage that I realised quite how many people were out there. Sneaking a peek from behind my counter, I was met with an endless sea of faces – more than 40,000 people were waiting to see their old friends from *Rainbow* resurrected. It was the biggest audience I had ever performed to in my life. Slowly, the platform I was sitting on was wheeled closer to the crowd. It was only then that I realised they were chanting 'Zi-ppy! Zi-ppy! Zi-ppy!' As Zippy popped up from behind the counter, 40,000 pairs of lungs roared as one, creating a wall of sound so overwhelming I could feel it hitting my hand and travelling down my body. If I still had any doubts that *Rainbow* was flying high once again, they were obliterated in that moment. Somehow Zippy had become a rock star.

Having witnessed *Rainbow*'s remarkable pulling power, it was perhaps inevitable that the suits at Fremantle Media began looking for ways to capitalise on the show's thirtieth anniversary. Our promoter, Guy, had been talking about his contacts in the music industry for some time, and now he was given the green light to put together a single.

Of course a single meant a music video, so Geoffrey, Malcolm, Mark and I would be getting together for a spot of location filming, just like in the old days – only this time for a rather different kind of adventure. We arrived at a street in Hackney to find an enormous blue Cadillac waiting for us, with a glamorous young woman behind the wheel who was providing the main vocals on the track. The video mostly featured the five of us driving up and down in the car, interspersed with a few nightclub scenes where grinning partygoers danced to the sounds coming from DJ Zippy's decks. I had already listened to the song, which had been recorded in a studio beforehand. It was catchy and relentless, a proper dance remix of the *Rainbow* theme tune with the additional thumping lyrics 'It's a rainbow, baby. Just like you it drives me crazy!'

The music video was to end with all five of us in bed together. To begin with, Zippy would be hidden under the covers, but after the girl gave a cheeky look to the camera he would emerge, wearing a bling dollar-sign medallion. Then Geoffrey would remark cheerfully, 'Take care, bye-bye,' just as he had a thousand times on the original television programme.

Although it all sounded rather glamorous on paper, the filming turned out to be anything but. In order to fit the puppets in the back of the car, part of the seat had been scooped out, with Mark and I crouched in a pool of rusty water for the best part of the morning. Still, it was fun to be filming with the rest of the *Rainbow* gang again, and Geoffrey was smiling from ear to ear at being back in front of the camera.

With our single about to hit the record stores, Fremantle had decided to capitalise on the *Rainbow* revival for all it was worth, bringing out new retro merchandise, anniversary DVDs and even a book – a spoof exposé going behind the scenes of the original programme, featuring 'interviews' with Zippy, George and Bungle. The company's publicists went into overdrive, organising events and signings to push the new merchandise. Most exciting of these was an appearance on ITV's *This Morning*, which gave me a chance to catch up with Phillip Schofield, who I hadn't seen since the *Dolittle* tour. Roy was also invited, to provide the voices of Zippy and George, just like the old days.

We arrived at ITV's London Studios at a hideously early hour, and as Geoffrey was rushed in to make-up I breathed a sigh of relief that my dishevelled, barely-awake face would not be making it on to camera. We were then walked onto the set, where the crew were preparing to start filming.

'Ronnie, it's great to see you!' shouted Phillip, rushing over and throwing his arms around me.

'Oh, do you two know each other?' asked Roy with surprise. For once, I was the member of the cast with the celebrity connections.

'Phillip and I worked together in the theatre,' I replied, emphasising the second syllable the way I knew Roy would have done.

'Oh really?' he muttered. 'How wonderful.'

No sooner had Phillip introduced himself and his

co-presenter Fern Britton to the rest of the troupe than we were sat (or in me and Mark's case crouched) down and the programme began. Phillip talked about *Rainbow*'s 'cult status' and showed some clips from an anniversary DVD that was being put out by Fremantle, including one from the very first episode of *Rainbow*, long before any of us had been involved with the show. 'That's not me!' Zippy wailed when Moony and Sunshine came on to the screen, and Fern remarked that he had changed his image over the years.

We did our best to plug the single and the various bits of merchandise that Fremantle had asked us to mention – the T-shirts, lunchboxes and miniature stuffed toys of all the characters. 'I'll give you a little Bungle when we're finished here, Fern,' Malcolm remarked cheekily. But the majority of the interview was taken up with the bizarre behind-the-scenes 'exposé', *Climbing High*, a book Fern described as 'raunchy' and 'not for children'. The best moment came when George was pressed on a section of the book in which he admitted to briefly dating Andrew Lloyd-Webber in the 1980s. 'Well, I thought he was a hippo,' Mark replied innocently.

Not long after our *This Morning* appearance, the phone rang with an offer I had never expected to hear in my forty-odd years in showbusiness: 'The BBC want you for *Top of the Pops*.'

It turned out that our single had entered the charts at number fifteen, earning us a slot on the show, and they wanted me and Mark to come and perform Zippy and George – apparently the stage was too small to accommodate Geoffrey and Malcolm as well as the singer and two dancers. Of course, I agreed to do the gig, at this stage feeling more bemused than excited.

I had barely hung up when the phone began ringing again, and I picked up the receiver to find a very excited Mark on the other end. 'I can't believe it, Ronnie!' he shouted. 'We're going to be on *Top of the Pops!*' Mark had been an avid fan of the show throughout his childhood, so for him this was about as big a deal as you could imagine.

As the day of the show drew nearer, Mark's enthusiasm began to rub off on me, and by the time our cab arrived at BBC Television Centre I was giddy with excitement myself. A runner greeted us in the lobby and led us down a labyrinth of curved corridors to a green room where we waited to be called on set.

Among those sharing the billing with us that night were Robbie Williams and Daniel Bedingfield, although there was no sign of them in the green room. Instead we found ourselves sitting next to a rather matronly Romanian woman with a heavy accent and two young girls in bright-gold hot pants. 'These are my daughters,' she proclaimed proudly. 'They are Cheeky Girls.'

'Oh, right,' I replied awkwardly, shaking the babushka's hand and smiling at her daughters. 'Nice to meet you.'

'We are Cheeky Girls,' the duo repeated in tandem.

'I bet you are,' muttered Mark, raising one eyebrow.

They certainly lived up to their name in the camera rehearsal, gyrating like mad in their flimsy gold outfits, while their mother beamed with pride from the wings.

Next it was our turn to run through our own routine. The BBC crew had set up some decks on stage, and Mark and I simply had to move around a bit behind them, lip-syncing to the pre-recorded audio on the single. It was child's play compared to what was expected of our singer and her two backing dancers. I'd never seen such an exhausting-looking workout in my life, and the poor girl had to sing (well, mime) along at the same time. Still, she seemed happy enough to be there – I suppose, like Mark, performing on *Top of the Pops* was probably the culmination of a childhood dream for her.

As the programme began, the studio was suddenly packed with bodies pushing and shoving their way to the front of the stage. When Robbie Williams came out to open the show with 'Feel' the crowd pressed themselves up against the barriers to get closer to him, while he danced up and down with a cane like an old-school crooner. Ms. Dynamite and Big Brovaz got them jumping up and down a bit before Daniel Bedingfield crooned them back into submission. All in all, I was surprised that the mood wasn't a little more raucous – but perhaps after my months on the university circuit I had come to expect a different kind of audience to that of a prime-time BBC show.

Then it was our turn. 'It's time for a nostalgia trip,' said the presenter, 'and this *is* a trip.' I didn't really know what to expect from the crowd, following on from a slow, heartfelt number, but from the moment the *Rainbow* theme-tune piped out at the start of our track they went wild, jumping up and down and screaming like maniacs. Wow, I thought to myself, they didn't do this for Robbie Williams. Our three-minute set seemed to go by in a matter of seconds, but the audience were so worked up that they wouldn't be quiet when the presenter tried to introduce the next band, Liberty X.

We might not have made the top of the hit parade (that honour went to Eminem, who did not attend) but as far as the night's entertainment was concerned, *Rainbow* was indisputably number one.

Chapter 18: Old dog, new tricks

With *Rainbow* flying high once again, my other professional family, the Little Angel, was struggling. After six years at the helm, Christopher Leith had moved on to pursue other projects, and with Islington Council repeatedly threatening to cut its funding the theatre was in a precarious position. The board of Potheinos Ltd, which ran the Little Angel, appointed a woman called Loretta Howells to take over from Christopher, and hopefully to put the theatre on stronger financial ground.

Loretta was a controversial choice – she was not a puppeteer herself, although in her previous position, at the Arts Council, she had helped fund training bursaries for puppetry – and she arrived with some bold new ideas for how to turn around the theatre's fortunes. Soon, many long-standing members of the board, which at that time was principally made up of grey-bearded puppeteers, had made way for a new wave of more business-minded individuals.

Loretta's most radical move was to persuade the board to restructure the Little Angel's financial set-up in order to make it eligible for more sources of funding. After John Wright's death, Lyndie had inherited the theatre company, which was run as a small business, while the actual theatre building was owned by Potheinos. Lyndie wanted to take more of a back seat in the running of the business, and neither of her children was willing to take the reins – Joe was now working as a television and film director, while Sarah had her own puppet company touring around Europe. Loretta suggested merging the theatre company with Potheinos to form a single, charitable company. Lyndie would have to give up her financial stake in the business, but she would retain ownership of her cottage and the theatre workshop as well as the existing collection of puppets, which she would loan to the theatre for revivals of the old repertoire. Lyndie agreed, believing it to be in the best interests of the theatre, but I knew it couldn't have been easy for her.

As it turned out, the board appointed Loretta at just the right time, because it wasn't long before all her contacts and management skills were called upon. Whenever I was in London I would pop into the theatre office for a cup of tea and a natter, and to put out my feelers for work on any upcoming shows. One day, I went to visit as usual, only to discover a distinctly sombre mood in the office. After years of subsidising the Little Angel, Islington Council had made good on their threats and finally pulled the plug on its funding.

Knowing my long relationship with the theatre, Loretta took me to one side to explain the situation. Without an alternative source of revenue, there were only two options available to her. The first was for the Little Angel to become a receiving house, picking up touring puppet shows but producing no work of its own – a heart-breaking prospect for those of us who had worked there for so many years. The second, even harder option, was to shut the theatre down – and that was what Loretta had chosen to do. 'We're going to have to go dark, Ronnie,' she told me.

I was stunned. In the forty years since I had started working there, the Little Angel had always soldiered on. But the figures were indisputable. The board had already decided that the theatre would have to close – temporarily, it was hoped – and the rest of the administrative team would be let go. Loretta planned to work unpaid for as long as she could while she tried to secure funding to allow the Little Angel to reopen.

With the theatre closed to audiences, the fundraising began in earnest. Clive Anderson's wife, Jane, a local doctor, started the Guardian Angel scheme, which soon began to attract donations. Meanwhile, Juliet Stevenson wrote a passionate piece for the local paper explaining how important it was to save the theatre, and Ken Campbell put together a special performance in aid of it.

I was keen to play my own small part in drawing attention to the campaign.

'The main thing we need is publicity, Ronnie,' Loretta told me. 'Do you think you and Zippy could help?'

Before long, I was posing for a photograph in the *Islington Gazette*, with Zippy crying into his hankie at the thought of the Little Angel's closure.

The campaign was a powerful grass-roots movement, and it soon gained momentum in the local community, which suddenly seemed to recognise the value of the little puppet theatre on their doorstep. As the months went by, with Loretta lobbying hard at local government and Arts Council meetings, and the new Friends committee begging for donations, I held my breath, hoping that all our efforts would prove enough. Losing *Rainbow* had been a difficult enough blow for me after so many years, but the thought of the Little Angel being gone for good was devastating.

In the end, the hard work paid off, and the theatre was brought back from the brink. With some generous donations from local benefactors and project-specific funding from the Arts Council, Loretta was able to reopen the theatre to the public.

I was overjoyed that John Wright's legacy was not going to be lost and that the Little Angel would continue

352

to entertain and educate the next generation of theatre-goers. But I had to smile when I thought how John would have felt knowing that Zippy – a crude, unsophisticated glove puppet – had helped save his beloved marionette theatre.

With the Little Angel back on firm footing, Loretta decided to move on, and a new artistic director took her place. Steve Tiplady was an intense, bearded man with the aura of a puppet guru. He was very much from the alternative end of the puppetry spectrum – his own shows involved manipulating trays of sand or reels of sticky tape, and on one occasion a fully nude performance behind a shadow screen. It was all rather new to me, but knowing my long-standing relationship with the theatre, Steve was keen to keep me as involved as possible in its productions, whether that be the traditional kids' repertoire or his own more experimental shows for grown-ups.

My first introduction to the world of alternative puppetry was a piece Steve had commissioned from the avant-garde theatre company Improbable. Like much of their work, the show was to be entirely improvised, and the 'puppets' we were using were just old items of household junk, flung around the stage for us to wander up to and turn into characters. This 'object manipulation', as it was officially known, was not something I had very much experience with, but Steve was reassuringly confident.

'You're a great puppeteer, Ronnie,' he told me. 'It doesn't matter if it's a marionette or a manky old boot, the job's the same, really.'

'Right,' I replied. I only wished I felt more convinced.

Steve arranged for me to meet with Phelim McDermott, the co-founder of Improbable, who would be directing the show. Phelim was a wide-eyed and wild-haired man with an infectious energy and good humour. He seemed a little eccentric, but he clearly knew what he was doing. Once the pleasantries were out of the way, he looked me in the eye. 'I've worked with puppeteers before,' he said, 'and often I find them quite blinkered. They only want to do their thing. You're not like that, are you?'

I shook my head nervously.

'Alright, good,' he replied. 'It's just that this show is unlike any other you will have worked on. You'll have to forget everything and have a really open mind, and go with whatever happens on the night. We don't rehearse. We turn up, take the temperature of the audience, and then we perform the show.'

'Um, and what exactly is the show?' I asked.

'Well, that's just it,' he replied. 'Who knows?'

The cast of the new piece comprised me and Steve on puppetry duties, plus a trio of performers from Improbable: a writer called Lee Simpson, who would improvise words on the spot, Phelim performing physical theatre, and Julian Crouch playing keyboards. Phelim had filled the stage with random objects, including some old toys, a cheese grater, pots and pans, newspaper, string and a load of empty plastic bottles. The thought of sitting there with this pile of rubbish and eyeballing the audience as they came in – well, for someone who was more used to hiding away behind a tabletop it was terrifying.

Phelim could obviously sense my anxiety. 'Don't worry, Ronnie,' he told me, 'you'll be fine. Is there anything I can do to help?'

'Well…' I began, wondering if I dared finish the sentence. 'I just thought maybe I could add something to the pile.'

'Yeah, of course,' Phelim responded. 'What is it?'

Gingerly I opened my rucksack and pulled out a plain wooden marionette. Phelim eyed it suspiciously. 'Alright, chuck it on the pile,' he agreed. 'But don't feel you have to use it just because it's there. And remember, Ronnie, I only want you to get up and do something if it really feels right. The audience can sit and watch nothing for half an hour, as far as I'm concerned. If it doesn't feel right, you don't do it.'

I was beginning to have a little more confidence in the idea, and as opening night came around and the audience filed into the theatre I started to imagine we could actually pull it off. Phelim began by walking on stage with a dictionary and asking the audience to pick out a page number, then he closed his eyes and pointed randomly to a word on the page before reading it out loud: 'Aggression.' Immediately Steve started scrunching a piece of newspaper into some kind of angry monster. I followed suit, while Julian began playing some discordant sounds on his keyboard. Before long the two monsters were facing off against each other, and I had almost forgotten the audience was still watching. This wasn't so bad – it literally felt like child's play.

Somehow I got through the whole of that first performance without once reaching for my marionette. But as the weeks rolled on, I found moments when it seemed right to use it, and just knowing it was there was enough to keep my nerves at bay the rest of the time. One night, we were improvising a scene about a criminal who was due to be hanged. Lee had already begun a story about the condemned man's final hours, and an image started forming in my mind. I gently pulled the little marionette up by the strings and began to walk him around in time to Lee's words: pacing the room, bravely facing up to his fate, and then succumbing to the hangman's noose, his little legs flicking slightly as the life finally left him.

I was aware that the audience had gone very quiet, and when I looked over to Lee I saw that his eyes had begun to water. What a great actor, I thought to myself, but as soon as we got offstage, I realised they weren't crocodile tears.

'That was brilliant, Ronnie,' he told me, putting an arm around my shoulder. 'I really felt like we were in it together.'

Unbeknownst to me, the hanging scene had also made an impression on a very important member of the audience. Peter Charlton was the chairman of the British Puppet and Model Theatre Guild and was in the process of deciding who should be given that year's Harlequin Award – the most prestigious prize a British marionettist can receive. A few weeks later, I received a call to say that the Guild had chosen to recognise me for my long-time commitment to string puppetry.

I was over the moon – I was used to living in Zippy's shadow as an anonymous puppeteer, but finally I was being recognised in my own right. Zippy might be a rock star, but now I would have the closest thing there was to a puppetry Oscar on my mantelpiece.

Under Steve's new regime, the Little Angel continued to move with the times, but the theatre's old guard were not forgotten. One cold, autumn morning I found myself standing at the hospital bedside of one of our longest-standing performers, Joyce Wren.

I remembered my first day at the theatre as a boy of fifteen, when Joyce the Voice, previously known to me only as 'the sea witch', had flung open the door and demanded to know what on earth I was doing there. She had always been so strong, such a vibrant personality, and now she seemed so quiet, so reduced – hovering between consciousness and sleep, at the border between this world and the next.

'It's nice of you to come,' I was told by a member of the family. 'But I'm afraid she probably won't know you're here.'

'That's alright,' I replied. 'I'd like to say hello anyway.' I drew up a chair by the bedside. 'Joyce,' I whispered. 'It's Ronnie here. I've come to see how you are.'

Her eyes opened and she stared for a moment as if trying to work something out. Perhaps she was attempting to match what she saw in front of her to some almost forgotten memory. 'Ronnie Le Drew,' she murmured suddenly, and her eyes became the piercing darts I had known as a boy. She took a deep breath. 'Good, better, best ... Never let it rest,' she whispered.

'That's right, Joyce,' I replied, almost choking up at the thought that she had remembered the embarrassing schoolboy rhyme I had recited all those years ago when she'd demanded that I name my favourite poem. They were words that had never left me, however simplistic they sounded.

I squeezed her hand. ''Til your good is better,' I continued quietly. 'And your better best.' Her eyes closed and she drifted back to sleep.

When Joyce died not long afterwards, generations of puppeteers came to her funeral. Although an actor by training, she had found a place for herself at the heart of the puppetry community – and her old-school, theatrical flair was sorely missed.

Meanwhile, the Wright family flame was burning brighter than ever. I was thrilled when Lyndie invited me to come with her to the premiere of her son Joe's new movie *Pride and Prejudice*. It was a star-studded occasion at the Odeon Leicester Square, with Keira Knightly, Donald Sutherland and Carey Mulligan all walking the red carpet, and I was delighted when Joe introduced me to his girlfriend Rosamund Pike, who played Jane Bennet in the film and had already made her mark in the most recent James Bond flick.

But despite the starry company he was now keeping, Joe never turned his back on the Little Angel. In fact, he returned to the theatre fresh from *Pride and Prejudice*, bringing a bit of Hollywood stardust with him, for a special gala performance of the theatre's old mainstay *The Little Mermaid*. The puppets would be the same ones we had been using throughout my time at the theatre – the same ones, in fact, that I'd seen there myself as a boy – but a new audio track was to be recorded starring the cream of the British acting crop, from Michael Gambon as the narrator to Judi Dench as the wicked sea witch. Christopher Leith had been called back to direct, while Joe would supervise the audio recording. I was to play the part of the prince, as I had done all those years ago during my first long stint at the theatre.

Before the new soundtrack was recorded, Joe and Christopher arranged for the new top-drawer voice cast to come and see a bit of the show. Then we all went to a studio in Soho together to make the recording.

Dame Judi – or just Judi, as she immediately insisted we call her – was the consummate professional. As soon as we got into the studio, the shoes came off, the glasses went on, and she got most of her lines spot on in a single take, dropping the pages of her script to the floor as she went along, like an old-fashioned radio star. Her sea witch was vicious and evil, but between takes she couldn't have been more sweet and friendly.

Michael Gambon was equally charming. He lumbered in, a huge and imposing presence with his bold, fruity voice, but his personality could not have been more unassuming. 'I'm just popping out for some bacon and eggs,' he'd told me when he arrived half an hour early for his slot. 'I'll be in the caff if you need me.' But as soon as we began recording, a whole other side of him emerged – suddenly he was grandeur and gravitas personified.

Of particular interest to me was Rory Kinnear, who would be voicing my puppet, the prince. He gave a great performance in the studio but it was one I knew I'd have to adapt my own work to. Rory's prince was much quicker and more edgy than the one on the recording I was used to, and the different energy really shook up the character for me. It took a few rehearsals to find my way into it but, when I did, I realised how much more fun the prince was to play like this.

My only regret about the entire production was that I couldn't sit and watch it from the theatre. Nonetheless, gazing down at the puppets from the bridge, or watching from the wings when I wasn't in a scene, I was as captivated as I had been all those years ago when I first saw the show as a boy of fifteen, sitting agog in the stalls and wondering if I could ever be a part of something so magical. It was an utterly spellbinding performance and my eyes watered at the sheer beauty of the spectacle, combined with the luscious new soundtrack. I knew that John Wright would have been so proud to see it.

Chapter 19: Full circle

After more than four decades in the entertainment industry, I was accustomed to the idea that a phone call out of the blue could change my life in new and unexpected ways. This time, though, it was not the latest bizarre job offer but something much more personal that awaited me.

I picked up the receiver to find my son John Phillip on the line. 'Dad, I've just been on a website called Genes Reunited,' he told me, 'and there's someone on there called Carol who seems to think she's related to us. She asked if I could give her your email address.'

'Yes, of course,' I replied, marvelling at the power of the internet and wondering who this Carol might be. Perhaps she was one of my father's relatives in Canada, I thought. He had never really kept in touch with them when he was alive, and I had only the sketchiest idea of the family out there.

A few days later, a message arrived in my inbox – and sure enough it bore the name Carol Le Drew. I opened it at once.

'I'm sorry for blasting into your life like this,' the email began. 'I've attached (the only) photo I have of who I believe to be y… *our* dad.'

As I clicked to open the picture, I almost choked on the coffee I was drinking. Sure enough, there was a picture of my father, looking very suave and stylish in an old black-and-white studio shot.

I thought back to the day, decades earlier, when Mum had received a letter out of the blue from a woman saying she was Leslie Le Drew's daughter. But that woman had been called Penny, and this one was Carol. How many secret siblings did I have?

Reading down through the email, I realised my mistake. It was the same person, after all – Carol was the legal name given by her birth mother and my father, while her adoptive parents had renamed her Penny.

'This is so difficult to write, Ronnie,' the email continued. 'I'm sorry if I've blown you away. I'm scared and excited.'

I thought back to the letter she had written before, and to the response Mum had sent her, making it clear we didn't want to have a relationship with her. I couldn't help feeling a pang of guilt. As I read on, I realised Penny had been feeling guilty too, for the upset she knew she must have caused my mum. As she put it, she felt her 'selfish curiosity' had already done enough damage – which was why it had taken so long for her to try contacting us again.

Reading those words, I felt terrible, and I was determined to offer Penny whatever help I could. I had gone along with Mum's wishes before, but now I had my own chance to get to know Penny, and to find out more about the year Dad went AWOL.

I hastily shot back an email saying that I was delighted she had got in touch and suggesting that perhaps we could meet up. Since she lived in Devon, we arranged to meet halfway, at Salisbury railway station.

As my train drew into the platform, I had butterflies in my stomach. What if we were nothing like each other? What if she wasn't really my sister at all?

I stepped off the train into what felt like a scene from an old black-and-white movie: for a few moments the platform was full of passengers, but as the crowd cleared, one blonde-haired woman remained, standing alone. I looked straight into her eyes and saw that they were just like my father's. There was no doubting this was my sister.

'Ronnie?' she asked me.

'Yes! You must be Penny!'

She beamed at me and took my hands. 'I'm so glad you replied. I hope I'm not causing too much trouble. It's been such a long time since I wrote before...'

I could see she was as anxious as I was, and after reassuring her that I was pleased to see her too, I suggested we go to the little station café for tea.

'So what have you been doing your whole life?' she

asked me with a nervous laugh, once we had sat down with our drinks.

It was hard to know where to start, but I filled her in as best I could, telling her about the Little Angel and *Rainbow*.

'Wait – you mean you're Zippy?' she gasped. 'I can't believe it!' Then she added, thoughtfully, 'So, in a way, I did grow up with you in my life after all.'

Penny told me she was a legal secretary, but that her real passion was surfing – she and her partner had travelled all over Australia in a VW camper van chasing the best waves.

I showed her some pictures I'd brought with me of our father.

'I've got something to show you, as well,' Penny said. She reached into her handbag and brought out a large heap of papers. 'These were the letters Leslie wrote my biological mother,' she told me. 'I thought you might like to read them.'

I instantly recognised the print from my father's old typewriter – one that I had inherited from him after he died. Glancing through the letters I was shocked to see that many of them had been sent from our old flat in Stockwell. Did that mean that Dad had started the affair while he was still living with Mum? I felt choked.

'She lived in Ramsgate, so they only got to see each other at weekends,' explained Penny. 'But they wrote to each other twice a week.'

This had been no fling, I realised, but a serious affair. The earliest document in the pile was a form from an introduction agency Dad had signed up with, dated August 1959, long before he moved out of the flat. He had not exactly been honest in his application – he had listed his age as thirty-eight (he was actually six years older) and claimed he was in the midst of divorce proceedings.

It turned out that Dad had been with Penny's mother Christine for over a year. Things had come to a head when she discovered she was pregnant, and after a terse and recriminatory exchange they had parted ways, with the baby being put up for adoption.

Penny had been brought up by a couple in Kent and hadn't learned about her true parents until she was older. After being rebuffed by me and Mum, she had been doing her best to trace other members of our family in Canada, and had succeeded in getting in touch with my father's brother's family. She had also tracked down her biological mother, who had given her the stash of old letters.

There was a lot to think about, and as I sat on the train back home my head was spinning. It was years since I had even thought about Dad's disappearance – his death, having come so soon afterwards, had always overshadowed it. It was hard to think of him having another life, let alone another family.

It was a few days before I began to properly look through the pile of letters Penny had given me. They were not easy reading; Dad wrote about how desperate he was to leave Mum – 'She is doing her best to hang on to me, I can't think why,' he wrote bitterly. It was clear he had really fallen for Christine, and that he felt a great affection for their daughter – he wrote of how much he wanted to hold the little baby when he saw her through the glass in the neo-natal ward. But for whatever reason, Dad felt that the depth of Christine's feelings didn't match his own, and this seemed to have driven a wedge between them. 'Thanks for waking me up from what was obviously a silly dream,' he wrote bitterly, in one of his final letters.

Although the whole story of Dad's affair was quite shocking for me to read, especially the part about him using a dating agency while still married to Mum, in a way it helped me feel as though I knew him better. He had died when I was just sixteen, and even before that he had been a distant figure, yet in his letters I saw another side to him – an emotional man who wrote about love and his hopes for the future, before things turned sour.

I felt desperately sorry for Penny, who had been the innocent victim in all this, but I also felt glad that I finally understood what had gone on in my family during those difficult years. I now knew why my parents had had all those arguments behind closed doors, and what had caused my father's mysterious disappearance. It wasn't pretty, but it was the truth.

My father might have died while I was still a boy, but his words had always echoed in my mind: 'You can try this puppetry lark for six months but, at the end of that, if they don't offer you a paid position you're going to have to get a proper job.' Over the years the spectre of the 'proper job' had always haunted me, driving me to work as hard as I could, never daring to stop for breath. But now I realised just how much I had outstripped his expectations. Forget six months – I had been a puppeteer for more than half a century! Losing *Rainbow* and being out of work in the nineties had almost crushed my spirit altogether, but I had come out the other side stronger, having learned to embrace the unpredictable nature of the career I had chosen. After bestowing on me the Harlequin Award, the chairman of the British Puppet and Model Theatre Guild – the oldest puppetry organisation in the world – phoned to ask if I would accept the position of president. Now I finally felt sure of my standing in the world of puppetry.

I was also financially secure enough not to need to work anymore, and I was certainly old enough to retire. Yet now I found I wanted to continue working for the sheer joy of it. I didn't need to prove myself to anyone anymore.

I no longer worried about the phone ringing, either, knowing that sooner or later it always did. Puppetry seemed to be experiencing something of a resurgence, with television advertisers keen to exploit its comic potential. As a result, I found myself constantly in demand for all manner of odd jobs, from operating meerkat puppets in a commercial for Compare the Market to creating a marionette version of the famous 'Diet Coke break' commercial.

I even managed to get my hands on a puppet I had worshipped since my earliest years: Brains from *Thunderbirds*, who was appearing in an advert for Drench mineral water. ('Brains perform best when they're hydrated,' was the slogan.) The conceit was that after taking a couple of gulps of the stuff, he would be so filled with energy that he would leap out of his chair and perform an incredible dance routine – everything from tap, to disco to breakdance. I was one of a team of puppeteers brought in to put the marionette through its paces, carefully copying the moves as a professional dancer demonstrated them each in turn. We ran through the routine in extreme slow motion, but even so there was no way we could get one of Gerry Anderson's famously stilted marionettes to match the fluidity of the living, breathing performer. Fortunately, the wonders of technology came to the rescue – with the help of some advanced computer software, our fumbling efforts were transformed into a perfectly poised dancing Brains, shaking his booty with even more style than the human dancer – and without a string in sight. If only all puppetry could be airbrushed to perfection!

In fact, despite the huge advances in CGI and motion-capture technologies, we puppeteers still seem to be needed by television and film companies. A couple of years ago, I spent several months at Shepperton Studios helping the animators work out how to make the character of the candlestick, Lumière, look realistic in the new live-action Disney film of *Beauty and the Beast*. I brought a simple wooden marionette with me, which they modified, removing the hands and replacing them with LEDs so that they could see how the light passed across the marionette's face when he moved his arms.

Nor had I seen the last of Zippy, either. Although the heyday of the *Rainbow* revival had come and gone, the gang were now firmly established as cult figures and, as such, were regularly brought out of retirement. Zippy and George graced the stage at Mr Gay UK – where George turned out to be something of an icon – and appeared on screen in *Ant and Dec's Gameshow Marathon,* as well as cropping up on Harry Hill's *TV Burp.* They even found themselves competing on the BBC game show *The Weakest Link,* taking on Soo from *The Sooty Show,* Roland Rat, Otis the Aardvark and more. (Predictably, Soo wiped the floor with the rest of us.)

In 2005 Channel 4 gave the two puppets their own episode of the list show *Favouritism* – following on from 'Michael Portillo's Losers' and 'Boy George's Queerest TV Moments', 'Zippy and George's Puppet Legends' saw the pair living the high life in a grand country manor, reminiscing about their prestigious career in showbiz and the many puppet legends they had rubbed shoulders with, from Roland Rat to Basil Brush. There were talking heads, among them Matthew Corbett and Phillip Schofield (credited as 'sidekicks' to Sooty and Gordon the Gopher, respectively), plus an interview with Orville the duck, who told Zippy and George that he originally met Keith Harris in a gay club.

Perhaps our most surreal outing was on the BBC's time-travelling drama *Ashes to Ashes*, where Zippy and George featured as emblems of Detective Inspector Alex Drake's 1980s childhood, appearing in a particularly disturbing dream sequence set in a police station. The director wanted something genuinely creepy, and Roy relished the opportunity to make the puppets as sinister as possible.

The emergence of YouTube also gave *Rainbow* an unofficial new outlet and helped to cement its cult status among adults. Roy's nudist camp prank and Jim Davidson's sweary dress rehearsal both found their way on to the video-sharing site, as did our infamous Christmas tape with the song about playing with our twangers. The deadpan performances of Geoffrey, Rod, Jane and Roger were so convincing that many people mistakenly believed it must have been a real episode, and were shocked to discover that the programme they remembered from childhood had apparently been so suggestive. One Christian group condemned the programme and threatened to launch a campaign against ITV, until someone quietly pointed out to them that the video was actually a spoof.

Soon other adult fans were inspired to reinvent *Rainbow*, redubbing and editing old episodes for comedy value. In the run-up to the London mayoral election of 2008 I tuned in to *Have I Got News for You* to see Zippy, George and Bungle on screen in what looked like one of our vintage episodes. When I turned the sound up, though, I realised something wasn't right. The three were bickering away as usual, but instead of their regular voices they had the mayoral candidates' soundbites popping out of their mouths: Zippy, grumpy as ever, was the belligerent Ken Livingstone, George the bumbling Boris Johnson, and Bungle the largely irrelevant Brian Paddick.

To this day, Zippy remains in demand. In recent years, I've been asked to make appearances on the BBC's *Children in Need* fundraiser and numerous late-night chat and panel shows, including *The Last Leg* and *The Keith and Paddy Picture Show*. In fact, Zippy and I have been so busy that Fremantle recently commissioned a new puppet to be made because the old one has faded from exposure to the limelight.

I was going online to check my email one day, when Zippy flashed up on the screen, along with the letters R.I.P. At first I couldn't work out what it meant, and in a kind of blind confusion I clicked on the link. There on the screen in front of me was an old black-and-white picture of Roy. I quickly scanned up the page to the headline: '*Rainbow* voice actor Roy Skelton dies'.

I caught my breath in shock, then quickly read on. I learned that Roy had suffered a stroke at his home in Brighton a few months earlier, and had finally succumbed to pneumonia.

Roy had always been such a huge presence that the idea of him being gone seemed unthinkable. I knew he had been nearly eighty, but somehow I'd never really thought of him as an old man. Another thought also crossed my mind: Roy was Zippy, and so was I – we were two halves of a whole. Without him in the world, a part of Zippy had died too.

Roy's death marked the end of an era, but although he was gone, the character we had shared seemed unlikely to be forgotten any time soon. When the government commissioned a survey to find England's most popular icons, I was surprised to see Zippy listed alongside the hymn 'Jerusalem', Routemaster buses, the King James Bible and the cup of tea. Meanwhile, I read in a BBC poll that *Rainbow* had been voted the 'Best-loved children's TV programme of yesteryear'. Improbable as it might seem, Zippy was now a national treasure.

But while Zippy is the puppet that has dominated my career, I've never lost touch with my roots. For more than half a century, the Little Angel has always been there for me, and I for it. Lyndie and I are both honorary associates of the theatre now, as well as board members, helping to steer the future direction of the place we love so much. She still makes puppets for Little Angel productions, while I regularly perform, direct and run classes there, teaching the next generation of puppeteers – making sure that the ancient art form of marionette puppetry, which John Wright loved so much, never dies out.

In October 2017 I got a call from the current artistic director of the Little Angel, Samantha Lane. 'A little birdie tells me you're about to turn seventy,' she said, 'and Lyndie's going to be eighty. We'd love to throw you both a birthday party here.'

I was touched that the theatre had remembered, and turned up expecting a few drinks and nibbles. But the team had surpassed themselves. More than 100 people were squeezed into the tiny space, its walls strung with fairy lights and marionettes from all our old favourite shows, and in the little workshop a jazz band was playing.

As all around me my friends from the world of puppetry laughed, sang and danced the night away, I remembered the nervous young boy of fifteen who had come knocking on the Little Angel's door all those years ago, hoping to be allowed into this strange, magical world. I felt so grateful that the door had been opened to him.

A note on the authors

Ronnie Le Drew is one of the UK's most respected puppeteers, and recipient of the prestigious Harlequin Award, the Oscar of the puppetry world. He has operated many of the most iconic children's puppets of the twentieth century – Zippy, Sooty and Sweep, Muffin the Mule, Bill and Ben, Brains from *Thunderbirds* – as well as working on classic puppet films such as *Labyrinth*, *Little Shop of Horrors* and *The Muppet Christmas Carol*. He continues to work regularly as a puppeteer in TV, theatre and advertising and also teaches at The Curious school of Puppetry, The Little Angel Theatre and the London School of Puppetry, which he co-founded in 1987.

Duncan Barrett and **Nuala Calvi** are the authors of a trio of *Sunday Times* top-ten bestsellers: *The Sugar Girls* (second highest-selling history book of 2012), *GI Brides* (also a *New York Times* bestseller in the United States) and *The Girls Who Went to War*. Duncan's other books include *The Reluctant Tommy*, *Men of Letters* and *Hitler's British Isles*, while Nuala's writing credits include features for the *Guardian*, the *Independent, The Times*, the BBC and CNN.

Acknowledgements

It's been a long and bumpy road getting this book published, and my thanks are due to everyone who has waited so patiently for it to come to fruition, and in particular, to those who helped shape it into what it is now.

It was Steve Tiplady who first suggested to Duncan and Nuala that they might like to write my story. I am grateful to him for the initial idea, and to both of them for their painstaking work on it over the years.

My family and friends have provided love and support throughout the process, as well as sharing their own memories – and jogging mine. In particular I would like to thank Caroline Astell-Burt, Sue Dacre, Linda Standfield, John Le Drew, Elizabeth Le Drew and Carol Le Drew.

Several former colleagues were kind enough to give up their time to share their memories of working with me, among them Stanley Bates, Malcolm Lord, Mark Mander, Nigel Plaskitt and Loretta Howells.

Some of the photos in the book were provided by Chris Clark, Peter Ball and Lyndie Wright, and I am grateful to them for sharing these. To Lyndie, of course, I owe a lot more – and I hope this book stands in part as a testament to the whole Wright family and the Little Angel Theatre. I am grateful to the current administration at the theatre for allowing us to shoot our crowdfunding video there, and for offering to host our launch party.

Olivia Grace Paolucci, formerly of Fremantle Media and now based at Boat Rocker Media, has been helpful and supportive, allowing me to use Zippy's closely-guarded image for the cover shoot and publicity photographs. At Unbound, Lauren Fulbright and her colleagues have expertly guided me through the process of publication.

Finally, thanks to those of you who pledged to fund the book, whose names are on the next page. Without you, this would never have happened.

Unbound is the world's first crowdfunding publisher, established in 2011.

We believe that wonderful things can happen when you clear a path for people who share a passion. That's why we've built a platform that brings together readers and authors to crowdfund books they believe in – and give fresh ideas that don't fit the traditional mould the chance they deserve.

This book is in your hands because readers made it possible. Everyone who pledged their support is listed below. Join them by visiting unbound.com and supporting a book today.

Chris Abbott
Alison Abedelmassieh
Terry Adams
Tamara Al-Bassam
Alison Alexander
Ian Allen
Stuart Allen
Paul Angus
James Arnott
Rob Ashman
Adrian Ashton

Caroline Astell-Burt
Nic Ayling
Dave Baines-Copping
Rene Baker
Peter Ball
Andrew Barrett
Michèle Barrett
Frances Barry
Jo Bater
Niccolò Becchi
Phil Beddow

Ted Beresford
Kim Bergsagel
Johnny Beskow
Sudakshina Bhattacharjee
Carolyn Birkbeck
Jayne Bishop
Keren Bobker
Sarah Bowron
Catherine Breslin
Martin Bridle
Kas Brown
Warrick Brownlow-Pike
Stephen Bruce
David Brunt
Nicola Buckmaster
Dave Burgess
Sarah Burgess
Joseph Burne
Andrew Burns
Lazlo Burns
Melinda Burton
Trent Burton
Veronica Calvi
Phillip Carruthers
Ana Cascon & Bill Shadwick
Nina Challenor
Amelie Chevalier
The Chimney Sweeps
The Cinema Museum
Holly Clark
Jo Clayton
Edward Cook
Adam Crosthwaite

Tania Czajka
Antony Czekirda
Sue Dacre
Martyn Daniel
Andrew Daw
Jorge Dickens
David Dmytriw
Alastair Doggett
Angela Doherty
Maureen Dominey
Lawrence T Doyle
Martyn Drake
Chess Dudman
Samuel Peter Dudman
Mark Dyson
Darren East
Barnaby Eaton-Jones
Jeff Elams
Judith Elbourne
Peter Elliott
Thomas James Elliott (@tje)
Richard Evans
Dr. Matthew Eve
Kate Eves
Kirsty Fantastico
Ian Ferrier
Stuart Fewtrell
Simon Fiddyment
Philip Fletcher
Stephen Foster
Penny Francis
Keith Frederick
Heidi Frost

Max Fulham

Fagner Gastaldon

Susan Godfrey

Paul Gouldstone

Ben Gray

Rachel Green

Robin Grey

Stephen Griffiths

Jimmy Grimes

Andrew Grundon

Ken Haines

Suzie Hanna

Daniel Hanton

Mike Harper

Jamie Harris

Barny Harrison

Polly Harrow Wright

Kevin Hatchard

Nik Hayward

Greg Healey

Larry Lee Hensel

Brian Hibbitt

Sheryl Hill

Steven Hill

Lori Hopkins

Stephen Hoppe

Darren Hopton

Michael Horsley

Tim Humphries

Kurt Hunter

Stephen Hunter

Jane James

Kate James-Moore

Kaja Jarosz

Paul Jeffery

Peter Jones

Andrew Keating

Laura Kelly

Liam Kelly

Chris Kendall

Kevin Kevane

Dan Kieran

Matthew King

Paul Kirrage

Dunstan Kornicki

Samantha Lane

Warren Lapworth

Liz Le Drew

Alain Lecucq

Fiona Ledger

Yuna Lee

Little Angel Theatre

Nick Long

Stephen Lonie

Dan Luck

Tasha Luxton

Karen Mace

Martin MacGilp

Jim Macrae

Sarah Mansell

Wayne Martin

Chris Martinez

Paul Matthews

Stephen McCarthy

Ryan McGivern

Simon Mclean

Will McNally
Jake McNeil
Julia Mealing
Richard Medrington
Jonathan Melville
Andrew et Reuben Michel
Kim Miles
Mervyn Millar
Hannah Miller
John Mitchinson
James Moorhouse
Dominic Morgan
Rebecca Morris
John Murdoch
Sue Mussell
Philip Nash
Carlo Navato
Hazel Nicholson
Freda O'Byrne
Helen O'Hanlon
Jonathan Owen
Paul Oxberry
Angie Parker
Carol Parker
Jill Parker
Rich Parkinson-Williams
Eddy Parnell
Nathan Pattinson
Bryan Peacock
Bianca Pellet
A Pellumbi
Penny
Suzanne Pentecost

Isabella & Sofia Petch
Ruth Petrie
Toby Philpott
Donna Phoenix
Karon Phoenix-Hollis
Miranda Pitcher
Mark Pitman
Justin Pollard
Andrea Poucher
Emma Powell
Sally Preisig
Fiona Putnam
Ellen Quach
Jackie Raggett
Peter Raggett
Andy Randle
Nimer Rashed
Melvyn Rawlinson
Natalie Raybould
Sabrina Recoules Quang
Stuart Reed
Shona Reppe
Anna Rice
Wyn Roberts
Andy Rolfe
Paul Ross
Lucinda Rowe
Kirsty Rowley
Alexis Rudd
Darren Rugg
Roy Russell
Gary Sanders
Nick Saunders

SUPPORTERS

Sarah Schofield
Lynsey Searle
Sukanya Shankar
Laurence Shapiro
Damon Shaw
Tamsin Shelton
Jenny Shirt
Dave Showler
Dave Sifleet
Tony Sinnett
Sheila Sky
Jonathan Sloman
Eric Smith
Maggie Southam Ferrari
Geraldine Spiller
Andrew Spooner
Linda Stanfield
Angela Stewart-Park
Ashley Stokes
John Styles
Philip Alexander Sugg
Rudy Sullivan
Brian Swann
Tim Sykes
Kevin Symonds
Kerrin Tatman
Ian Thom
Hattie Thomas
Samuel Toogood
Karen Torley
Kirsten Treasure
Charlie Trimmings
Garry Vaux

Mark Vent
Elizabeth Vermeulen
Antony Wainer
Martin Warren
Tessa Waterhouse
John A Watson
Nenagh Watson
Hannah Webb
Ray West
Jonathan Westwood
Robert Whelan
Joyce Wilburn
Rebekah Wild
Nick Williams
Jamie Wilson
Stuart Witts
Andy Wood
Ian Woods
Darryl Worbey
Steve Wright
Syd Wright
Christopher Wylie
Soledad Zarate